BROTHERHOOD OF THE SKIES

WARTIME EXPERIENCES OF A GUNNER OFFICER AND TYPHOON PILOT

David Ince DFC

GRUB STREET · LONDON

Published by
Grub Street
4 Rainham Close
London
SW11 6SS

British Library Cataloguing in Publication Data
Ince, David
Brotherhood of the skies: wartime experiences of a gunner officer and typhoon pilot.
1. Ince, David 2. Fighter pilots – Great Britain – Biography. 3. World War, 1939-1945 – Aerial operations, British
I. Title
940. 5'44'941'092-dc22

ISBN-13: 9781906502645

Cover design by Sarah Driver

Typeset by Pearl Graphics, Hemel Hempstead

Printed and bound by MPG Ltd, Bodmin, Cornwall

Grub Street Publishing only uses
FSC (Forest Stewardship Council) paper for its books.

CONTENTS

FOREWORD

In the decades following the end of World War II, many books were written on all aspects of air warfare. Often, those earlier books fell into the Boys' Own category, and were none the worse for that, given a public appetite for accounts of the deeds of those directly involved in operations. Even as the rate of publication abated, it was becoming clear that such books had not always done justice to the circumstances surrounding the gallantry and sacrifice that they portrayed, Very often written for a lay readership, they tended rather to gloss over the context in which men were sent into battle, their preparation and their training.

David Ince has avoided this pitfall. He writes both movingly and with great insight into the exploits of a Typhoon squadron in battle, from

Normandy to the Elbe. He writes with firsthand knowledge of the demands and stresses of life as a ground-attack pilot and he paints a very convincing picture of the highs and lows of his experience in a costly but highly successful campaign. His style is both distinctive and graphic. He is a keen observer of human behaviour and has the ability to describe events with an immediacy that will commend itself to the reader. He is, however, uniquely qualified to expand his approach to the subject beyond the limits of more familiar earlier treatments. In many ways, that is the most important aspect of this book.

David Ince draws on his own experience as a former army officer, a highly successful fighter-bomber pilot, a test pilot and engineer, to tackle areas such as tactics, operational training and equipment which have very largely been neglected by other authors. His analytical powers are much in evidence in his observations on these matters which deserve the attention that he has given them. His account of the dearth of structured weapons training and his views on operational training are of particular value.

Perhaps it is in the final reflective chapters of this book that there is most to digest and to admire. David Ince's own personal odyssey from what he honestly describes as intense hatred for his foes in 1945, to his embracing of reconciliation with the former enemy in later years, is sensitively and powerfully described. He has been instrumental in handing on the traditions of the short-lived Typhoon squadrons of the 1940s to members of today's nascent Eurofighter Typhoon Force at RAF Coningsby. This book will provide a permanent and powerful reminder to them and to later generations of what it was like to fly and fight in the conditions of the Second World War.

Air Vice-Marshal A.F.C. Hunter CBE AFC MA LLB DL

CHAPTER ONE

CLOUD PAVILIONS WHITE

Typhoon 1B. About to become airborne with two x 1,000lb bombs. Arguably the best fighter ground-attack aircraft of World War II.

Jumping from our jeeps we dived under the camouflage netting and scanned the operations map for evidence of change. There seemed to be no movement at all on the approaches to Caen and progress amongst the hedgerows of the Bocage and the foothills of the Alpes Normande appeared to be as limited and difficult as ever. The rumble of guns, clearly audible, was continuing evidence of slow progress on the ground and we knew that the Germans were still capable of mounting a major counter attack.

Yet there were no feelings of unease. Rather there was a sense of satisfaction that we were back in France. In growing strength, thanks to the miracle of Mulberry, the artificial harbour which had been towed in sections across the Channel. We were here to stay – amongst the first RAF squadrons back on the Continent – supporting our ground troops in the liberation of Europe and somewhat frustrated that it all seemed to be taking so long.

It was sweltering in the heat as we crowded round the CO studying the target photographs. The aiming point was the middle of a tiny village, overlooking a wooded escarpment, some twenty-five miles inland from the Normandy beaches. "We'll run in this way and go down to port. Remember our boys on the ground are very close and ready to go in. No, repeat no, undershoots are permitted!"

The sunburned face, under its mop of curly dark hair, seemed confident – almost relaxed. He looked at us thoughtfully, then glanced at his watch: "Press tits at fourteen thirty – Good luck chaps!" Nothing to it really, just thirty-five minutes chock to chock and back in time for tea. I glanced at the others. Some of them had been with the squadron for a long time. Did they feel as I did, fulfilled beyond my wildest dreams, flying a Typhoon to war? Did they savour the preflight tension, the challenge and uncertainty of every sortie and, in the background always, fear to be mastered? Questions which were never asked – although for most of us the answers would have been in the affirmative.

I look back on the period of my life and recall the words of another airman:*The fact is I enjoyed the war... it became my driving force because it had a purpose and I accepted the risks, the excitement of combat, survival and retrospect.... We all did... with faith and courage*[1].

In from the coast a belt of well developed cumulus reached upwards, dazzling white. Where they merged together the clouds formed deep canyons of clear air, framing a distant landscape of sunshine and shadow. They grew higher, closing in on the formation until we were flanked by walls of shimmering vapour – sitting ducks for the gunners waiting below. And with the thought a salvo of black oily bursts materialized from nowhere as the aircraft moved into echelon for the attack. "Bassett Leader going down now!" Another salvo – closer still – shredding and gone in a moment. In the same instant we were plummeting earthwards, strung out down the sky, gunsights tracking onto the target as it emerged from the shadows far below. A picturesque almost alpine scene – wooded heights, tortuous winding roads and a deep gorge – bathed in brilliant sunshine. And there the similarity ended. Where the village had once been was just a vague cruciform shape, its outline merging into a sea of rubble. A charnel house of pulverized limestone and flickering fires where a Panzer unit had dug in its tanks and guns.

An umbrella of white shell bursts formed over the ruins, a lethal, seemingly impenetrable, screen. Then the diving aircraft were through and still unscathed – cannon smoke trailing – and each pilot conscious of the tracer rising lazily upwards and accelerating violently towards him, willing himself to press home his attack.

Bombs gone. Moments later they erupted across the target area. There was an angry red explosion and a new and violent fire began to rage amongst the wreckage. The enemy gunners redoubled their efforts and the air was torn by a maelstrom of flak. The dark cloud base, low above our heads, tilted crazily as we weaved and jinked in the gloom trying to evade the deadly searching fingers of tracer. And time stood still.

As suddenly it was all over and we were back in the sunlight, climbing hard, moving into battle formation and setting course for home.

The intelligence officer was waiting, pacing up and down, as the aircraft taxied in. Seemingly oblivious to the clouds of dust, the clatter of PSP[2] tracking, and the dying sounds of our engines as one by one we swung to a stop and shut down. A typical academic, with his steel rimmed spectacles and a map tightly rolled under his arm, he must have found our light hearted banter difficult to accept as we gathered round him. Yet he listened patiently enough and quietly inserted his questions.

"So it had been ABTA[3]? And with what results....?"

"What else had we seen....? And the flak....?"

That was our cue and we responded as always with a touch of the Noel Coward's – brave and ever so slightly effeminate: "The flak Gwyn! My dear the flak!... and the noise!... and the people!..."

And somehow honour was satisfied, even if we said it too often in those far off days, for only those who had been there knew what it was really like.

Time to spare a thought for the Canadians working their way up the escarpment against those dug in tanks, and the superb Panzerfaust[4] and

Zipp Button has a touch of the Noel Coward's.

infantry firepower of the German army. There was, thank God, a strong impression that we had hit the defenders really hard.

For me at least, the drive back to our tents in the orchard was, as always, to relive each sortie with its powerful mix of images and emotions. Like today, with strong defences – ready and waiting – and a cloudscape which had helped them as much as it hindered us, the odds were hardly in our favour. Yet Johnny Button's up-sun positioning – his instant attack and our aggressive follow through, had helped to swing the balance – to penetrate the fearsome light flak barrage unscathed.

During those last vulnerable moments pressing home the attack – feeling the g and clambering for altitude and safety, the enemy gunners had tried their utmost to claw us out of the sky and had failed.

Something to learn from all that. About luck? Well certainly a reminder about how a really determined attack could upset the defenders and reduce their effectiveness. Something else too, which would grow and become clearer with experience. Immensely valuable when the time came to lead others into battle. About maximizing the impact and minimizing the risk – perhaps even about helping to create one's own luck. The very opposite of a gung ho approach. Sometimes of course it was just not possible. But on many occasions it worked.

And, not least, the sheer inspiration from the guys around you – their unspoken mutual support. Utterly impossible to let them down.

As the adrenaline drained away, so did the images, the fear and the excitement. And I found myself back in the real world surrounded by the very chaps about whom I had been thinking and with whom I was flying day in and day out – British, Canadians, Australians and New Zealanders. All of us motivated by that marvellous unspoken feeling, almost tribal in its intensity, of belonging to the best squadron of all.

Time indeed for tea, to record another operational sortie in our logbooks, and enjoy the moment of returning without loss and the warm feeling of life and survival until next time.

And they are fortunate, who fight
For gleaming landscapes swept and shafted
And crowned by cloud pavilions white;
Hearing such harmonies as might
Only from Heaven be downward wafted
Voices of victory and delight[5].

CHAPTER TWO

NEW PERSPECTIVES

On our farm a mile or so below Hadrian's Wall, in the mid nineteen twenties, we lived to the sounds of pipeline milking. A rare sound in those days – but father was ahead of his time and his name was already in the herd book. Twice a day the yard across the lane, where Boodie worked with his cows, echoed to the clack of pneumatic pulsation and the clatter of aluminium buckets. In summer there was haymaking on the fells and at harvest time great mugs of tea and wedges of bread and butter – family and helpers sitting amongst the stubble below the slats and belts of the threshing machine. An idyllic existence in which to grow up – brought to a sudden and unhappy end when farm and livestock were sold and we moved to Glasgow.

Glasgow in the early thirties was full of disturbing images. Squalid tenements and shawlie womenfolk gossiping in the doorways. The unemployed, standing around in their cloth caps and mufflers, at every street corner, their poverty, seen for the first time, was an affront. Made worse by the tragedy that so many of them were survivors of the Great War – the blinded, limbless, and horribly disfigured amongst them – literally begging for a crust. There were ex bandsmen too, with their treasured instruments, and others with performing monkeys and hurdy-gurdys[1].

I hated them for being there, for showing how little the nation cared for its heroes, yet admired them beyond words for their courage in defeating what I was already learning to think of as an arrogant and warlike foe. Their music added to my confusion – jazz and the soldiers' songs which I loved, mixed with the brass band sounds from their yesterdays which filled me with a strange longing – to wear a uniform, to stand tall and go marching.

My father had ended the Great War as second in command of the 18th Durham Light Infantry – a Pals Battalion – and I had spent many fascinated hours poring over his photo album. His wartime pictures concluded with the laying up of the battalion colours in Durham Cathedral and there he was, on horseback, leading that last ceremonial parade through the crowded streets. Although he spoke rarely about life in the trenches, I knew that he had almost accepted a permanent commission, and I soon came to realise that the annual reunion was a most important event in his life. When he talked about the Durham miners, who had formed the bulk of the battalion and its reinforcements, it was in words of great affection. And I came to equate them with those tragic Glaswegian urchins of war. It made a profound impression on me from an early age.

I greatly admired my father. Our relationship was more like that of an older and a younger brother. Years later – during his second war when we were both in uniform – I told him so and he was pleased that we shared the same feelings. But there was another side to that relationship. The sale of our farm and the move to Glasgow had been occasioned by my grandfather David Dunn Warren who ran a successful business in distributing explosives and sporting ammunition throughout Scotland. His vast home, his Rolls-Royce, glazed roof motor house, Wishart the chauffeur, a sombre but kindly man who washed his car every day (with cold water only!), and the bevy of servants betrayed all the trappings of wealth.

Pampa was a lovely man, larger than life in every sense, with a wicked sense of humour. One night, when we were staying at Westbourne House, he set me up in advance of a dinner party at which I would appear very briefly and, when the moment came, I responded to his:

"And what happened to your train David?" with the words,

"It's all buggered up Pampa."

At which he sat rocking with laughter – ample stomach heaving in the midst of a long and shocked silence. For such freedom of expression was not acceptable in those far off days. For my sister on other occasions it would be: "Jessie – a small glass of wine for Miss Rosemary", (then aged five!). No wonder we thought he was the bee's knees.

But sadly his family – four daughters and a son and the most domineering stepmother imaginable for his wife had died in childbirth – were totally dysfunctional. And here was the problem. Grandfather was not well, and he did not trust his son to take over the business, so he had invited my father to sell up the farm and join him. It was a recipe for disaster, made far worse when our lovely grandfather died as the Great Depression of 1929 was just getting under way. His executors panicked, his fortune vanished, and the whole family was at loggerheads.

For me, I just knew that my parents were very hurt. My mother was placed in an intolerable situation. She remained utterly loyal to my father who, for his part, continued to work for the family business and never once complained at the way he was being treated.

Our house was sold, the car and the Labradors disappeared. We moved into a very small flat where I apparently filled my room with so many model aeroplanes that mother could not clean it! Hence I suspect her early opposition to my aviation interests although she gave up the struggle in due course and was eventually secretly quite pleased at my efforts.

Things were so bad financially that the plans for our education barely survived – and only then because my late godfather's family came most generously to the rescue. Fortunately things got easier as the war approached. My father joined the Territorial Army and commanded a searchlight battery – which gave him a new and absorbing interest, and took him away during hostilities. Soon afterwards, and to great relief all round, Imperial Chemical Industries took over the family business and really sorted things out.

When my mother's family was around I had great difficulty in keeping my mouth shut. And it is hardly surprising that I took refuge in war, and things military, during my school days. That happened immediately at Aysgarth, in the Yorkshire Dales, a marvellous escape from Glasgow for nine months in the year. There, like Hugh Dundas[2] before me, I too discovered the *Times History of the Great War* in the school library.

Before long I had become totally absorbed by the bitter struggle and any earlier childhood ambitions soon gave way, Biggles like, to the images of an aviator. I tracked down every book written by his creator Captain W.E. Johns – an ex RFC pilot himself – and read them from cover to cover. A piece of decking up in the trees, across the steep little valley which contained the school rifle range, became the cockpit of my Sopwith Camel or SE5 as I climbed aboard to fight the dreaded Boche again and again.

Aysgarth had a school tower. A sort of modern angular brick-built folly, three stories high, with a single class room on every level. From the top you could see the Hawker Audaxes in the circuit at RAF Catterick. I wasted hours watching them when I should have been revising for exams. There were other pleasures at Aysgarth. Like the roller skating rink in front of the main school buildings where we blew off steam between classes. And the swimming pool where you started life as a new boy, wearing a pair of dark blue serge pants, (if a bit older we would have called them passion killers!) and the school had devised a cunning scheme to encourage athletic endeavour.

Swim an observed 1/4 mile and you were issued with pale blue slips – 1/2 mile and they became orange – complete the speed test and they became silver. This arrogant youngster went for orange in one, made silver two weeks later – and was singularly unpopular for a time. Things got much better after I was totally defeated by the next test which involved picking up a scattering of clay pigeon discs from the bottom of the pool!

Came the great day when the school caught fire. It burned prodigiously, the roof fell in and we left it to the fire engines and went home for the Easter holidays almost a week early. Returning some four weeks later we found the rebuilding already started and the nearest playing field covered in wooden huts. Unheated, it was summer term after all, they had somehow been fully plumbed and were to be our dormitories for the next three months. The classrooms, dining hall and kitchens were undamaged – as indeed were our headmaster's study and his cane!

By the end of the summer holidays all had been completed, including a new fully tiled open plan bathhouse with six enormous baths. Early, on the first morning, we could hear them being run. Shortly afterwards we were roused – told to remove our pyjamas, to form orderly queues approaching each bath and plunge in one by one. The water was stone bloody cold! Thanks to the fire our splendid headmaster had found a new way to make us stronger and healthier. At least so he informed us.

Rugger was a great enthusiasm with the added fun of fixtures against other schools at home and away – and especially at Ampleforth. There was something about the soaring buildings, with their wonderful interior woodwork and the austere yet welcoming monastic atmosphere which appealed hugely – quite apart from the mug of beer at supper after the game. Visiting Ampleforth was a special privilege.

However flying was the real obsession. I had to experience it for myself. Eventually, during the summer holidays, a member of the Renfrew Flying Club agreed to take me up. An ex Royal Flying Corps pilot, and partially disabled in his right arm, he was anxious to assure me that he could cope in the air and especially that he could land safely. But I was far too excited to listen. Caught up in the ritual which was to become so familiar in later years and the precisely repeated words of command:

"Switches off! – Suck in! – Throttle set! – Contact!"

Unless you too have experienced the tang of burnt oil and the slipstream in your face and felt the transition from bumpy take-off to smooth flight and itched to get your hands on the controls – you've never lived.

So it was with me, late on that summer's day so many years ago, as the Gipsy Moth lifted into the air and swung northwest towards the Clyde.

Work and life had returned to the shipyards and the open hull of the new Cunarder[3] was clearly visible in John Brown's yard. It was truly awesome, like the skeleton of some huge stranded whale, swarming with ant like figures, illuminated by the flashes from myriad welding torches. Little did I know then that I would travel in her across a wartime North Atlantic.

Up river lay Glasgow, dimly visible under its regular pall of smoke. To the north and west the evening sun lit up the distant mountains, and the dying cumulus, in a magnificent display of colour. Our brief flight took us across the estuary, towards the long shadowy reach of Loch Lomond, turning for home as the light began to fade. Then down and down, the dark air full of smuts and burning smells from the shipping and yards below. Down the long slope of the cemetery, with the headstones slipping past, until the grass field loomed out of the dusk.

At Cheltenham the memories come crowding in... with my friends John Slatter and Peter Holmes, beside the duty pilot's van, watching the yellow Hart trainers flying circuits and bumps. We had been amongst the first to join the new OTC[4] Air Section at Cheltenham College, belonged to the same House, and shared a love of flying and rugger. Our visits to the FTS[5] at South Cerney were intended to instil a basic knowledge of radio, armament, and navigation. But we escaped from the stuffy lecture rooms at every opportunity.

On the last two Empire Air Days, as the war clouds gathered – we stood together near the tuck shop, looking out across the playing fields towards the chapel. Almost exactly where we had stood immobile in the chill of poppy day morning – as the maroons echoed distantly in the sky to mark the eleventh hour of the eleventh day and there was utter silence across the land. Only this was summer and, watching the massed formations passing overhead, we saw ourselves in the years to come as part of that great Service – fighter pilots in another war...

...at summer camps where we were soldiers again – our make believe battles on the scrub-covered slopes above Tidworth enlivened by the presence of an occasional Hawker Audax or Hector. Local army co-operation squadrons demonstrating the art of air support. So highly developed it was said that some of the aircraft were even being flown by army officers seconded to the RAF. On a late evening exercise we watched them against the sunset – engines throttled back, dropping low to launch a weighted bag almost into our laps or picking up a message slung on a cable between two poles – marvelling at their skill in the fading light...

...becoming part of the OTC band. Practice sessions in the wooden hut on the middle of the old parade ground. Underneath was the miniature rifle range, scene of much winter activity, culminating in the annual public schools' Country Life Competition. Cold as charity as the captain endeavoured to direct his team onto near invisible targets scattered across a large black and white landscape. Somehow it worked and, although we never actually won during my time we were usually in the first five or six. It was encouraging to be selected for the cadet pair and subsequently for the eight in my last winter.

In the summer, cycling to the open air range at Seven Springs in the hills above Cheltenham – a long climb weighed down by our rifles – and the need to recover your breathing as soon as you got to the top. From then on it was all go – manning the targets – firing at different distances – and that ultimate torture the Marling. Where you leapt to your feet as the target came up, ran a hundred yards, flung yourself down and tried to fire two rounds before it disappeared again. This process started on the 600 yards butts and ended at 100 yards, by which time the long-range target loomed huge, but you were almost too winded to hit it!...

...and the day, around the time of Chamberlain's useless visit to Adolf Hitler in Munich, when we were busy filling sandbags and experienced a fit of utter madness. Saved up our blank cartridges – arrived on the range very early and went into the woods at the far end where pheasants were reared in their hundreds. We shot a couple of the wretched birds at point-blank range, hid them in our saddle bags and persuaded Thomas Plant, the school outfitter, to hang them in his cellar...

...as for the band – I never made first cornet! Yet it was great on those spit and polish occasions – trousers soaked and put under the mattress could produce a knife-edged crease, webbing blancoed to perfection, puttees wound just so. Absolute replicas of our fathers' war! Even the rifles and bayonets were standard 1914-18 issue!...

...field days were another matter. Exhausting. Always attacking uphill. The umpires had a flair for it. Even when the defenders were required to counter attack. So everybody wanted to crew the Vickers heavy machine gun. A great brute with its water-cooled jacket, massive tripod and belt-fed ammunition. Always moved by truck. What could be better? That it could only fire a maximum burst of five blank rounds at a time mattered not at all.

At the end of the day, marching back to the bus, we were knackered. Until drums and brass filled the air with sound – echoing off the tree-lined Gloucestershire lanes, setting the pace and drawing it together. The well loved tunes working their familiar magic:

> "Bollocks was all the band could play!
> Bollocks! They played it night and day!
> Bollocks! Tra La La Bollocks!
> And supper seems so much less far away!"

Summer 1938. Gloster F5/34 eight-gun monoplane fighter. The stuff of dreams.

Of all those memories the most treasured were the stolen afternoons at Hucclecote, home of the Gloster Aircraft Company, cycling over from Cheltenham surreptitiously photographing the aircraft on flight test. And the golden day when Frank McKenna, the general manager whose son Kevin was also at Cheltenham, took us round the factory. On the production lines were Sea Gladiators for the Royal Navy and the Hawker Henley light bomber converted to target towing. I could not understand why. In the air it looked so much faster and more agile than the big and heavy Battle.

The golf course beside the airfield was disappearing under a raft of concrete as a shadow factory began to take shape. Soon it too would be producing a new and still secret bomber, the Armstrong Whitworth Albemarle.

In the flight shed was Gloster's latest, the F5/34, a unique opportunity to explore the cockpit of an eight-gun monoplane fighter. I sat there trying to take it all in, surrounded by the aroma of cellulose dope and hydraulic fluid, grasping the throttle lever – hand on the spade grip, head in the clouds.

A few days later I watched as the elegant prototype accelerated across the grass airfield, tucked its leggy undercarriage out of sight, and climbed away into the autumn sun, far out over the Severn estuary. From then on a career in the Royal Air Force became my dearest ambition.

In a matter of weeks circumstances beyond my control were to change all that. At No 1 Central Medical Board in London I failed the eyesight test. However war was fast approaching and there must be some other way. Back in Glasgow once more I applied to join 602 Auxiliary Squadron. After meeting the CO, Squadron Leader Farquhar, it seemed likely that I would be accepted, but there was another medical

Judging height by perspective. An unrecognised skill.

to face. When he had completed his examination, the medical officer looked at me and shook his head: "I'm afraid you could never land a Tiger Moth, let alone a fast fighter like a Gladiator, and as for low flying you'd kill yourself."

Strange that he should say Gladiator when the squadron was replacing its Gauntlets with Spitfires. Was he, by deliberate choice of words, seeking to underline how far I fell short of the standards? To deter me from ever trying again.

Something happened about that time which had a profound effect on what was to occur later. In my frustrated enthusiasm I had started to draw aircraft – in all sorts of situations – but especially low flying, approaching to land and taking off. As I struggled to learn and apply the rules of perspective, and looked at the results, it stood out a mile. Perspective itself must be the way to judge height. Not some continuous squinting and refocusing process on the texture of the landing ground beloved of the aero medics.

I could not change their belief – nor the tests derived from it – which always tripped me up. But it seemed obvious that I could land an aircraft and go low flying, as well as the next chap, and the coming war would surely give me an opportunity.

Our last real peacetime family holiday together was in the late summer of 1938 – grouse shooting, near Hawick in gorgeous August weather. Angus Macfarlane-Grieve had rowed with my father in the College boat and served with him in the 18th DLI – now he was master of University College Durham. His family had owned the estate and shooting box, with its director's railway halt at nearby Shank End, since Victorian times.

Well over six feet tall, thin, not a grey hair on his head, with a central parting like my father as was the fashion in their day, he much enjoyed being addressed as Uncle Angus. Although the kindest of men, modest to the point of diffidence, he was totally intolerant of the least bad behaviour. There was about him a steeliness which was quite disconcerting. Made worse because he was extremely short sighted and wore very thick pebble glasses. So that when he went quiet, and fixed you with a long look, it was difficult to read any message in his eyes let alone what was going on behind them. I was very fond of Uncle Angus. After my father died in the sixties he made a point of inviting my wife Anne and I to dine with him annually in his London club. They were rather special occasions, full of old world courtesy.

That holiday was one to remember. Unbelievable breakfasts – starting with coarse, lightly salted, porridge with cream, served in a wooden bowl with a horn spoon – loads of fruit and several nourishing courses to follow. Important he said, for our survival, should the picnic lunch prove inadequate! Wonderfully energetic, mentally relaxing days, walking the fells, winding through the little coniferous woods and fording the burns – gun dogs and grouse, wily weaving snipe. Then back in time for tea and crumpets, changing for dinner and evenings round the fire. The end of an era – whilst our world rolled on towards war, and over the hills to the north the mortar ranges rumbled and banged through day and night.

CHAPTER THREE

FIELD GUNS AND FRUSTRATION

Almost a year later when war broke out, I had already enrolled as a first year student in mechanical engineering at Glasgow University. Thinking that if for a start I couldn't fly them perhaps I could shoot them down, I applied immediately for anti-aircraft and coast defence. But the army rightly considered that ack ack and CD was not for youngsters and sent me, six months later, to field artillery.

Life in a training regiment is mostly spent breaking in new recruits, as practised by armies everywhere, and the unit near Harrogate was no exception. Long days – up at six, PT, square bashing and gun drill – a punishing routine. To which, very soon was added guard duty – two on and four off – throughout the 24 hours, for three long days on end.

Gun drill provided the battery sergeant major with a special way of bending us to his will, because boots have to be broken in as well. By a long established process combining polish, spit, a toothbrush handle and much elbow grease you could produce a mirror finish – especially on the toecaps. Kneeling on the gravelled parade ground surface, around the guns, could create untold damage if you were careless and our sergeant major was utterly pedantic in perfecting our kneeling positions – and so ensuring that the worst happened. Back in our barrack rooms, as we set to work once more, we cursed him endlessly.

But we were young and fit, life was fun in spite of it all, and the spa town of Harrogate was only five miles away. So three of us spruced ourselves up – blancoed and polished – and took off to sample its delights. We were in for a rude awakening.

First port of call was a rather plush looking cocktail bar. We marched confidently in, chatting noisily, sat down and looked at the price list. Realising that more than two rounds would put us seriously in debt, we ordered the cheapest drinks on offer. Taking a large mouthful of my whisky and orange I looked round and nearly choked. Apart from the threatening silence there was an air of serious and ostentatious wealth about everyone in the place – especially the female majority – although most of them were too old to be of interest. They looked us up and down with varying expressions of disgust. It was quite clear that they were much put out by our presence. The war, already disrupting our lives, had barely touched them as yet until our arrival on the scene.

From there it was all downhill. The idea of three young gunners in boots, and rough khaki battledress, was obviously as unacceptable to them as their wealthy arrogance was to us. We finished our drinks and moved out to the nearest pub to be welcomed rather more warmly.

This varied introduction to military life happened to coincide with the run up to Dunkirk, and we almost failed to realise its significance, until our 1918 style eighteen pounders were taken away to help re-equip the returning troops.

The growing risk of airborne invasion brought a change of scene, to Yeadon, for airfield defence. A party of the longest serving trainees, those who had been at Harrogate for almost three months, together with several NCOs and an officer, moved into the empty RAF quarters and prepared to hold out against all comers.

From our main defensive position, on a hill overlooking the airfield, the place looked like a morgue. 609 Squadron, the local auxiliary unit, had left to take part in the aerial battles over southern England and the Avro shadow factory, which would eventually be producing Lancasters in their hundreds, only existed on paper.

For company we had three local brickies. Large, muscular, beer bellied and totally idle. They were supposed to be building the pillbox in which we might have to fight for our lives, and theirs too, come to that. But they were not bothered at all until the sergeant major made some very pointed remarks about putting his bayonet where it would hurt!

Our weapons were pretty limited, rifles, Molotov cocktails[1], and the crudest imaginable dummy gun on which we continued to practice our drills. That the latter, which had been constructed from the wheels, axle and shafts of an old farm cart, surmounted by a rusty length of stove pipe would have deceived the enemy seems highly improbable. As for machine guns, there were none at all.

The domestic site and sleeping quarters were on the edge of Otley, a small Yorkshire textile community, where the pubs were friendly and the locals enjoyed their beer. They responded with enthusiasm to the victories against the Luftwaffe in the south and there were some mighty parties. One of our number, himself a local, found temptation all too great and arrived regularly on our nightly stand to parade rather the worse for wear.

Although he managed to conceal this fairly well, his little weakness had been spotted by our detachment commander. An unpleasant character, with a permanent chip on his shoulder, who was always looking for some unfortunate on whom to vent his spleen.

And so on an August evening, after the air battle had gone rather well, the defenders of Yeadon were treated to an episode of high comedy. Our hero, trying desperately to avoid swaying, confronted by his officer who knew that he had cornered him at last.

"Gunner Bloggs you're drunk!"

"Me? – not me sir!"

Incredibly he had pulled himself together and was standing rigidly to attention. Then the faintest trace of a smile as, in his drunkenness, he almost succumbed to dumb insolence. So they stood, facing each other at close quarters, officer and man, a ludicrous tableau, as the daylight slowly faded, until the sergeant major's voice broke the silence in scarcely veiled tones of contempt.

"Dismiss the parade sir?" And we fell out in the darkness – collapsing in silent, helpless, laughter.

The army moves in mysterious ways and a batch of OCTU[2] postings came through with little evidence of any selection procedure. The 'lucky' ones transferred to a requisitioned hotel in nearby Ilkley, wore white bands on their forage caps, and started to learn how to be officers and gentlemen for the duration. No gun drill now, but there was plenty of physical training and route marching, to help make good the ravages of life at Yeadon.

It was back to school with a vengeance, lectures and tests, and a need for at least some 'homework' in the evenings. An introduction to the mysteries of MT included motor cycles – on one of which I nearly wrote myself off – and driving instruction on heavy vehicles with crash gearboxes. Years later, when I bought an ancient Alvis big port beetleback, attracted by its sporty styling and an engine which could still take it up to fifty-three in third per the maker's handbook, the experience proved invaluable.

Amongst the more durable memories of Ilkley, was a stand-too early one September morning, one of the rare occasions when church bells were rung during the war. It lasted for hours and hours and no weapons were issued, not even rifles and bayonets. Were we to fight those German paratroopers with our bare hands for God's sake? Nobody could tell us what we were supposed to do. Even when the parade was eventually dismissed, and confined to camp for the rest of the day, there was no explanation.

When the course ended, in time for Christmas leave, three of us had been posted to the 27th Army Field Regiment stationed at Melton Mowbray. We were joining a regular unit which had been evacuated at Dunkirk, and about to become its first wartime trained subalterns.

The officers of 24 Battery lived in a requisitioned Edwardian house which served as the mess. Due to a shortage of rooms a few of the most junior, which included the new arrivals, were billeted out. We probably enjoyed greater comfort than our seniors but, as a way of breaking down barriers, it was not a good idea.

Our gun crews billeted in the Coleman (of mustard fame) family's stables – beautifully built in the most durable quality materials – were like pigs in clover. They had never had it so good. It has to be said that they accepted their new and raw subalterns more easily and readily than did their officers – at least initially – and in time honoured fashion the senior NCOs helped to guide and educate us and keep us out of trouble.

To prewar soldiers like Major Mead, the battery commander, and Aubrey Buxton, the senior captain, the arrival of two temporary and very raw second lieutenants must have been viewed with misgiving. Their attitude, quite unconsciously, tended to suggest that they regarded us as inferior beings; whilst the new arrivals, for their part, had little enthusiasm for peacetime customs and courtesies and were inclined to find their amusements elsewhere given the least excuse. An uneasy relationship – which gradually improved as we grew into our jobs and came to respect the traditions of the Regiment.

The first of many moves to come ended close to the Yorkshire coast after a long detour westwards for practice firing in the Brecon Beacons. Out on the ranges, particularly in the mountain-top observation posts the cold was intense. Mine was the last shoot before dark, at the end of a long day, and it was hardly a roaring success. Every ranging shot seemed to land out of sight, echoing loud and long from the far side of some distant ridge, to the great amusement of my comrades and the detriment of my slender reputation. It was hardly fair because we had been fortifying ourselves at intervals with neat whisky, trying to keep out the cold, and mine as I said was the last shoot – and the light was failing.

Hedon, a few miles to the east of Hull, was a pleasant change from the rigours of South Wales. It marked the beginning of a period during which the regiment was to lead a nomadic existence in the coastal areas of the East Riding. Our arrival coincided with the height of the night blitz and, although there were frequent air raids, the pubs and clubs in the town centre were still doing a roaring trade.

One night, for no good reason at all, the subalterns of 24 Battery left their favourite spot at an earlier hour than usual. The first bombers arrived overhead as we reached the mess, and the nocturnal hate seemed worse than usual, but nothing much happened at Hedon. Just a few sticks of incendiaries in the grounds and the pressure waves of an occasional landmine. In the morning it was a different story with all the signs of a major disaster. A pall of smoke hung over the city of Hull and an acrid smell of burning filled the air.

Later in the day, with Spitfires and Beaufighters cruising overhead to drive off any Hun reconnaissance sorties, we took a truck into town. It was a distressing sight, houses burned black and smouldering still, others with their interiors open to view – floors teetering, treasured possessions exposed for all the world to see. Whole streets were cordoned off, restricted to military and rescue vehicles, and dust-covered figures toiled in the wreckage or struggled with landmines swaying lethally on the end of snagged parachutes.

Approaching the scene of our early departure the previous night almost nothing was recognisable, hardly a building was standing. Just masses of scorched and shattered rubble. I thought of the others who had stayed on, of the cheerful band to whose music we had danced on many an occasion, and turned sadly away.

A mile or so down the road from our mess was the headquarters of a balloon barrage unit. Running into some of them, in the local pub, they invited us over for drinks on the following evening.

As it happened the Luftwaffe had chosen to go elsewhere that night and the little gathering in the Romney hut turned into an almighty thrash. Inciter in chief was Flying Officer Len Harvey, ex heavyweight champion boxer, who set a punishing pace. A splendid boozy occasion, just the tonic we all needed after the events of the last few days. But it still hurt that there was no way in which a field regiment could hit back at the enemy bombers. Even our balloon-flying hosts, with their ungainly charges, were playing a part in the air defences.

During that period of intense bombing and, following a long and tedious train journey, in April 1941 I arrived on leave very tired to join my mother and sister in the gardener's cottage near Gartshore House. The latter being my father's searchlight battery headquarters at the time. A sharp raid developed around midnight, several sticks of incendiaries fell very close, and I disgraced myself by sleeping through the lot, while mother and Rosemary were out in their night clothes dousing the flames with earth and buckets of sand.

Gartshore was not far from Grangemouth in the Forth/Clyde valley and, all that the week, there were Whirlwinds flying around. They looked fast and purposeful. A painful reminder of my intention to become a pilot which seemed to be getting nowhere.

When the RAF finally announced that aircrew volunteers were being sought from the army it seemed entirely appropriate. In point of fact it was an obvious reaction to the situation developing in 1941. Greece and Crete had fallen, ground fighting was limited to the Western Desert, and the air war against Germany had become number one priority.

This was the moment. The standards now could well be lower or less rigidly enforced, and I got down to serious eye exercises, to help with the test which had caught me out before. This time luck was on my side. A few outright lies to distract the examiner at the critical moment – talking about my prewar pilot's licence and flying the Percival Mew Gull, a pretty hot racing aircraft with a high landing speed. Perhaps he was just a sympathetic medical officer who didn't believe a word of it. No matter. I had done it. I was through.

But there were more hurdles to come. A few months passed and then an official letter arrived. It informed me that:

RAF aircrew needs have now been fully satisfied, and all further transfers from the army have been suspended... Volunteers are invited for training as army glider pilots.

Which was not the idea at all!

What to do next? And then I remembered those prewar seconded army officers flying Audaxes and Hectors. Was it still possible? A visit to the adjutant's office to look through KRs[3] and ACIs[4] – and there it was, in amended wartime form. ACI 152/40.

The object of the scheme is to produce for Army Co-operation Squadrons a number of pilots who are also trained as army officers....

It was necessary to have a minimum of eighteen months service *in a theatre of war* – whatever that might mean – before one's training could start. Another eight months to go. Better late than never. I applied at once and was accepted. The game was still on.

Whilst I had been pursuing my lonely fight much had been happening to the regiment. Shortly after the heavy air attacks on Hull there was another invasion flap and we moved up nearer the coast. Our elderly, much modified, 18/25 pounders were run into camouflaged emplacements a couple of miles inland from Withernsea. Trail arcs were dug and false angles of sight computed to give the old guns some much needed extra range. An observation post was located in the cliffs overlooking the sea. Fixed barrage lines were established. For weeks on end there was a stand-to at dawn and dusk. The legendary First Corps of which the regiment was then part, spearhead of the British Expeditionary Force in 1914 and again in 1939, had set the stage for one battle which never happened.

Soon new equipment began to arrive – 25 pounder gun/howitzers, more potent and flexible than the old 18/25s which they were replacing. Morris and Guy Quads, powerful, toad like, four-wheel-drive gun tractors – proper military vehicles to replace the requisitioned cars and vans – new and better radios. We were beginning to look like professional gunners once more.

Our CO, Lieutenant Colonel Dorling, no doubt enthused by this revival in our image, decided that it could be improved even further.

Thereafter each troop – until then identified by its letter in the rather dreary phonetic alphabet of the period – *Ack, Beer, Charlie...* became known as *Attack, Battle, Challenge...* As he said, when he was putting the idea over to us: "Do you really want to go into action calling yourselves Charlie Troop?"

When these names began to appear on our vehicles we were subjected to a fair amount of ribaldry from other units in the area. They were a bit of a mouthful on the radio. But we found a way round that and soon began to take a pride in being different as well as better. With hindsight our colonel knew his public relations.

From time to time we pulled out of our gun pits and took off on manoeuvres. Once, when so engaged, our newly christened 'Challenge' Troop was caught by the RAF. Out on a flank, standing at the ready with megaphone and director, I watched the Quads come to a halt and the crews tumbling out, swinging guns and limbers into action.

As they did so the sudden snarl of diving aircraft almost swamped the words of command and four Spitfires came slanting down out of the sun. Twice they came back, eight cannon and sixteen machine guns, against just one Motley[5] mounted Bren on a 15 cwt truck. It was an unmistakable message conveying the savage potential of fighter ground-attack.

I first met Pierre in the bar of the Beverley Arms. He wore a pilot's brevet and the word 'Belgium' on the shoulders of his blue tunic. We had much in common. Waiting for an event which would change our lives.

For Pierre it would be the liberation of his country, whilst I could hardly contain my impatience at the delayed start of pilot training. Our chance meeting turned out to be the first of many.

Once he took me up in a Blenheim, far out over the North Sea. It was a grey day, with occasional shafts of feeble sunshine penetrating the cloud. The water below looked cold and uninviting, lumpy and streaked with wind lanes. We flew on and on in silence, and then: "This is the nearest I can get to Belgium, it must do for now, but one day I shall fly above my house again."

We turned back towards the ranges off Flamborough Head, emptied our guns into the angry sea and came home through the rain and low cloud of an approaching warm front. Pierre never lived to make that flight of his dreams. When the end came on a last shipping strike, I pray that it came quickly. Now only the memory remains and his name, with all those others, on the memorial above Runnymede.

Soon after Hitler turned his armies loose on Russia the regiment left the Yorkshire coast. A visit to the ranges at Larkhill more than made up for Sennybridge the previous winter. When my turn came to control the shoot it was almost perfect. Even against moving targets the rounds of gunfire were hitting every time. As the instructors said, it showed great promise or, more likely, just beginner's luck.

We talked to them at length about the German development of air burst ranging, which enabled their artillery to go straight to fire for effect, without any prior warning or time for their opponents to take cover. Extremely effective, particularly for counter-battery work during the retreat to Dunkirk, and our chaps had hated it.

So what about giving the Huns a dose of their own medicine? Not so easy it seemed. Air-burst ranging depended on the availability of high accuracy theodolites. These were in short supply, and only issued to survey regiments, who were most unwilling to part with them or to get involved in anything so vulgar as the accurate aiming of field guns!

From Larkhill we moved into suburban south London and then at the beginning of 1942 on to Rye harbour on the Sussex coast, breaking our journey at an ancient country house overlooking the Weald of Kent.

In a scene that was almost Dickensian we sat down to our evening meal by the light of an immense log fire. The sap crackled and banged, the port circulated to an aroma of wood smoke, and the atmosphere was relaxed and friendly. A final turn around the rose garden failed to break the spell. It was one of those nights when the sky pulsed with stars and the sounds of patrolling aircraft seemed to be magnified, a thousand times, in the frozen stillness. America was in the war, the German army had ground to a halt in front of Moscow, and my departure to the RAF was drawing near. I retired to bed contented.

With the approach to Rye harbour, on the following afternoon, our spirits fell with every mile that passed. A flat and dreary landscape, which looked like the end of the world, and the first sight of our destination was not much better. A small railway siding, an isolated cluster of mean-looking houses and rusty sheds overlooking the quayside, and beyond, two hundred yards or so towards the sea, a Martello tower.

Our quarters were totally uninsulated and icy cold, there was barely sufficient accommodation, little to do and nowhere to go. Fortunately, thanks to my enthusiasm for unofficial modifications, I was otherwise engaged. After the episode of the four Spitfires, I had been looking for ways of strengthening our anti-aircraft defences, and had found a possible answer in the Motley mounting itself.

Comprising a rotating seat – to which was attached a spring-balanced arm carrying a single Bren gun – the design was such that additional guns, up to four in total, could be added by the simple expedient of cannibalising other mountings. There were problems of course, such as how to operate the multiple triggers and counterbalance each extra gun, but none were insuperable.

We built a prototype double Motley, took it to the ranges near Dungeness, fired it against a number of balloon targets and proved that it worked. The next step was to assemble a total of four double units, and install them in weapon pits, with a landline to the observer corps post in the Martello tower. After further practice firing, the gun crews were thoroughly drilled in aircraft recognition, and we were ready to go.

For three weeks, during a period of almost continuous frost and east wind, we manned those guns from before dawn until dark. There was an occasional alert – but we never saw a thing or fired a shot.

We made two more trips to the ranges. The first was to try out my *pièce de resistance*, a quadruple Motley unit, on which the guns were to be fired and reloaded in successive pairs. Unfortunately the inertia of four Brens was too great for any normal gunner to handle. What we really needed by then was several four-gun bomber turrets with a hydraulic power take-off driven from a stationary engine!

The second occasion was an official demonstration of ground strafing with cannon and machine guns. A party, which included officers from all over the command, watched as twelve Hurricanes systematically demolished a line of old cars and lorries. Even with empty petrol tanks, and no fires or explosions, it was most impressive. The silence, as we moved around inspecting the results, was tribute enough.

Shortly after we left Rye harbour I was sent to Aldershot on a messing course. Amongst other delights we learned how to generate surprising amounts of heat, for cooking in the field, using old engine oil and water.

At the abattoir a poleaxed bullock and the infantry officer standing next to me collapsed at the same time. The latter recovered quickly enough, but how on earth would he cope in battle?

The best part of that course was to learn just what could be done, by keen and conscientious cookhouse staff, using standard army rations. From then on I made it my business to watch what went on and urge the cooks to do better. Surprisingly they rose to the challenge and started to take a renewed pride in their culinary skills. Their customers were pleased, my colleagues quietly amused, and it really was rather satisfactory.

By early spring the regiment was under orders to move overseas. A quick check revealed that, if I left the UK, my secondment to the RAF now only three months away would automatically lapse.

The whole process would have to start all over again – 18 months after arriving in India, where it was rumoured that the unit was going. After an appeal to the colonel fortunately reason prevailed. I was posted Officer i/c Home Details.

Amongst the forty or so who remained behind was Adam de

Hegedus, Hungarian journalist, writer and student of human nature. In a book[6], published about three years later, he accused me of running a commando regime.

He was absolutely right and our camp surroundings were perfect, with a wooded hollow which echoed to thunderflashes and blank cartridges, as I put my OTC field day experience to good use and ensured that every attack was made uphill. Actually it was important to keep a mixed bunch of men, including several known criminals, occupied and out of mischief. As most of them were posted afterwards to the artillery depot at Woolwich, where conditions were reckoned to be tough, my so-called commando training can have done them no harm at all.

CHAPTER FOUR

BROON FOCKERRS

For my final spell of army life commonsense triumphed splendidly over bureaucracy. In May 1942 I was to be attached to an army cooperation squadron for unspecified liaison duties. It was an admirable solution. In the event it turned out far better than I dared hope.

Twinwood Farm, on the edge of a low plateau overlooking the River Ouse, had once been considered as a municipal airport for Bedford. Now a satellite of Cranfield, home of 51 Operational Training Unit, it was used for night fighter training and shared with the unit to which I was about to report.

613 City of Manchester had been a peacetime auxiliary squadron. Until recently it had been based at Doncaster. As high speed single-seat fighter reconnaissance had become the norm, replacing the slow and vulnerable Lysanders which had taken such a beating in the Battle of France, the squadron had re-equipped with Tomahawks and then Mustangs. Now it had become the reconnaissance squadron of 9th Armoured, commanded by General Horrocks, and each aircraft carried the division's black and white panda head painted large on the forward fuselage.

Most important, for my alleged liaison duties, enquiries revealed that the squadron had a Tiger Moth, a Master III and a Battle on strength. Even better, after discovering that I was destined for pilot training, George Buckley – commanding A Flight – consulted the CO and they decided that this should commence forthwith.

From then on, whenever conditions were suitable, I was airborne in the Tiger. Ron Smith and Reggie Trapp, a golf professional from Newton Abbott, were my unofficial instructors. Despite the pressures of Mustang training they were generous with their time and, before long, I was almost ready to go solo.

One day, during the usual midday lull in Bisley circuits and bumps, the squadron commander took me for a check. After stalling and spinning we returned to the airfield where, using the triangular patch of grass between the runways, I managed to pull off some reasonable landings. As we taxied in I heard his voice through the Gosport tubes: "Technically there's no reason at all why you shouldn't go solo, but I can't send you off, I do hope you understand. I'm very sorry."

It was disappointing, but I did understand. Just to imagine the aftermath of an incident with the squadron's Tiger, flown solo by an unqualified army officer, was enough! Never mind. My day would come.

In all I must have flown about fifty hours, more than half in the Tiger. Reggie, who was elected aerobatics instructor, nearly put me off for life by pulling an inordinate amount of g on the recovery from his first demonstration loop. He apologised profusely, explaining that he had not aerobatted a Tiger for some time, and thereafter all was well.

A few weeks later he invited me to spend a weekend with him and his family in Devon. They were kindness itself, and the meals were unbelievable – even to the clotted cream. They must have been saving up their rations for weeks. At lunch on the day we left I watched him sitting there, his wife and children around him, and thought of the time, not far distant, when he could be taking his Mustang into action. And I thanked my lucky stars that I was still single.

One trip, wind finding in the Battle, confirmed my feelings about this underpowered monster. Thank goodness Ron was upfront – comfortable and relaxed. I trusted him absolutely. But he seemed miles away under the long glasshouse and everything, except landing, seemed to happen at about 120 mph. The initial climb was alarming in the extreme. When the driver selected coarse pitch the whole contraption almost fell out of the sky. Once again I determined to find out more about it – and the Henley.

The rest of my flying at Twinwood was in the Master. On each occasion there was some allegedly important communications purpose. Ron was up front but I did most of the flying, and practised pilot navigation, from the rear seat. It was pleasant, bowling along at 180 mph behind the smooth running Wasp engine, learning one's way around England.

Once we were trapped by weather at Snailwell and I was able to see a Typhoon, for the first time, at really close quarters. 56 Squadron commanded by the same Hugh Dundas of my Aysgarth days – 'Cocky' to his friends – was first to be equipped with the new fighter. He invited me to explore it and somehow I knew that it was for me. Still wingless and in army uniform I told him so with all the arrogance of youth.

He looked at me sadly, listed their problems, called me an idiot, and started talking about the spate of engine failures from which they were suffering, and the pilot who had crashed that very afternoon. He had tried to stretch his glide and stalled in just short of the boundary.

Although there was no fire, the remains were not a pretty sight and, in the mess that evening, the Sabre's reliability was the subject of much adverse comment. Cocky never liked the Typhoon. In one sense he was right. It takes time to sort out a new engine/airframe combination and the Typhoon was all of that. Later I would learn much more. However I had seen enough of the Typhoon to convince me. I had to fly it on ops.

On another cross country we were already aboard for the return flight and the aircraft was being refuelled by a WAAF. As the bowser moved off she sat on the starboard wing root and replaced the filler cap. Then she slid towards the trailing edge, right over the blade-shaped undercarriage indicator, and we had visions of a major disaster. Fortunately all that happened was an expression of great surprise on her face and a massive tear in the crutch of her battledress trousers. She explored the damage, her standard issue 'passion killers' clearly visible, then clutched herself together grinning sheepishly as Ron ran through the starting drill. It was a hilarious return trip on what turned out to be my last flight with the squadron.

613 had been marvellous. They had welcomed me from the start as one of themselves – insisting on sharing their aircrew meals with a wingless 'Brown Job'. More important, they allowed me to prove to myself that, whatever the medicos had said in the past, I could land an aircraft.

As a result I was able to face the pressures of grading school in November 1942 with that major uncertainty resolved and some useful flying experience under my belt[1]. I shall always be in their debt.

13 ITW[2] was a happy interlude, in good company, the South Devon coast at its autumn best and Torquay still preserving much of its prewar charm. There was even a genuine – if elderly – palm court orchestra and a clientele reminiscent of the cocktail bar episode in Harrogate, if a deal more threadbare and careworn, for the war had taken its toll. However, although we were now commissioned and numerically stronger, the 'Tea Dances' were not held at a very suitable time of day and it has to be said that they did not appeal. It was to the pubs that we directed our steps – warm and relaxing – especially on Saturday nights.

We were an unruly course, seconded army officers and RAF aircrew remustering as pilots, out for a bit of fun with a determination not to conform or to be treated as new recruits. The honours were pretty even. We defeated the officers outright. They had little enough experience and no idea how to handle us. The NCOs were made of sterner stuff, the drill sergeants in particular being adept at conveying well known expressions like "You horrid little man – SIR!" without ever putting them into words.

It was a pity that our first trial of strength had to be with these professionals, but it was almost inevitable. The idea of drilling again like a bunch of rookies was offensive. Perhaps we could encourage them to have second thoughts by putting on an immaculate performance. So that the whole thing would be seen as an utter waste of time.

Unfortunately we counted without 'Nobby' Clarke. Lanky and seemingly uncoordinated, with rather bent features, Nobby was an odd ball. Giving an impression of cluelessness which he elaborated by expressions such as "It jolly is!" and "I jolly won't!" A natural comedian who was accident prone. Never, let it be quite clear, in an aeroplane. But quite deliberately as part of the image.

Early one morning, just as we were getting well into our stride as the faultless drill squad, Nobby had a genuine and disastrous accident. He saluted to the left with his left hand! Our instructors had a field day – suggesting that if one highly trained officer could make such an error there would be others. Bad habits, picked up on war service, must be eradicated. On second thoughts our special course might be in need of even more square bashing than usual. The message was clear. We had lost.

In reality the drill instructors were a good bunch, who took pride in their work and earned our respect. At ITW, dealing with aircrew trainees impatient to be on their way, they had an unrewarding task.

In the classrooms we battled with the intricacies of navigation, stripped and rebuilt the .303 Browning until we could do it blindfolded, and sweated to make twelve words a minute at Morse. Meteorology, with hindsight, was treated surprisingly in the abstract. For our future safety in the air might well depend on a good practical understanding of the subject – and particularly of frontal systems.

Almost from the moment of our arrival a state of warfare had existed between Pat Garland, at thirty-six the old man of the course, and the CO. The latter, portly and slow witted, was no match for Pat's rapier-like charm and determination.

When his brother won a posthumous VC, attacking the Maastricht bridges, Pat decided to transfer to the RAF. Now en route to Mustangs it never occurred to him that he was well past the age at which most fighter-recce pilots would be retiring from ops.

As the weeks went by the relationship between Pat and the CO got steadily worse. Matters came to a head one Saturday night when the regular pub crawl, returning to base, found that the bar had just been closed. Pat's *bête noir* was there, large as life, smiling at our discomfiture. When he refused to reopen the bar there was near mutiny.

The next morning Pat put his troops to work and shortly after dark everything was in place. A light-fingered character had dealt with the lock on the French windows to the CO's office. A large and smelly ewe, 'borrowed' from an unsuspecting local farmer, had been herded in for the night. And just to be sure that she was comfortable we left her with a supply of hay and water and a large amount of straw bedding.

It was a great pity that the CO's reaction could not be recorded for posterity. But it was enough that the whole course was summoned to view the results, presumably in an effort to get someone to talk, and to see for ourselves that the wretched man was speechless with rage. He left no stone unturned in his efforts to find the culprit. Every vehicle on the place, service and civilian, was checked for sheep droppings, and the local farmers all received a visit. But he drew a complete blank.

Around this time the seconded army officers acquired a collective name. It may well have arisen from the episode of the sheep. Less offensive sounding, when spoken in the Scottish vernacular, we adopted it as a sort of backhanded compliment from our RAF colleagues. From now on we were the "Broon Fockerrs!" – BFs for short.

My most vivid memory of ITW concerns a game of rugger, sometime in October. That game which has attracted me so much over the years – from Aysgarth and Ampleforth to Cheltenham and the House team – where John Slatter and Peter Holmes were so much better built for the scrum and I became a wing forward. Above all, until that moment, the treasured events of December 1939 when my cousin Alastair put together a scratch fifteen – all boarding school types – and we licked the local teams, with some mighty parties to follow, before going off to war.

This one was to be BFs vs. the rest. A challenge we couldn't resist. We gathered on the sports field, down by the Grand Hotel – white shorts and coloured tops, red for the army and blue for the RAF.

About halfway through the second half, when we were all beginning to feel the strain, there was the snarl of an unfamiliar aero engine and an Fw190 streaked low overhead and pulled up into a steep climbing turn.

Everyone scattered and dived madly into the boundary hedge, regardless of thorns and scratches, as the Hun fighter lined up. Cannon and machine guns winked viciously. The cover was thin and we must have been clearly visible in our sports kit, yet he missed – his shells raking the turf some yards away. Then he was gone, swinging up and round for a second pass.

I cringed to the ground, convinced that my last hour had come. But no, the same thing happened again and then, as he pulled up, a flame appeared under the fuselage. He continued climbing and jettisoned the canopy, simultaneously rolling inverted, but the nose dropped before he could get out. Later we learned that a bombardier from the nearby coastal battery, armed with a single Lewis gun, had shot him down – and probably saved our lives into the bargain.

A few weeks later we were on our way to Desford, near Leicester, exchanging the mellow South Devon air for the harsher feel of approaching winter.

No 7 Elementary Flying Training School had become a grading school. A filter through which those who passed were accepted into the Empire Air Training Scheme and those who failed could be 'returned to unit' without further cost to the taxpayer. Grading involved some twelve hours flying, mostly dual, and two 'Flying Aptitude Assessment Tests'. In addition we understood that it was necessary to go solo in less than ten hours.

Messing and sleeping quarters were in a hut which had belonged to the Leicester Aero Club. The timbered interior, with its close pitched bunks and porthole windows, was reminiscent of an ocean-going yacht gone to seed, grossly overheated and ill ventilated. But the food was good – nicely presented and served – and sleep came easily after a day in an open cockpit.

We were fortunate with the weather. It was anticyclonic throughout the whole of our course, and the fog usually cleared to allow several hours of intensive flying. A brisk walk across the airfield to the sound of Merlin engines, as Reid and Sigrist readied their latest batch of Spitfires for testing, made a pleasant start to the day.

Then the pressure was on. You pushed into the crowded flight hut, scrambled into your flying kit, and attempted to corner your instructor. There was a bit of 'first come, first served' about it all, particularly post solo. With luck you might even persuade him to book you out, in a spare Tiger, after a quick dual circuit.

Memories of Desford are of calm, cloudless days, with hardly a sign of turbulence, and the haze so thick in the circuit that it was barely possible to see the assembly sheds against the winter sun. Overhead, and on the approach, the place swarmed with Tigers. An occasional Spitfire would sweep low over the field, pull up steeply, lower its wheels while still inverted and roll out on a precise curved approach all the way to touchdown. A glimpse of what the future might hold if you made it.

The girls from the factory, with their turban-like head gear, would call at us over the fence when they came out at lunchtime. They would appear later in the local pub all spruced up – loaded with lipstick and sexually voracious – trying to lure us back to their digs. But we had the flying bit between our teeth. Then we would think again. They were doing a great job building those Spitfires in their parallel wartime lives – and they were fun. So we chatted them up, lived dangerously, and somehow survived.

Like all good things Desford came to an end. The BFs got through safely and my time with 613 paid off handsomely. But it would be almost three months before our training got under way once more, on the far side of the Atlantic.

CHAPTER FIVE

CANADA

The journey to Canada began at Hooton Park, Manchester in December 1942. The dreariest of transit camps; where there was little contact, and almost no relationship between the permanent staff and those who had the misfortune to be sent there to await a ship. Inoculations and vaccinations appeared to have the sole purpose of setting us up for the duration and flu-like symptoms abounded. We were confined to camp, allegedly to be ready for embarkation at very short notice. This was no hardship at all, as the outside world looked equally unattractive, and it never seemed to stop raining!

The train which took us north – blackout and blue bulbs through the long winter's night – stopped and shunted endlessly, and eventually delivered us to a dockside some eighteen hours later where we boarded a tender. We were tired, unwashed, and extremely hungry. Across the river, at the Tail o' the Bank (Clydeside speak), was our transport to North America.

The *Queen Elizabeth* towered above us, almost merging into the grey winter afternoon and the misty hills beyond. Embarking down near the waterline – and climbing forever – we dumped our baggage and went in search of food. It was like entering a new world. Stewards in spotless uniforms, immaculate white table linen and napkins to match – masses of freshly baked bread and slabs of fresh butter, and a meal such as we had not seen in years.

As part of the Anglo-American deal, for the wartime operation of the two *Queen* liners, catering was provided by the USA. On that westbound journey, as we enjoyed the benefits of a totally uncrowded ship, they certainly did us proud. There were perhaps fifty officers, and a couple of hundred other ranks, en route for pilot training and a small military mission bound for Washington. So we wallowed in luxury and, when a storm hit us on the third day, it was even better as the numbers were depleted by sea sickness.

At the height of that storm, in the fading light of a winter's afternoon, we talked our way on to the bridge and marvelled at this huge thing –

all 80,000 tons of it, pitching dramatically and almost taking it green over the bows! For speed was the key to her unescorted crossings. That and the information from a most secret Bletchley Park, quite unknown to us then, which must have helped to keep her clear of the U-boat wolf packs.

Arriving in New York in early January 1943 was an extraordinarily clandestine affair; extraordinary because the United States had already been in the war for some time. Security was totally over the top. We were ordered below decks and out of sight in our cabins. Only when the short winter afternoon gave way to dusk were we allowed to disembark. To be surrounded immediately by a posse of New York police, who escorted us through a myriad of underground passageways and railway tracks, until we reached the sleeper train for Canada and Moncton, New Brunswick. More food, and comfortable bunk beds, saw us through the night to a most excellent breakfast which started with blueberries and cream and ended with waffles and maple syrup.

We stayed briefly at Moncton, a simple rustic town in the grip of winter, and the transit camp was a world better than Hooton Park. Our EFTS[1] postings soon came through, with just enough time to visit Quebec for a couple of nights, to climb the heights of Abraham, discover the unpleasant effects of frost bite and confirm that the police (required to be bi-lingual) were most unwilling to address any English serviceman in his native tongue. Then it was off again through the snowfields, warm and comfortable aboard, with the huge locomotive up front, all cowcatchers, bells and whistles to lead us on the way.

The Empire Air Training Scheme was an outstanding achievement. In Canada alone the basic facts were impressive enough. The first course opened in April 1940, four months from a standing start, and by mid 1943 the number of schools had risen to ninety-two. Even more remarkable was the way in which the standards of flying training and airmanship were maintained in the face of such a huge expansion. So much depended on the instructors and it was they, above all, who made the system work. Mostly locked in for the duration as a result of age, or skills which could not be spared, the great majority would have given their eye teeth for a posting on ops. Their contribution has never been properly recognised.

Roy Waigh was one of them. He commanded one of the flights at 35 EFTS Neepawa, to the west of Winnipeg, and I was incredibly lucky to have had him as my instructor. For nothing, before or since, has had such a positive influence on my flying. A modest man, not much given to small talk, Roy was married and lived off the station. I never got to know him socially. Even so, in the short time that we were together, he was much more than just a gifted instructor. In the ways of the air and of airmanship he was my guide, counsellor and friend.

It was Roy who introduced me to the snow-covered airfield, and the winterised Tiger Moths with their canopies and skis. I flew occasionally with other instructors. But it was he who took me through the whole range of exercises, who set the standards, and taught me to be analytical about my flying.

Neepawa, where the skies were a brilliant blue and the snow was bright and clean. Where the sun always shone (well almost) and we flew morning, noon and night. It was not unusual to be airborne three or four hours a day, for several days on end, and I once managed to put almost five hours under my belt. There was a freshness about EFTS. An awakening sense of discovery almost like early childhood. As if life was starting all over again. Twinwood Farm and Desford had become part of an earlier era. And always my growing passion for the air beckoned me on.

Climbing out over the prairie for a session of aerobatics, the atmosphere was clear as crystal. The checkerboard landscape stood out against the snow, extending far beyond the horizon. Here and there a group of grain elevators, or a township, bordered the railroad track. Otherwise there was nothing. Just miles of open country, devoid of cover, the heartland of Canada's cereal farming in the iron grip of winter.

4,000 feet and a stall turn to start the sequence. Hold the dive and pull through into a loop. Up and over. Another loop. And again. Pushing the learning curve. Aware of the chief flight instructor's test to come. Now a slow roll – horizon, snow and section lines slewing horribly across my vision. It was bloody awful... I could almost hear the familiar voice ringing in my ears: "More top rudder! Keep the stick forward!"

The next one was better. And the next. But I must still talk to Roy about my rolls. A change to forced landings. Cut the throttle and swing earthwards in a long descending arc. You're getting too close to the field! Remember to warm the engine. You're still too close! Another quick burst of power. Down and down in a long slipping turn... You're too high!... More sideslip!... Then up and away before the snow can catch your skis.

My chosen field, exactly one mile square and flat as board was too easy by far. But there was no better alternative, they were all the same, hundreds of them, as far as the eye could see.

A first crack at low flying. On an afternoon when Roy was feeling benevolent. Real scenery, for a change, in the foothills of Riding Mountain. A fascinating sense of speed, as the countryside flooded past like a river in spate. Features on the surface – a farmhouse, a group of tall trees, or a sudden escarpment –rushed at you destructively.

We all longed for the day when we could practice it on our own. But the RAF knew better. They understood the dangers, the impetuosity of youth, and the deadly temptation to fly ever lower. Our time would come at OTU and not before. Unauthorised low flying was, and still is, the most heinous crime in the book. It could finish your flying career in a number of different ways, all of them unpleasant. Better by far to rely on the presence of an instructor.

Amongst that album of memories there is a vivid picture of night flying. The last landing at the end of a session. With my eye well in and my finger out. Cross wind on the final turn. Flares guttering against the snow. Green all the way on the glide path indicator[2]. The round out neat and precise. The touchdown smooth as silk. A rare moment of near perfection. I felt like a god and the mug of hot chocolate, on my way to bed, tasted like nectar.

Pride comes before a fall. And mine happened soon afterwards. One evening, towards the end of the course, the mess was almost deserted. Just the three BFs and an instructor who invited us to join him in a drink. After several double whiskies, and some prairie oysters, he announced that he had to carry out an air test before dark. He must go and do it forthwith. Would one of us like to join him?

It seemed a good idea at the time. But his air test soon developed into an impromptu aerobatic display. His loops and rolls got lower and more dangerous. Apart from the risk of sudden death this performance could mean curtains for two flying careers. There was no difficulty in feigning immediate and violent air sickness and to my great relief he took the hint. Never have I been so glad to step out of an aircraft.

On the following morning as we walked together across the snow-covered tarmac, Roy looked steadfastly into the distance:

"You were flying yesterday evening." It was a statement, not a question.

"Yes, Roy," I said, "and it wasn't much fun."

We had arrived at the aircraft. He turned and studied me carefully, more in sorrow than in anger:

"That's what I thought. I hope you'll never do it again."

The weather broke only once during our stay at Neepawa, with a blizzard which lasted for several days. Apart from that one occasion we rarely suffered from much in the way of wind, which was just as well. Skis on an icy surface could be tricky, and it was sensible to keep a close watch on the windsock. Taxiing, even in moderately gusty conditions, soon became impossible as the aircraft slithered sideways and weathercocked out of control. For the airmen, who rushed out to hang on the wing tips, the combination of cold, slipstream, and wind chill must have been quite horrendous.

During the final week of the course in early April, in the midst of cross countries, winter suddenly gave way to spring. There were problems in landing away because some of the destination airfields thawed out faster than others. Our Tigers were back on wheels, while Neepawa was still covered in snow, and my first ever runway landing occurred solo on an out and return flight to another school. Completely thrown by the dark ribbon of tarmac, in total contrast to the surrounding brilliant white, I held off much too high. A quick burst of throttle saved the day, and fortunately Tigers are strong, but it was an untidy arrival to say the least.

Two weeks later we gathered outside the hangars to arrange ourselves for a photograph in front of the obligatory aeroplane. Number 80 course was over.

Rolling across the prairie again, on the journey to Vancouver, Canadian Pacific continued to provide the best of North American rail travel. The weather had turned unexpectedly hot and ice by the hundredweight was shovelled into the long containers under the passenger compartments to keep us cool. The big coaches, equal to the best of Pullmans by day, and the upper and lower bunks which swung into place when required, were as comfortable as one could have wished. In the mornings, after the usual relaxed night between freshly laundered sheets, there was that unbelievable breakfast again – blueberries and cream, eggs sunny side up, waffles and syrup, rounded off with excellent coffee.

Then, if so disposed, you could repair to that chauvinistic delight of the North American railroads, the club compartment. A retreat where male passengers could take their ease undisturbed by the ladies. It certainly brought out the worst in our colleague Lieutenant Kenneth Morris. On his first and only visit Kenneth pushed open the door, stood for a moment like some latter day Goebbels, to whom he bore more than a passing resemblance, peered through the smoke, homed in on the spittoons and said loudly: "How absolutely disgusting!" And that from somebody who smoked his cigarettes so wet that he absolutely disgusted us.

We tried to convey silent apology to the other occupants and hustled him out before he could do any further damage. But relations were strained for the rest of the journey.

We had encountered our first government liquor store, back in February, after crossing the border between Quebec Province and Ontario. As the train slowed our fellow male passengers had started to behave most oddly. Bunching up at the doors and jumping out before it had even stopped. Joining them out of curiosity, we got swept along to a small wooden hut close to the railroad station, where they were queuing to buy a quantity of the hard stuff and offering an official looking card to be stamped.

Canada was essentially dry but you were entitled to a monthly ration, based on the province in which you lived, and a card to record your purchases. Yet by some oversight – or was it intentional? – travellers could acquire another full ration and liquor card in every province on their journey. The liquor stores were ideally placed to satisfy this arrangement. But it seemed that the railroad company had made little allowance in its schedules. Hence the mad rush to be served.

Now we knew the form – and on the way to Calgary, where we had planned to stay overnight and celebrate the first successful stage of our training, we bought our full liquor entitlements en route. The hotel was beside the railroad station, so no problem with that – and they knew the form too.

"Are you from England? And over here learning to fly?"

And they put us in rooms on the party floor.

Next morning we caught the train to Vancouver to enjoy the comforts and hospitality of Canadian Pacific Railways yet again. All afternoon we stayed in the observation car taking masses of pictures. Then another splendid meal and so to bed.

There was a reception committee at Vancouver station ready to take care of our leave. I teamed up with Geoffrey Bensusan, an infantryman of theatrical bent, to stay with a middle-aged couple whose sons were in England with the Canadian army. Their house was detached, an attractive modern chalet bungalow, with an elegantly landscaped garden full of spring colour. They were kindness itself, gave us a complete run of the place, invited us to come and go as we wished, gave us breakfast every day and were always available if we needed anything.

They were extremely proud of their two boys – who had fortunately missed the Dieppe raid with its casualties – and were desperately afraid of what the future might bring. We longed to bring them some comfort but there was so much war to come. In the end we gave them two bottles of good whisky, purchased from the bootlegger, (the hotel party at Calgary having consumed all of our earlier supplies) and promised to keep in touch. But somehow, to our shame, we never did.

After that leave in British Columbia, we returned through the Rockies, to Calgary and 37 SFTS[3]. To find that most of the BFs – sent to different places for elementary training – were back together again. A few of our fellow pupils had come straight from American flying schools where they had failed to make the grade. As was customary, and frequently successful, they were being given another chance in Canada.

Some of their stories were quite extraordinary. Trainees on the most junior course were required to eat 'square meals', following a dogleg route from plate to mouth. Marching round the perimeter track in full kit and parachute during the heat of the day, or sitting on the 'T' after flying was over, were typical punishments for quite trivial offences. Instructors often shouted in the air and threatened physical violence. Maybe this worked with the average American flight cadet, but it went down rather badly with our chaps.

In contrast to this brash American scene I was singularly fortunate, once more, in the matter of instructors. Ossie Ossulton had almost never been known to raise his voice in anger and his easy manner concealed a highly professional approach. He had a remarkable way with him – which pushed and encouraged his pupils and yet, almost paradoxically, exercised a powerful restraint on their youthful exuberance.

We set out to master the Harvard's complexities – variable pitch propeller, retractable undercarriage and flaps – sitting in the cockpit and running through the drills until we knew them by heart. First solo came up in less than five hours and we were soon well into the new training programme.

The Harvard had a tailwheel with a very small positive castor angle and a rudimentary form of steering. The makers, North American Aviation, obviously approved of this arrangement because it appeared on the Mustang in a slightly different form. Described in the pilot's notes thus:

Steerable tailwheel, this springs into engagement with the rudder so that, when taxiing or in gradual turns, it can be used for steering. If a sharp turn is made, the tailwheel can spring out of engagement, this will occur more easily if the stick is not held back.

What they did not explain was that if a swing started on landing and this was corrected by differential braking, which in turn caused the pilot to apply an unintentionally large rudder angle – the tailwheel could unlock and precipitate a ground loop. It sounds worse than it really was. But for all that it was a feature which I did not like. In other ways the Harvard was pleasant and easy to fly. Our Mk II version was said to have a more docile stall than the Mk I. It still spun very positively and would do splendid flick rolls.

Geoffrey Bensusan, my mate in Vancouver, good looking with dark ginger hair and a luxuriant moustache, could easily have modelled for the 'Two Types' of the 8th Army cartoons. He had coped well with the Tiger Moth. But the Harvard defeated him. It was as if, by nature, he was too laid back to master its added complexities. When he was RTU (returned to unit) it hurt him, and it hurt us too, because he was a very decent and amiable fellow.

Shortly after soloing the Harvard I visited the largest store in town.

To my surprise they could supply sun glasses to your own prescription. Better still, one of the frames on offer looked almost identical to the standard service issue. I had solved the problem of flying in spectacles, should I wish to do so (because they were not vital) without being found out.

As the course progressed some of the flying took place from Airdrie about a dozen miles north of Calgary. A dry featureless sort of place where you could sunbathe between flights, and take photographs round the airfield, which would have been out of the question back at base. After a night flying session it was customary to sleep there and the round trip was sometimes completed with an early formation practice on the way home.

Hardly a tremor in the air. Not a cloud in the sky. The climb out steady as a rock. The mud brown hills, bordering the prairie, looked parched and dusty – the mountains beyond in strong relief against the distant blue. Each time the formation swung into a turn the morning sun came flooding across the cockpit, blinding you with its glare. Working hard to hold station beside the leader you were aware, as always, of his instructor watching you like a hawk. Distrusting. Ambivalent. As if warning you to keep your distance and in the same breath challenging you to do better.

Later, whilst we sweated to fly accurately in the heat and turbulence of the day, small cumulus filled the sky. When the air was more unstable those harmless fair weather clouds grew into thunderstorms which swept across the countryside in the late evenings. It was in such conditions that Ian Stewart lost his life.

Flying night circuits from Airdrie he got caught in a line squall, blinded by heavy rain and low cloud. His aircraft must have been thrown around by the violent turbulence, toppling the gyro instruments and disorienting him completely. He ended up in a spiral dive from which there was no recovery. A few days later six of his fellow BFs were pall bearers at his funeral.

Incensed at the instruction to carry his coffin at the 'trail' instead of shoulder high, to avoid offending the locals, we had argued strongly against it: "To hell with Canadian practice," we had said – "Ian was our friend, not theirs." But the station commander was adamant.

It was an arid service, in a soulless modern church and the committal was hot and dusty. A sad waste of a young life. We took ourselves back to the mess for one of our better parties, a spontaneous gathering of the hard core BFs, in farewell to the first of their number to get the chop.

After that we needed a break – and what better than Banff, just eighty miles away in the Rockies. It had looked marvellous on the trip to Vancouver and the reality was even better. The spacious Banff Springs

Hotel, a huge echoing edifice reminiscent of southern Germany, was comfortable and uncrowded.

Lazing around a swimming pool was never my idea of fun. But this one was fed with hot mineral waters and the glass walls looked out on the Cascade Mountains. Besides which we had brought a good supply of rye whisky. Alcohol and altitude are a heady mixture often, in my experience, without the penalty of a hangover. For much of the time I was gently inebriated and totally captivated by British Columbia. Even to the extent of thinking about bush flying there after the war, if that ever came to pass.

When we got back to Calgary an army of graders and road making machinery was hard at work, building a runway to the west of the airfield. The first Airacobras and Kittyhawks started to use it before it was even finished. They came straight in from the south in loose gaggles, without any pretence of a circuit, and were gone in the morning before we were up and about. Their numbers increased day by day and soon there were bombers as well. Aid for our Russian allies and tangible evidence of the massive production capacity of the American war industry.

With the end of the course in sight the pace quickened. Formation flying, navigation and gunnery were the order of the day, together with long sweaty sessions under the hood. Anson sorties were an unwelcome chore more appropriate to navigator training, and the staff pilots were given to practicing evasive action whenever one of the 'hands' went aft to relieve himself. The BFs evolved a punishment to fit the crime. An ambush in the dark and a jug of iced water delivered precisely into the front of the perpetrator's trousers.

Just after the final flying tests my logbook was taken away. It would be returned, bound in leather, on Wings Parade. The custom at Calgary for those who came top of the course. I thought with gratitude of 613 Squadron, of Roy Waigh and Ossie. It was very much their show.

CHAPTER SIX

PRELUDE TO BATTLE

At Moncton, waiting for the next boat home at the end of August 1943, I spent much of the time with David Tomlinson. Already making a name for himself on stage and screen, his past had caught up with him, and he was being urged to leave the RAF and return to acting. He could, they said, make a greater contribution to the war effort by playing in patriotic films, and yet he desperately wanted to fly on ops. We talked about it often during those idle weeks and I argued that, as an actor, his knowledge of the RAF and service flying would be invaluable. And so it proved to be, for his portrayals of aircrew, in later wartime releases, were quite masterly.

When our sailing orders came through it was the *Queen Elizabeth* again, out of Halifax, and crowded with American troops bound for Europe. With some 15,000 on board the enlisted men had to share bunks, on a rota basis, which must have added considerably to the discomforts of the voyage. Meals were served in an endless series of sittings, and we soon got brassed off with the nonstop tannoy messages: "This is the third call for dinner. All with white cards form your line."

In fact there was only time to provide each passenger with two meals a day. So the wise made up a bacon butty at breakfast, to fill the midday void, then slept and read the long hours away until the next call came round.

All day long, a mass of American soldiers surged round the halls and stairways. Little groups huddled in every available corner playing poker or shooting craps. The air reeked of cigars and the decks were littered with empty tins of Coke. Fortunately the weather was calm and for much of the time our presence was concealed by thick banks of fog. Only the occasional glimpse of an escorting Catalina, or a sudden burst of fire from the twin Bofors high up in the superstructure, broke the endless monotony of those four long days and nights. It was a merciful release when the ship reached her anchorage in the Clyde.

An account of the *Queens'* trooping activities during the war alleged that the huge passenger loads rendered them barely stable. Had an enemy appeared violent evasive action would have been quite impossible. Sometimes it is just as well to be ignorant.

Bad enough to return from the peacetime comforts of Canada to the winter of 1943/4. Worse still to be faced with a period of enforced idleness, at the Aircrew Reception Centre, and Harrogate had taken a distinct turn for the worse since my gunner days. It was a transit camp like Hooton Park, no games or organized activities whatsoever, no personal contact with the staff who deliberately kept a very low profile indeed. The worst time of all. A brief interlude with the Aircrew Officers School at Sidmouth, a sort of post-graduate ITW, helped to keep us occupied and was actually welcomed. Escape and evasion had been added to the syllabus and, amongst other delights, we were shown how to break the neck of a German sentry with his own coal scuttle helmet. It was said to be very easy, but practice was forbidden!

Small arms training was also included, to help us play an effective part in airfield defence, but not to increase the firepower of friendly resistance fighters should we be shot down amongst them. Our duty in those circumstances was to evade and get home. Not to stay and fight.

As we practised with rifle, bayonet and sandbag dummies, and carried out firing practice on the Sten, that explanation began to sound less and less likely. Maybe there was a more sinister purpose behind our spell at Sidmouth – like a last minute transfer to the RAF Regiment or as infantry reinforcements for the second front. Difficult to judge, because we only knew the RAF side of the story, and mostly by rumour, but it was alarming enough.

The surplus in single-engined pilots was now so great that the vast majority, apart from the BFs who were lined up for fighter-recce come what may, were likely to become reinforcements for Bomber Command. Worse still the AFU[1]/OTU pipeline was running in excess of squadron needs and we might be stranded at Harrogate for months on end.

From the moment of our arrival at Peterborough these fears were all forgotten. A first glimpse of the airfield on a frosty December afternoon – yellow flare path lights in the dusk, Masters on the approach like geese against the sunset – was more than enough. The BFs were back in business. No 7 (Pilot) Advanced Flying Unit was a place of contrasts. In the depths of a British winter, our flying hours built up even faster than they had done in Canada. A tribute to the way in which the unit was run, the standards of aircraft serviceability, and above all to the instructors. On the other hand there was little evidence of objectives and there were no progress tests.

I wondered, at first, if the sole purpose was to keep us in flying practice until an OTU, somewhere, was ready for another intake. So why the deliberate pressure? Why were we into pair flying, crossover turns, and the rudiments of battle formation – all flown solo with an instructor leading – when type conversion was barely complete? Why the urgent cut and thrust around the blackboards in our smoke-filled crew rooms – moving on, forcing the pace – focusing on the next stage? Extraordinary when you think about it. We were longing to complete our training and move on. They were preaching to the converted.

No question about the somewhat open-ended syllabus with its strong emphasis on tactics, evasion and more. Advantage of height. "Hun in the sun – thumb to the sun" (the latter bit of doggerel with palm downwards giving the best finger four orientation with two pilots looking in the most dangerous direction). Max power when breaking into an attack. Warnings about low speed – avoiding negative g manoeuvres and the advantages of deliberate skidding under fire. All this backed up by air-to-air camera-gun sorties, practice interceptions, and attacks on 'enemy bombers'.

The message was clear. The BFs, heading for fighter-recce, had joined a pre OTU course for fighter boys in the traditional mould. Not really as bad as it sounds. A solution was certainly possible – more flexibility and a gently massaged programme which would have been equally acceptable to us and also to the ground-attack fraternity who would be needed in greater numbers.

The instructors were a great bunch. In the circumstances they could not have been more helpful. Many of them had been around for a long time. Like those in Canada, they longed to fly on ops. It was rotten luck.

Conversion to European conditions was taken seriously and the need for night training brought an introduction to the joys of Two Stage Amber, known as 'sodium flying'. The former was largely a matter of navigation, learning to cope with a mass of ground detail, poor visibility, the absence of section lines, and a careful introduction to the hazards of a maritime climate.

Sodium flying, monitored by an instructor/safety pilot, turned brightest day into darkest synthetic night. It was an unpleasant exercise and, like most of us, I disliked it intensely. The sodium goggles were cumbersome and uncomfortable, and nothing was visible except the instruments and flare path. Fortunately we were never subjected to it again after leaving AFU.

After my inexperienced encounter with the Master at Twinwood Farm, it was surprising to discover that it cruised a good deal faster than the Harvard, and had a much higher rate of climb. The stall with wheels and flaps down, and the rear canopy raised, demanded respect, as the aircraft flicked inverted without any warning, and the heavy ailerons were a disappointment.

There were many reminders of a changed world. Not least in the crowded East Anglian skies of USAF daylight ops and Bomber Command air tests. Day after day the P38s[2] from nearby Kingscliffe assembled overhead, squadron by squadron, before winging their way to war. We watched them returning seeing the gaps in their ranks.

One came home with an entire engine missing. Difficult to imagine how such a massive object could have broken away without total destruction. He passed low overhead, long after the rest of the wing had landed, escorted by his wingman and another.

Peterborough, grass and rather narrow, flanked closely on its eastern side by a range of large industrial buildings and the main London North Eastern Railway, was not the sort of place you would choose in an emergency. Particularly if you were flying a Marauder[3] with its high wing loading and tricycle undercarriage.

Arriving low and fast, our visitor landed heavily, throwing up a great shower of mud and water. The surface was wet and the deceleration minimal. Fortunately or otherwise, depending on your point of view, there was a large pillbox blocking the exit. The Marauder stopped instantly, looking much the worse for wear, and a train which was leaving Peterborough continued happily on its way. The crew bailed out, almost unhurt, with a few cuts and bruises.

When the blood wagon arrived they insisted on being taken to the officers' mess, where some kind soul opened the bar, and they were given a round on the house. Later that evening, when their transport arrived, they departed full of good cheer.

On clear nights East Anglia was lit up by a vast array of bomber airfields. Each one, with its flare path and circle of lead-in lights, resembled a faintly glittering compass. A welcome landscape in the darkness. You could tell when it was like that, long before your turn to fly, by the relaxed atmosphere in the crew room.

When marginal weather coincided with the heavies taking a break you groped around, beacon flying, and worried like hell if the flare path disappeared. With good reason too, there were no navigation aids. Radio was dubious and, unlike the bomber boys, ours was no Drem lighting system[4]. We had to make do with a few gooseneck flares[5], on a grass strip, and the river with its constant threat of fog was only a mile away.

That dangerous combination almost caught me out on 28 January, 1944. Just once, but it was enough. My return to base had been unpleasant in the extreme, ending low down, with a tight turn on to finals. Trying to judge height, with a single flare path, was difficult at the best of times. Now even that had been reduced to a few flickering patches of brightness flowing towards me out the murk. My hold off was fast and high, no question of going round again in those conditions, and the last moments of flight were alarming to say the least. The buffet warning, the starboard wing dropping violently with the onset of that lethal stall brought me out in a cold sweat, as we hit the ground and slewed away from the flares. It had been much too close for comfort.

Alf Warminger was an AFU instructor who had actually flown on ops. In later years he was Sheriff of Norwich and we would become gliding colleagues and good friends. At Peterborough his calm and experienced approach could not have been bettered in preparing this exuberant sprog for his first flight in a Hurricane.

One day cruising southwards in that ancient fighter, it had been built in 1938 no less, I managed to stalk a P38. The air was full of brickwork smoke, burnt blanket smelling muck, and the visibility at cloud base very poor. Easy to creep up behind him until my propeller was only feet behind his tail. I sat there, looking along the length of the twin-booms with their big air scoops and down through the transparent rear of the humpbacked canopy, and wondered if he had fallen asleep. Suddenly he rolled onto his back faster than my ancient kite could ever follow, and pulled away in a long vertical dive.

Another twin-boom shape slanted across my bows. But this one had a bulbous fuselage and no propellers. The de Havilland Spider Crab, forerunner of the Vampire. I watched in fascination as it swept upwards and out of sight.

The Hurricane was an exciting reminder of operational flying to come. An idea which proved too much for one member of our little band. The fumes in the cockpit made him feel faint, yet no one else was affected, and carbon monoxide checks revealed nothing amiss. Quite suddenly he vanished – 'returned to unit' – the ultimate disgrace. Was he really LMF[6] at its worst? Had he deliberately applied for a pilot's course, to spin out the time before he had to face the enemy, hoping that the war might be over by then? His fellow BFs would never know.

One of us was the very opposite. Partially disabled, due to sandfly fever of the hip, he could fly OK. But getting to and from his aircraft, and climbing aboard, was difficult, very painful, and obviously getting worse. Came the day, despite sympathetic instructors and helpful ground crew, when he could no longer cope. He left us broken hearted.

The BFs moved on, in late March, to a satellite of 41 OTU on the Duke of Westminster's estate south of Chester where the approach was totally different. We flew fighters, but we were no longer fighter boys, our aircraft were means to a different end. From now on it would be singletons or pairs – with a little preliminary refresher on battle formation and crossover turns. Surprisingly, considering our future role, the first exercise was in a decompression chamber, half a dozen of us at a time, up to 30,000 feet, for a demonstration of anoxia. Much hilarity as we took it in turns to remove our oxygen masks – becoming totally incompetent and semi-conscious, with no subsequent memory of what had happened. It was a useful lesson.

After a dual check, in an elderly Mk I Harvard, it was assumed that you knew how to fly. Type conversions were to be made with a minimum of fuss. Demonstrations after that were brief and to the point. Given the basics you were expected to work things out for yourself.

Spring had come. The scent of freshly mown grass filled the air. On the Welsh mountain peaks the last of the snow had gone and the banks of the Dee beside Eaton Hall were ablaze with daffodils.

A springtime of wonderful memories. Soon after our arrival a batch of Hurricane IIcs appeared straight off the production line. With their metal-skinned wings and more powerful engines they were better than anything we had flown before. The four unfaired 20mm cannon looked suitably functional. And the essence of their newness – unblemished cockpits, smooth control mechanisms and the aromatic mixture of factory fresh materials and recently applied dope – was an added pleasure on every flight.

There was something immensely satisfying about the rugged feel of a Hurricane. The sturdy wide track undercarriage, the straightforward handling and the commanding position from which you viewed the world at large. So what if it was slower and less elegant than the Spitfire – this was a man's aeroplane in which you would have been content to go to war. But the Hurricane's fighting days were almost over. I recalled the Typhoons of 56 Squadron, which had so attracted me almost two years before. Yet how could the Hurricane's successor play any part in my future, as a seconded army officer, indelibly labelled 'fighter-recce'?

Fighter-recce – for a start our navigation had to be improved until we could find our way to an exact position and it had to be straight in and out again, otherwise you greatly increased the risk of being caught by flak or fighters. 'Pinpointing' was easy to set up, given a large-scale map and a prewar tourist guide. It was an exercise that came in two versions. Start out with a map reference and bring back the description of a building or other feature, or the reverse, with a photograph to look at beforehand and a defined area in which to search.

For Tac-R[7] training we could hardly have been better placed. The roads south from Glasgow and Liverpool, and to the west of Birmingham were carrying large numbers of troops on their way to the concentration areas for 'Overlord'[8]. These military convoys were used to teach us the principles of medium and low level tactical reconnaissance. Valuable undoubtedly, yet there was surprisingly little evidence that our reports were being monitored by instructor check sorties, or in any other way.

Nor were we given any serious training with ground troops using camouflage, or in minimising the risks from flak or, for that matter, in being bounced by enemy aircraft. For the latter an occasional sortie by one of the instructors, with an otherwise idle Mustang, would have been more than sufficient to keep us on our toes.

One hot and hazy afternoon David Hurford and I were briefed for a practice Tac-R sortie. By now we had put in some twenty hours apiece on the Hurricane. Flying it was becoming second nature. Even selecting undercarriage 'up', which meant changing hands on the stick, had become a practised art.

Our departure was neat and tidy, no porpoising to spoil it, as the wheels tucked themselves away. We moved quickly into battle formation, riding the turbulence, climbing through the murk, into air which was calm and clear. The haze layer, falling away beneath our wings, had a well defined upper surface. It veiled the landscape in shades of purple and bronze, and thickened into the distance, until it became another horizon hiding the earthly one below.

Our task, searching the roads along the Severn valley, would not be easy. But, before long, there was something very different to distract us.

Interference on the radio, faint and disjointed at first, then louder and unbroken. The great rolling cadenzas filled my earphones. Beethoven's Emperor Concerto. An unforgettable experience which I shall treasure always.

I pulled closer to my companion and admired the powerful hump-backed shape and the spinning disc of the big constant speed propeller drifting towards me. David, in the rostrum of his cockpit, visibly conducting with his left hand! "Where's your baton, David?"

We dropped briefly into the murk, towards the river bridges below, looking for signs of movement and his reply echoed my thoughts: "Absolutely super! Shall we turn back and hear the rest?"

The nobility of the heavens seemed all around us, as we cruised on, accompanied by those fading sounds from a distant age. And the magic of our Hurricanes added to the spell. Winging across the years...

The Luftwaffe, in its great defensive battles over *das Vaterland*, knew how to use the power of music to motivate its pilots. Just as today's America Cup contenders and others, with their modern audio systems, apply the same techniques to blast and hype their way to victory. Much easier to understand after that memorable sortie above the River Severn.

Low level Tac-R was something else again. Down on the deck, you hugged the contours, watching for power lines, checking your track. In a Tiger Moth the countryside had flooded past like a river in spate. With a Hurricane it became a raging torrent. Slowing as you lifted briefly over some obstruction, accelerating violently as you dropped close to the ground on the other side. A familiar illusion which never failed to excite. Low flying was and always will be an addiction, an exhilarating pastime, requiring skill and absolute concentration.

The lethal temptation, to fly lower still, was always present. There was an issue of 'Tee Emm'[9] – with a picture displaying the remains of a Hurricane, just to remind us! A trail of wreckage littered the length of an open field and, where it ended, a larger collection of debris surrounded a battered Merlin engine and a bucket seat. That the pilot, incredibly, had survived almost unscathed was beside the point. The total disintegration of his aircraft was enough.

An isolated line of wooded hills marked by the ruins of Beeston Castle, guards the eastern boundary of the Cheshire plain. On many a day we hurdled that ridge – aiming for the distant Victorian outlines of Eaton Hall – red brick amidst surrounding green. Hard back on the stick, as the Dee glistened through the trees, and into the circuit, curbing the Merlin's song. In the wake of our passage lay a rich dairy farming countryside, large estates and well set up Georgian houses. Long after the drum roll crescendos of our low flying Hurricanes have become a distant memory, they will still be there.

Once, on my own, I was contour chasing near the borders of Shropshire and Offa's Dyke, where mountains give way to wooded hills, and castles mark the scenes of ancient wars. Suddenly I came on a long unbroken ridge, the edge of a lofty plateau, which stood high above its surroundings facing west. Something made me look closer, and there on top was a blister hangar, locked and silent, and the faint impression of a landing ground in the heather. Slowing down I could almost sense the wind striking that escarpment and the fragile sailplane shapes, poised in the updraft overhead, as I had seen them at Sutton Bank before the war.

A moment more to absorb the scene, and then out into the valley again, back to the world of Tac-R, and the roads leading south towards Hereford and Gloucester. Other times and other skills – I vowed that someday, somehow, I would be back.

Our Hurricanes were equipped for oblique and vertical photography and after a single Harvard sortie, to demonstrate the technique, you were sent out on your own. It was an effective approach because each exercise produced its own immediate results; wet prints to study whilst the flight was still fresh in your mind, and this led to a rapid improvement in performance.

The instructors had their moment of fun, demanding a vertical pinpoint of Ince Hall, a decaying country seat, which they had unearthed on the Wirral peninsular. The photographs were duly displayed, with captions suitably worded, to suggest a close family connection. All quite untrue. It was owned by the National Coal Board and demolished soon afterwards.

Squadron Leader Majumdar was our mature student. A prewar Cranwell cadet he had returned home, to early command of No 1 Squadron Indian Air Force, where he had won a DFC fighting the Japanese. Proud in the best sense of the word, a powerful character, Karen Krishna Majumdar had given up a staff appointment and dropped a rank in order to broaden his experience by flying on ops in Europe. A splendid man. In the words of that earlier war: 'One would have been happy to go over the top with him.'

But that was hardly the situation as we taxied out together and lined up for take-off. Combat was almost the last exercise before our conversion to Mustangs and, to my delight, I had been chosen to joust with this formidable adversary. Drawing the short straw perhaps, but there was much to be gained from such an encounter.

15,000 feet, and we were rushing towards each other almost head on. A brief glimpse of a grey-green shape standing on its wing tip, as it hurtled past in a violent turn, and the sudden onset of g – vision momentarily fading. Within moments we were locked into a winding match, throttles wide open, pulling on the limit... and this man was good. Almost ten years my senior and he was doing his utmost to reel himself onto my tail.

Escape from that turning contest was almost impossible, although both of us kept trying, for our aircraft were equally matched. And so, as our height drained away, we worked and sweated, and endured the g. Only the threat of cannon shells was missing as we strove to break each other's will. After what seemed an age, but was probably only a matter of minutes, our battle was deemed to be over. Inconclusive perhaps – but for me at least, as we clambered down from our aircraft and walked across to the NAAFI wagon for a much needed mug of tea, it had been a most valuable sortie. A vital stage in learning to fly an aircraft to its limits.

And yet we had only scratched the surface. There was much more to learn about combat as I was to discover. Was it pride that prevented us from being more exploratory, or more innovative? The thought that if you broke away from the winding match, the other guy would be on your tail in a flash, winning the battle. I am sure that it was, and equally, that it created an important missing link in our training.

My adversary went on to complete a tour on 35 Wing, with 268 Squadron where he clearly made a profound impact. The wing intelligence officer writes of him as:

> "(of) proud spirit and contemplative reticence... by common consent one of the elect amongst his companions... his whole

> desire was that the Indian Air Force should attain the standards of efficiency to which his prowess in action testified... one whose friendship touched me deeply."[10]

He was awarded a bar to his DFC, and then returned to India. Soon after I was saddened to hear that he had lost his life in a flying display.

Mustang conversion took place at Hawarden. We were allowed rather less than two hours general handling, plus a forty-minute sortie to be flown mainly in cloud. After that it was all gunnery mostly air-to-air, for a further eighteen hours, of which two were devoted to rather gentle camera-gun combat. Understandable that our exercises were set up in favour of applied flying at this stage. But the Allison-engined Mustang was a very different beast to the Hurricane – heavier, faster, underpowered for its weight and wing loading and fitted with large-area camber-changing flaps. At the very least we needed briefing on these features, and their effect, on operational flying and combat. Although our instructors were experienced pilots, who had flown on ops, this never happened.

The laminar section was alleged to be the main reason for its low drag wing and long range. But later investigations showed that the excellent radiator design was by far the most important factor. For the new wing section did not provide much benefit at Mustang Reynolds numbers (i.e., speed). Although it subsequently did rather well on high performance sailplanes.

The handling was good if rather bland, with greater longitudinal stability than the Hurricane and, as I was to realise later, other British fighters. I always preferred the latter for their greater manoeuvrability but the Mustang must have been more acceptable for long-range escort duties. The cockpit was clean, with a proper floor, no missing tools! The instruments and secondary controls were generally excellent, including the multi-position switch for the electric propeller mechanism. But the absence of a standard RAF blind flying panel was difficult to understand, as it had been designed to a British spec, and the seating position, although more g tolerant than its British counterparts, did not feel quite right. Like going to war in a bath as someone commented rather rudely.

Perhaps I was biased, but I had reservations, and for other reasons as well. Like the multi-section canopy, reminiscent of the so-called 'coffin jobs' on the earlier Typhoons, and the Harvard-like combination of toe brakes and tailwheel lock. This let me down on an early flight, when it failed at touchdown, and I ended up going backwards down the runway at about eighty mph!

Later, as one of a pair, I found myself trapped before take-off by an

ATA Beaufighter which was being given absolute priority. He ran off the runway on three successive attempts to get airborne – before ultimately making it in a cloud of dust and grass mowings. We were forced to watch while he parked beside us, studying his pilot's notes at some length before trying again, and our engines overheated. It was humiliating to shut down and wait for a tractor to tow us in. Perhaps this was the flip side of the low drag radiator.

The Mustang was exceptionally well engineered, with a forgiving stall, pleasant handling over the whole speed range and nicely harmonized controls. It did everything well but never engaged my emotions. That is until I got my hands on a P51D with its Packard Merlin engine.

CHAPTER SEVEN

TYPHOON

Then everything went pear shaped. Our course of seconded army officers was posted to the Naval Bombardment Pool in late May. We were to observe and direct the fire of naval guns during the invasion. Or that at least was the idea.

It ignored the fact that our training in ArtyR (artillery reconnaissance) had been perfunctory in the extreme. For the Air OP squadrons, with gunner officers flying Austers, were already taking this over.

The most that we could recall was a single afternoon, on the so-called 'Sand Table', at Hawarden. A large hessian landscape – marked with roads and rivers and a scattering of model trees and houses, which had been slung over some simple frames to create a three-dimensional effect. Underneath, sweltering in the heat, was an unfortunate corporal whose job in life was to smoke endless cigarettes and puff upwards at the correct time and place to simulate the fall of shot.

It was about as far removed, and as helpful, in developing naval bombardment skills as one could possibly imagine. So what? If it was our only way to war, we had better grab the opportunity while it lasted.

The CO took a different view. He was already well aware that we were totally lacking in the right sort of operational training. His two RAF squadrons, 26 and 63, were equipped with ancient Spitfire Vcs – clipped, clapped and cropped[1] – and he was under strict instructions to conserve their flying hours for maximum effort come the invasion. They were not to be used for type conversion. We were stuck. The words: "You can't fly a Spitfire 'till you've flown one!" ringing in our ears.

Then we discovered that John Irving, an RAF direct entrant who had trained with us in Canada, had joined one of the squadrons from a Spitfire OTU. Still wet behind the ears in our view, lucky John had been cleared to fly escort whilst we, much more service experienced and highly qualified fighter-recce pilots (as we saw ourselves!), were grounded.

We hung around hugely frustrated, watching the navy at work and, it has to be admitted, with not a little admiration. Making sure that we did not get caught out, through ignorance of orders, became important. For we were on unfamiliar ground – not so far removed from the days of canvas and cannon – of rum, sodomy and the lash!

Be that as it may, in our self-imposed reading we came across some remarkable statements: *Engines are not to be run up close to the apple trees as this will blow off the blossom* and, I kid you not: *Personnel on duty who need to cycle on the perimeter track must do so with extreme care – because of taxiing aircraft – and Wrens so doing must wear bell bottoms for the sake of decency.*

Lee-on-Solent was home to no less than six squadrons, four of Fleet Air Arm Seafires, plus our two RAF units. It was crowded and uncomfortable. The wardroom, grossly overheated for late spring, was full of sailors – the aviators in heavy white roll neck sweaters, with an aura of endless naval tradition and bull which made us feel even more bolshie.

During those pre-invasion weeks, with the station almost cut off from the outside world, its occupants were involved in their own private battle. Pilots unable to fly, and deprived of the delights of Pompey[2], were apt to live it up in the bar. Elderly staff officers who regarded the wardroom as a civilised place, clearly objected to such behaviour, and some even expected to find the paper of their choice neatly folded beside their recognised breakfast places. We considered such practices arrogant in time of war and did our best to disrupt them.

Geoff Hartley's contribution was more personal. As the senior flight commander he had led the two RAF squadrons to Lee-on-Solent. On arrival he had made himself known to the duty officer who looked him over and asked him if he was in charge. Geoff agreed that he was – to which the reaction was pretty blunt and unwelcoming: "You chaps had better watch it here. There's a limit on wardroom bills for those below the rank of lieutenant commander."

Geoff, a Yorkshireman, whose relaxed and affable manner belied a forceful personality, was absolutely livid. He got his own back, by operating a system which isolated the evening supply of gin from his naval adversaries before they could even get in on the act. Night after night he arrived at opening time, accompanied by his pilots. They bought tots of gin in advance of consumption, stored the contents in a large jug and so, in his words, prevented the navy's limited supplies from falling into the wrong hands.

The surrounding area was packed with troops preparing to embark for the invasion. Security was tight. There were signs galore: 'Do not loiter; Civilians must not talk to troops.' The forbidden Spitfires were being painted with black and white stripes. History was in the making and, unless something happened soon, we would be left sitting on the sidelines.

Fortunately our plight had been noted and we were posted at the beginning of June to 3501 GSU[3] at Cranfield for Spitfire conversion. It seemed almost like peacetime after the rigours of Lee-on-Solent. A different world which, nevertheless, held its own wartime secrets as I was to discover years later when Enigma and Bletchley Park finally hit the headlines. The latter, with billets in the area, was also to cause me some embarrassment.

Nearby, in the village of North Crawley, the Crawley Arms was said to be a decent country pub. We paid it an early visit, to discover that the lounge bar was full of Wrens. In those days of 'careless talk costs lives' it never occurred to us to wonder why they were there – and to ask was simply not done.

One of them was rather attractive, and in due course I offered to walk her home, but she declined. The big house, where she was billeted, was just down the road. But we agreed to meet on the following evening. Fast forward twenty-four hours to when she was getting undressed and talking to the girl in the next bed. The conversation went something like this: "Met such a nice young pilot in the pub last night and saw him again this evening. Of course I'm so tall that when he wanted to kiss me good night he had to stand on a pile of bricks!"

"Good heavens! What was his name?"

The questioner was my sister Rosemary who operated one of the 'bombes' at Bletchley Park and she tells that story against me at every conceivable opportunity!

At Cranfield there seemed to be most variants of Spitfire, including the new and rare low altitude Griffon-engined Mk XII, but we were only to fly the earlier models. The Mk Vc with its clipped wings and low altitude blower, for all its age and lack of performance, charmed us from the word go. The Merlin, bulging aggressively, limited the forward view and positively demanded a curved approach, and the narrow undercarriage called for some care, especially in cross winds. But the easy handling and well harmonized controls encouraged the least adventurous to upgrade his aerobatic and combat skills. The Spitfire, we agreed unanimously, was the fighter boy's fighter of all time. No wonder it has been loved by so many for so long.

The Mark IX, more potent especially at high altitude, grew on you with experience, even if it had lost something in the purity of its handling due to the increased torque and gyroscopic effects of the more powerful engine. Both were a joy and we lived in a world of our own, for days on end, quietly hogging the hours.

On my last sortie from Cranfield I went on a solo battle climb, upwards through sunshine and shadow until the cumulus dwindled into the distance below, and the supercharger thumped as it changed gear. Soon half of southern England lay spread beneath my wings. The Channel coast and the Isle of Wight were clearly visible, and my thoughts returned briefly to the invasion, wondering what the future had in store.

Letting down, on the way home, a familiar airfield came into view with its runways and dispersal areas shimmering in the heat. There was no sign of activity, no aircraft in the circuit, perhaps they were all asleep. Temptation stirred. My Spitfire was unmarked. They would never be able to track me down. I came out of the sun diving fast and low, battering the crowded dispersals with sound, and sweeping upwards into the blue – almost three vertical rolls into a hammerhead stall. Immensely satisfying. I never took a Spitfire into battle. But the memories remain, bright and beautiful like the summer skies over Bedfordshire where for a brief moment I learned to fly and love it.

Just before we were due to return to Lee-on-Solent there was a change of plan and we found ourselves posted to 84 GSU at Aston Down. A pity in one respect that we never returned to those spotter squadrons. It would have been a splendid line shoot for the BFs: "We are army officers seconded to the RAF, who hold commissions in both services and direct the fire of naval guns!"

As for the naval bombardment sorties, according to Geoff Hartley they got off to a bad start. The first targets were coastal gun emplacements and the navy used armour-piercing ammunition exclusively, even for ranging. After a number of pilots had returned with nothing seen, the penny dropped and they started using HE[4].

Naval spotting then became a much more rewarding activity. The large calibre high explosive shells were easy to see, the opening shots were usually close to the target, the corrections were rapid and precise, and a salvo produced the most satisfying results. In fact the whole thing worked so well that it was quite possible to continue hitting enemy tanks and transport as they struggled to escape.

But my thoughts were firmly elsewhere. For Aston Down supplied replacements, pilots and aircraft, for the squadrons of 84 Group 2nd Tactical Air Force. Scattered around the airfield were Spitfires, the odd Mustang, Austers, a few Ansons and those Typhoons of my dreams. Now, if ever, was the moment; with my army background almost invisible amongst all those other pilots. There was no time to waste before my fighter-recce posting came through. I sought an immediate appointment. The wingco would see me after lunch.

My arguments were well rehearsed, based on an index finger which had been mangled in an accident years earlier. This, with some truth, was a decided disadvantage when pulling g on a Mustang and attempting to press the trigger on its pistol grip control column at the same time. A problem which did not exist with the spade grip and thumb-firing button on British fighters – ergo what about a transfer?

I spoke carefully, avoiding any reference to the army, and the wingco listened in silence. Then he looked up, staring me straight between the eyes, as if seeking the truth. Was there the faintest hint of derision in his expression? Did he think that I was LMF? Should I be on my way within the hour to wherever they sent such unfortunates? For an awful moment I thought that I might have overplayed my hand – and then at last: "The Typhoons have been suffering casualties. They need reinforcements. Would you...?" A wintry smile crossed his face.

"Yes sir! I would like that very much. When can I start?"

I felt myself grinning like a fool.

Before the afternoon was out I had presented my credentials at the Typhoon flight and found an aircraft to explore. Now I was seated high above the ground, pilot's notes in my lap, absorbing it all.

Much had happened since I had sat in that early Typhoon at Snailwell beside Cocky Dundas and, in my enthusiasm, had told him that it was the aircraft for me. I well remembered how he had looked at me through the open cockpit door more in sorrow than anger: "We've lots of problems," he said "and you're an idiot!" Since that conversation Cocky had fought in Malta and had been given a Spitfire Wing in Italy. He had risen to be the youngest group captain in the Royal Air Force. In those same two years the Typhoon problems had been largely sorted out.

The most visible changes surrounded me now. A glazed rear fairing had appeared almost immediately. This despite Sydney Camm's insistence that his new 400mph plus aircraft was so fast that its pilots did not need to see backwards. The unloved main hood assembly with its car-type doors – the so-called coffin job – took much longer to replace. But the final teardrop sliding canopy, which set a new standard in all-round visibility, was fitted to all squadron aircraft before D-Day. The bomb racks and rocket rails were a squadron fit not normally seen on GSU aircraft.

Other changes were less visible but pretty fundamental. The concern about carbon monoxide poisoning, as the cause of some early fatal accidents, had led to the mandatory use of oxygen from start up to shut down on every flight. It was on my list of vital actions for the morrow.

The vibration was said to be so bad that you would become infertile if you flew Typhoons for too long. Probably quite untrue for there was no sense of emasculation at the time. Nor later when many of the survivors got married and produced offspring!

Canopy progress and an outstanding final design.

In reality the pilot's seat was very close to the engine bearers with little intervening structure to act as a damper. Spring seats helped considerably. But they bottomed when you pulled g. Fortunately the last major modification – a four-bladed propeller which needed the larger Tempest tailplane for longitudinal stability reasons alone – reduced the vibration considerably.

Worst of all had been the fatal accidents arising from rear fuselage failure at the transport joint. This had been reinforced by a strap, then by fishplates, but the accidents continued.

Eventually two things happened. An elevator mass balance bracket broke before take-off and a pilot diving at high altitude was thrown out – and survived – as his aircraft pitched nose down and broke up. Fatigue failure of the offending item had been diagnosed in each case.

When the bracket was modified there were few subsequent accidents and all was thought to be well. But, as Hawker's later, and privately, admitted there never was an absolute cure.

There were many sleeve-valve failures on the early Sabre engines. Air Commodore Rod Banks, widely respected for his prewar work on Schneider Trophy fuels and wartime Director General of Engine Development, was a man of some determination. This was a crisis. He

Typhoon laid bare. Vibration and fertility rumours.

insisted that Bristol engines, with their successful range of sleeve-valve radials, should work flat out to help Napiers.

The problem was speedily solved. Even better, there was a suitably sized forging in production for the Bristol Taurus. Enough were machined to make sleeves for a trial installation and a modified engine for type test. Six months later the Sabre had become one of the most reliable engines in service.

Suffice it to say that the operational progress of the Typhoon had been equally difficult, not to say harrowing. Now it was ready. With its four 20mm cannon plus rockets or bombs, and flown by a changing breed of fighter pilots who were mostly learning on the job, it was about to become the outstanding ground-attack weapon of World War II.

By the spring of 1944 the newly formed 2nd Tactical Air Force had acquired its full complement of eighteen Typhoon squadrons and increasingly these were being directed at the German coastal radar installations and V1 launching sites. Good training for the precision army-support operations to come. But their targets were strongly defended and they were taking casualties. The day of the Typhoon had arrived.

On its way to ultimate success, the Typhoon had built up quite a reputation. To Winkle (Captain Eric) Brown, well known Farnborough test pilot, it was, "A great brute of an aircraft – large, heavy, fast and somewhat alarming!" A slight overstatement. Otherwise he was absolutely right and, as I was soon to discover for myself, it was all of these things. Except that I never found it alarming.

Why then, and especially after being utterly charmed by the Spitfire, had I remained so determined to pursue the Typhoon before I had even flown it?

Why indeed was I soon to join my future comrades in gently mocking the Spitfire as a 'boy's aeroplane' – and in reflecting rudely about its pilots, most of whom refused to volunteer (so it was alleged) when calls went out for Typhoon replacements?

Like so many of us at that time as our training came to an end, as we saw the casualty lists and the awards for bravery and heard the tales of derring-do – we longed to be there at the sharp end. Not in any sense of bravado. Rather the reverse. To prove to ourselves that we had the courage – the guts – what the Yanks called 'the right stuff'. In the early summer of 1944 the Typhoon, in that sense, seemed to offer a pretty unique opportunity.

There were more personal reasons. The aesthetic and emotional ones which had attracted me from the word go. It was truly massive for a fighter, at seven tons all up almost twice the weight of a Hurricane. There was an aggressive, purposeful, elegance about it. In the thick, slightly cranked wings, the deep chin radiator and the four very visible 20mm cannon. The wide track undercarriage added to the effect like the claws of some ravenous bird of prey. In the air it looked strong and powerful – ready to pounce and to deliver, and bring you safely home. The thought of flying it into battle sent the blood coursing through my veins.

There were other very practical reasons. The Luftwaffe was in decline. The Wehrmacht was still there in force and I wanted to fight low down. It suited the Typhoon and somehow it suited my temperament as well. Above all, as a seconded brown job, I wanted to be there supporting the army in the battles to come. That could only mean ground-attack; and ground-attack as surely meant Typhoon.

I might have thought otherwise at the time. Yet, in reality, this was only the end of the beginning. I had to master the brute, to join a squadron and to win my spurs. Little did I know it then, but we would be together for some fourteen months, in the forcing house of war, and the Typhoon was to give me the time of my life and opportunities more than I could ever imagine.

On the following morning it was for real. Climbing aboard once more, there was so much to betray its Hurricane ancestry. Already, after that brief session the previous afternoon, the cockpit was familiar – everything was positive – reassuringly Hawker.

Here too was a British fighter with the undercarriage and flap controls positioned on the left – no more changing hands on take-off. And, on the starboard side, close to where they might otherwise have been fitted, was an array of switches and engine instruments dominated by the big cylinder priming pump.

The splendid frameless canopy, the high seating position and the gunsight arranged to reflect directly on to the armoured windscreen, provided the best view ever from a piston-engined single-seat fighter. Within months every other manufacturer, British and American, was trying to follow suit.

Starting the big Sabre, for the first time, was a rare and emotive experience. Having pressurized the fuel lines you grasped the priming pump handle – aware that each stroke would send a load of petrol/oil mixture sloshing into the cylinders and that the correct amount depended in some mysterious way on the indicated oil and air temperatures. Get it wrong, or touch the throttle, and the whole thing might erupt in flames as you pressed the booster coil and starter buttons.

And there, just to remind you, was an airman – standing well back from the prop – fire extinguisher at the ready and waiting for this Typhoon tyro to boob. If you did he shouted "Fire!" and you switched off everything within sight and stuck both hands as far as possible out of the cockpit. Whereupon he would go through the most extraordinary procedure – putting his head inside the radiator intake, carefully opening spring-loaded doors and peering inside for evidence of flames.

A raucous bang from the Coffman starter – the engine coughed, hesitated, spewed sheets of smoke and snarled into life. A marvellous sound, like a multitude of thrashing chain-drive transmissions. Taxiing out, conscious of the instruction to wind on full port rudder trim, to watch the powerful swing to starboard... and I was off.

At +7lb/in^2 boost pressure and 3,700 rpm the sense of power was exhilarating. The acceleration fairly pushed you in the back. The airspeed and rate of climb seemed to rocket upwards before you could get the wheels and flaps up.

This was intended to be a wary introduction to the fighter of my dreams. For the sheer size and weight, and the performance, demanded respect. All went well until an Oxford appeared below and to port, skirting the clouds – perfectly placed for a quarter attack. The temptation was too much. I rolled into a descending turn, eased off a bit of power – pulled too much g and flicked onto my back.

It was creep away laddie and lick your wounds. Climb up to a decent height and start exploring things more fully. The Typhoon was easy and responsive to fly – the ailerons a bit heavy at speed and the change of (rudder) trim with power was quite marked. The stall, thank goodness was not quite as unforgiving as I had imagined at first. The spin was fairly violent – and aerobatics, although rather satisfactory, took up a lot of sky. And boy was it fast! I also have to thank the Tiffie for giving me some of the best slow rolls of my flying life – always slightly barrelled because nobody wanted to risk negative g and oil starvation on that engine. But confidence was coming fast, and all the time an inner voice kept urging me on.

"You're going to war with this one! Learn to fly it to the limits, like you did with the Hurricane."

Downwind in the circuit and the yawing effect from the undercarriage was quite pronounced. There was a marked increase in drag when the big twenty-four cylinder engine was throttled back and the flaps were very powerful. Steep approaches would become the order of the day. Not this one though – I came in sedately, using plenty of power and wheeled her on with her tail high in the air.

It was now the 25th of June and within a couple of weeks I would be joining a squadron. Except that I had only practised dive bombing briefly on a Harvard and rocket firing not at all. It was obviously essential to learn as much as possible from other members of the Typhoon flight while there was still time.

Perhaps my fighter-recce training might help to compensate for a lack of experience in weapon delivery. And indeed, much later, after months on ops and an armament practice camp behind me, I reckoned that I had been no worse off than those who had followed the normal route to a squadron. Their OTUs had concentrated on Typhoon conversion with typical 'fighter' emphasis and insufficient attention to target finding and weapon training.

So I pushed for more, in the short time available, and type conversion merged immediately into the most intensive applied flying imaginable. Day after day, the pressure continued – lead follow all over the sky, battle formation, and crossover turns, one to one air combat, contour chasing low down.

You felt the Typhoon's weight and its heavy ailerons at speed and sweated with the effort. But it was OK. In addition there were two vitally important dive-bombing sorties without bombs.

By quizzing the others beforehand, and following them carefully through each simulated attack, a basic drill began to emerge. Run in was at 8,000 feet, with sections in finger four, changing to echelon at the last minute. The formation leader rolled almost vertical as the target disappeared below his wing, allowing the nose to fall away until he could bring his sight on to the aiming point. Properly executed this was a precise and comfortable manoeuvre which would line up the target exactly on the desired heading – important if it was a bridge or a ship, with only minimum positive g adjustments to centre the gunsight bead.

Aiming off was required to compensate for the trajectory after release. As the Typhoon pundits put it:

> "Continue the dive until approaching a height of about 4,000 feet, pull through the target, pause briefly and press the tit. If the dive is shallower pull through further and pause longer."

Once again there was a marked difference between the well understood techniques of flying training and the less certain approach to applied flying. My unofficial and impromptu conversion to ground-attack was in no way an OTU. However it highlighted yet again, the limitations and the problems of operational training.

Air-to-ground firing with the four 20mm cannon down on the saltings near Weston-super-Mare brought all this to an end. That wonderful gun platform – especially in rough air... feeling the recoil... sensing the punch... seeing the shell bursts. The flat trajectory and visible impact made for rapid aiming adjustments and accurate shooting. A positive and satisfying conclusion.

Almost immediately after my defection to ground-attack one of the fighter-recce squadrons began to re-equip with camera-carrying Typhoons and I was rostered to deliver the first of these to Odiham on 11 July. There was a deep depression heading in from the Atlantic but the warm front, so the Met man said, was not expected to cause any problems until mid afternoon. Through the window behind him, as he sat over his charts, the cloud was thickening fast and the windsock pulled and trumpeted. If I was to make Odiham today, whatever the local experts might think, there was no time to lose.

Airborne soon afterwards I wondered if the most ancient Typhoons were being quietly dumped on an unsuspecting fighter-recce. This one was down on performance and there was a great deal of vibration. So much in fact that it seemed prudent to keep a really close watch on the engine.

The weather got steadily worse with sudden flurries of rain, and the tops of the Berkshire Downs were already in cloud. A brief diversion eastward and it should be possible to take the Thames valley through to Reading. What a stupid idea! The hills closed in on either side and I was reduced to creeping along with 30° of flap and the canopy wide open. The cockpit, no longer insulated from the miserable world outside, was cold, wet, full of exhaust crackle and altogether less secure.

A Walrus loomed out of the murk ahead going in the same direction. He seemed to be standing still as I squeezed my way past him. If the weather became really impossible he could cut the throttle and drop down onto the river below. Lucky old Shagbat!

The cloud over Reading was lower still and the rain had become a deluge. Flying a circuit to pick up the line to Basingstoke, trapped above the roof tops, was sheer claustrophobia. In my anxiety I missed it first time and had to go round again.

After that it was easier, following railways through the flat countryside. Only the Sabre, rough as ever, in contrast to the exhaust which crackled reassuringly through the open canopy, and a few overhead power lines stood between me and my destination. Except at the very end. The airfield was on rising ground. It was touch and go once more as I slid round a minimum altitude circuit, drifting in and out of cloud, and dropped thankfully onto the sodden runway.

268 Squadron were not best pleased with their new acquisition, it was clapped out, heavy with added armour, and down on range compared with their Mustangs. A few days later the engine which had vibrated its way from Aston Down finally gave up the struggle. On subsequent deliveries one felt distinctly unloved. Each Typhoon was just another embarrassment to be tucked away in a corner of the airfield until they were forced to use it.

In the midst of these trips to Odiham I was summoned to meet Denys

Gillam, then Group Captain Commanding 20 Sector, at his Tangmere headquarters. At first he seemed withdrawn, almost to the point of diffidence, but the interview soon revealed a very different man.

The steely determination was unmistakable. You would cross him at your peril. His questions were searching and to the point. Why had I joined the army and then seconded to the RAF? Why the switch from fighter-recce? How many hours on Typhoons? What experience of bombs and RP? At last he seemed satisfied and pronounced my fate – a posting to one of his bomber squadrons.

Hurn, when I got there, was warm and peaceful. The air was full of New Forest smells and the drowsy murmur of insects. The war seemed far away. As the evening shadows lengthened the airfield began to stir, watching and waiting. And suddenly they were back, eight or twelve at a time, sweeping down across the threshold, their engines shaking the ground.

Moments later they were strung out high on the downwind leg, curved approaches swinging into a tightly spaced stream landing. It was stirring stuff.

My first social occasion with 193 Squadron remains a vivid memory. Watching them relax, in the bar of a nearby pub, with their tankards held close to the shoulder, mark of the clan to which they belonged. As a newcomer you sensed the camaraderie and the elitism of a fighter squadron at war. Thrown together at a dramatic moment in time they had become comrades in arms, respecting each other's skills and buoyed up by the mutual confidence which comes from sharing the risks of battle. Bonds, stronger than any discipline, which could turn a bunch of young pilots into something much greater. It happened time and again.

Johnny Button the CO in non regulation dark blue shirt and silk scarf, battle dress cuffs turned back at the wrist, was the timeless fighter leader, dominating them all with the strength of his personality. So like a throwback to 1940 that you half expected to see his blower Bentley parked outside the pub.

That evening I met two other members of the squadron who would remain lifelong friends. The first, Charlie Hall, when it was my turn to buy him a drink, answered in pure Colonel Chinstrap (from a popular BBC series of the day). A deliberate, slightly inebriated: "I don't mind if I do."

Typical of this chubby extrovert, with his unruly moustache, that he should wish to put a stranger at his ease. Jimmy Simpson did too, in a different way. A Londoner, born and bred, he was more mature than the rest. His manner was direct, almost blunt, but the integrity and strength of purpose were unmistakable. There was a sensitivity too, a feeling for the needs of others. An ideal man to introduce you to ops.

193 Squadron, and 146 Wing to which it belonged, seemed to be in a state of organized chaos. Flying to Normandy for operations during the day – partially based at Hurn and partially under canvas at Needs Ore Point. It was a clear indication of our limited toehold on the Normandy beachhead. Although there was some practice flying for the new boy, this situation enabled me to roster myself for a cross country flight, and thus to get a message to my family about my imminent departure to war.

My flight plan involved a landing at Bradwell, recently vacated by the airborne forces and virtually empty. They were bored to tears, welcoming me without question, and by now I had no qualms about starting the Sabre or running out of cartridges. A quick canter across a couple of fields brought me to my Uncle Monty's back yard, where the old boy almost had a heart attack – but recovered himself, gave me a cup of tea and listened to my (somewhat censored) story.

All went well after that except that he could not grasp the idea that I would be back at Hurn in less than twenty minutes. I made a low pass after take-off and he waved at me in the most bemused fashion. But the message got through. He was not a scout commissioner for nothing!

There was another cross country which I never made. John Slatter, from my Cheltenham days, had flown a tour on Wellingtons. Now he was instructing on Mosquitoes at Bassingbourn. A quick trip from Hurn and we would lunch together. It would be great. I hadn't seen him for years. Two days beforehand I received one of the most distressing letters of my life.

It was from his wife, they had been so happy and she was expecting his child. He had lost an engine on take-off. Oh John! Not you! We had shared so much together.

CHAPTER EIGHT

BEACHHEAD NORMANDY

I simply had to get airborne. So it was fortunate, although quite unexpected, that 25 July found me rostered for Normandy at last. First impressions were dramatic. The narrow coastal plain looked like a vast construction site, littered with dumps – tanks, guns, bridging equipment ammunition and fuel – the whole paraphernalia of war. Advanced landing grounds (ALGs) added to the congestion, their dispersals and makeshift runways visible for miles. Huge highways had been bulldozed across the countryside, swathes of bare earth swarming with traffic, each convoy throwing its curtain of dust high in the air. Until, as they neared the battle area, the vehicles slowed and the telltale clouds subsided.

To port through the thickening haze a brief glimpse of Caen, shattered buildings open to the sky, the flicker of distant fires, and as suddenly the Bocage countryside below was empty, devoid of movement, threatening.

A brief command, a swift formation change, that familiar rolling entry to the dive and our target lay below. Cannons thumped, and thanks to those training sorties at Aston Down the rest came almost automatically – pull through, pause and press the tit. A quick glance back to check the bomb bursts, then it was over, and we were climbing steeply away.

What an anticlimax. There had been no sign of the enemy. No fleeing soldiers, no flak, even the bombs looked puny. I felt cheated. All those years, waiting and training just for that. Later I would see more, but never much. Enemy skills in camouflage and concealment, except on rare occasions when they were forced to move by day, were too good by far.

Such had been the pressures to move the squadrons to France that the landing grounds were operational within range of enemy guns and sometimes under fire. Advance parties, flown in by Dakota, were reduced to living in foxholes for more than a week. One day, as the servicing commandos were preparing their aircraft for action, the pilots saw two milkmaids riding back to back on a donkey. They headed for the corner of the airfield, found their cows, unhitched their buckets, sat down on their stools and got to work.

The donkey stood waiting, calm, almost immobile. Yet something – perhaps the odd shell burst or Sabre sound – had excited his masculine feelings. They became dramatically, not to say massively, obvious. The milkmaids finished, loaded up, and prepared to ride away quite unconcerned. There was no change whatsoever in the state of the donkey.

The pilots looked at each other helpless with laughter, until one said:

"Look at that bloody donc!" and another replied:

"That's not a donc you Nana. That's a willie!"

And in that simple way the squadron had conjured up a new name which would last for the duration.

As the situation improved 146 Wing and its four Typhoon squadrons, soon to be joined by a fifth, settled in at St Croix sur Mer. B3[1] had a single PSP runway, laid across the stubble, and an orchard where our tents were pitched amongst the apple trees. The shattered casemates of the German beach defences, beside the airfield, looked out across the coast towards Arromanches and Mulberry – a scene of never-ending activity with men and materials continuing to flood ashore.

Wing ops was located on the edge of the orchard in two trailer vans parked close together, covered in camouflage netting, their awnings protecting the briefing area from the worst of the weather. Here, if not airborne, were to be found Denys Gillam, now commanding the wing, and the wing leader. Here too were the army/air liaison and intelligence sections. This was the nerve centre – where sorties were planned and the squadrons were briefed – situated on the boundary between the two parts of our lives. The orchard and the air.

A large-scale map under perspex showed the whole beachhead and the battle areas. It was covered in chinagraph markings – the bomb line, inside which nothing must be attacked, and the enemy units beyond. Crack divisions, SS and Panzer, stiffened the defences. The elite of Hitler's armies. In Normandy they faced a stronger enemy, who possessed devastating air superiority, and we could not but admire their tenacity and courage as they strove to hold the line.

The enigma of the German nation, their fanaticism, their willingness to fight and die for such an evil cause, occupied many a conversation with Neville Thomas. Usually in the late evenings, catching up on his battle map. It was a subject which fascinated us both, but we never reached any conclusions.

'Tommy', the senior intelligence officer, was old by our standards. He must have been all of thirty-five, round and balding, and the future bank manager was just beginning to show through. Very much at the centre of things, shrewd and capable, he had learned to keep his own counsel. Just occasionally he might unburden himself, to an audience of one or two, especially if there was a bottle around. Because Tommy enjoyed nothing better than a quiet session with a few intimate friends.

The orchard at St Croix sur Mer will always recall the legend of Reggie Baker. For it was there, after his grave had been found, that Jimmy Simpson told the story again. A wing show which he was leading, late in the day, had run into intense flak. Hit and diving almost vertically out of control he had called his squadrons – calm and confident on the radio – and turned them away from the murderous barrage in the last moments of his life.

As Jimmy's voice died away the bursting shells were all around us... and the glowing streams of tracers.... and a single Typhoon hurtling earthwards.... What a way to go!

Those who were privileged to serve under his command recall an extrovert, hell raising wing leader. Who feared no man, had no respect for bureaucratic authority or stupid senior officers. His voice on the telephone, shaking the canvas walls of his tent on the airfield:

"Baker! BAKER!... B for Bastard!... A for Arsehole!..." When the occasion demanded he had his own phonetic alphabet.

Above all they remember his last show. And those whom he led on that occasion have a more personal memory. The groan which went up at briefing when he announced that they would be going in at 4,000 feet, and his response, so poignant in retrospect:

"What's wrong! Do you want to live forever?"

A very gallant gentleman. He was awarded a posthumous DSO.

Before we turned in, Pete Langille, A Flight's tall gangling Canadian told me another story about Jimmy's battle to get on ops. Difficult enough, after two years at Cranwell instructing on twins, without the major crash which he had only just survived. It had left him unconscious, for almost a fortnight; with no memory of the flight on which it had happened or of anything else immediately beforehand. But Jimmy was tough and we were singularly fortunate that we had acquired him or, more correctly perhaps, that through his own determination he had managed to acquire us.

That night was typical of many. Silence in the orchard, just a faint rumble of gunfire in the south, the distant explosions throwing a moving curtain of light across the horizon. Before long we slept. Moments later, or so it seemed, all hell broke loose.

An air attack on the beachhead and, as usual, the occupants of the orchard were in more danger from the defences. A tent and bedroll offered no protection from shell splinters and as these rained down, you sweated it out in bed, tin hat protecting head or crutch. The alternative – braving the chill night air to sit upright and protect both at once – was unthinkable.

Our ground-attack predecessors in the Great War were said to have thrown out the 'bath tub' of armour, which added some twenty-five per cent to the Camel's empty weight, and reverted to the dubious protection of sitting on flattened steel helmets. With hindsight we could have done with a couple of these apiece when the nights got noisy!

Sleep returned briefly, as the air attack died away, only to be interrupted again by the arrival of a heavy calibre shell. Others followed at intervals as the enemy kept up his nightly hate. The gun in question was eventually located in a railway tunnel near Pont l'Évêque. A low level attack by 197 Squadron, led by Johnny Baldwin who had taken over as wing leader, effectively blocked both ends of the tunnel and stopped that nonsense for good.

For the most part, in July and early August, we hammered away at the enemy around Caen and westwards. Strongpoints, troop and tank concentrations, headquarters, fuel and ammunition dumps. There was a wild and savage beauty about those sorties which lives forever in the memory. Beauty and death.

Down below were the killing grounds of Normandy. Marked by lurid bursts of flame, and tenuous clouds of smoke, which drifted across the woods and fields and shattered stricken villages of the Bocage. Beauty and death in the choreography of wheeling and diving aircraft – in the lazy rising tracer and the clouds of bursting shells – in the last stricken moments of a friend, usually in silence. Sometimes a few words of shocked surprise, suddenly cut off, like 'Wee Mac': "I've had it! Second tour too!..."

One day a huge bomber stream came sweeping in from the sea. For almost an hour it darkened the sky, a procession of Lancasters, Fortresses, and Liberators, escorted by Spitfires, on their way to pound the enemy positions around Caen. The start of Operation Goodwood, another round in the fight to break out of the beachhead.

We watched in awe, and then sudden concern, as a Liberator went out of control in a dramatic sequence of tail slides and stall turns. In moments the orchard was full of silent figures, willing the crew to bail out, and praying that their aircraft would hold together until they did. When the first parachute emerged, and the rest followed, there was an audible sigh of relief. Until we saw that the falling bomber was scything back and forwards amongst those helpless swinging figures. After half a dozen heart-stopping passes it fell away below them and disappeared from sight.

Soon afterwards the weather broke, and became completely non operational for days on end. The attack on Caen petered out in a morass of bomb craters, mud and rubble on the northern outskirts of the city. Once again the resilience and tenacity of the Germans had been remarkable, and there were growing doubts about the wisdom of using strategic bombers in this way. It seemed too much like Monte Cassino all over again.

Non flying weather and we were off to explore the local area – Jimmy Simpson, Pete Langille, and myself, and at the wheel, 'Killy' from Ulster, Flying Officer Kilpatrick. The only pilot known to have survived after losing the tail of his Typhoon. He remembered diving at high altitude – the aircraft beginning to pitch violently nose down and then in a flood of words which made it quite impossible to discover whether he was angry or surprised: "Woke up flat on my back. Surrounded by great potato plants. And my parachute wrapped around me. Thrown out through the roof I was and the Lord *Jaisus* pulling my ripcord – for I never did." Then – in words of utter disbelief: "And there wasn't a Tiffie in sight!"

To warnings of fifth columnists, and snipers in the rear areas, we buckled on our pistols, and set off at suicidal pace, while Pete and Killy argued about the route. Jeep trips were always spiced with danger. But this one was like some manic motor rally as our driver, slithering on the muddy surface, weaved between tanks and lorries to a steady accompaniment of: "T'is this way Pete. T'is indeed! Get out of the way you fat bastard!"

To Jimmy and myself, hanging on grimly in the back, it was soon apparent that there would be little opportunity for sightseeing. Whenever we entered a village, Killy remarked that there might be a sniper in the church tower and his foot would go down even harder. Eventually, on the way back to B3, he was persuaded to stop in the middle of Banville and again for a photograph beside its damaged church.

No manufactured goods of any sort were to be seen in the village shops. But there was plenty of local produce, cut off from its traditional markets in areas still occupied by the Germans. Butter by the kilo, big discs of Camembert, even bottles of raw Calvados from under the counter in exchange for a few cigarettes, if you were lucky.

The locals were mostly old men, women and children. The others had gone to forced labour or underground with the Resistance. Those to whom we spoke seemed bemused. A few were almost hostile, others not unfriendly, glad that the Germans had gone, but still cautious. For us the breakout from the beachhead was a foregone conclusion, simply a matter of time. The Allies had almost total air superiority and overwhelming material resources. The enemy was forced to move under cover of darkness or face almost total destruction by day. For the inhabitants of lower Normandy it was very different. They had experienced the Germans triumphant in 1940, had suffered four years of occupation and now the Anglo-American forces had ground to a halt. Not surprising if they were still worried about the outcome.

The prime minister's visit in the first week of August could hardly have been in greater contrast. One day, as the weather began to improve, a Fieseler Storch appeared low in the circuit. Harry Broadhurst, AOC 83 Group, under whose command we were temporarily operating, had arrived with Winston Churchill.

We gathered round him as he climbed out of the aircraft, seeing the familiar figure in raincoat and nautical cap, pleased that he was on the beachhead and had found time to visit the wing. Winston was in his element, splendidly informal – full of deliberate mispronunciations and good humour.

"We've got that barshtard Hitler and his Narzees on the run!... One more good heave should see them orf forever!" He spoke from the heart, with a marvellous feel for his audience, as if rolling back the years to take part in the battle himself. Inspiring and deeply moving. When the time came for him to leave, and Denys Gillam called three cheers for the prime minister, we cheered him to the echo.

With the return of flying weather the Americans broke out southwards from the Cherbourg peninsular. As they went over to the attack the left flank of the advance swung east in a giant hook to take the Germans in the rear. To Tommy's dedicated map watchers it was frustrating that the British and Canadians were making so little progress against the enemy divisions massed against them in the Caen sector.

A few days later the map showed an astounding change, with a massive German thrust aimed towards Avranches. Most of Panzer Group West was being thrown into an all-out drive, to cut off the advancing 3rd US Army from its bases in the north. Amongst them were those same crack German divisions which had been holding the line around Caen. Admire them we might and yet one of our worst fears was that of being taken prisoner by the SS. Bad enough, as a ground-attack pilot, to be captured by front-line troops but to fall into the hands of an SS unit, with their reputation for unbridled brutality, would be a thousand times worse.

It happened to Killy in the closing stages of the battle for Mortain, when the Typhoon squadrons were locked in combat with the panzer spearheads, and through sheer guts and that deceptively carefree Irish manner he turned it to good account.

Hit by flak near Vire he forced-landed half a mile behind the German lines and managed to evade the enemy foot patrols by hiding under a tank for almost four hours. From this exceedingly dangerous position, with the crew moving around a few inches above his head, it was perhaps fortunate for him that he was seen by a German officer, and forced to surrender.

Dispatched to Luftwaffe headquarters, with an escort of two riflemen, travel was only possible at night and the overcrowded roads made progress very slow. For nearly a week he was on the move – collecting a number of American POWs in the process. On the sixth day, close to an SS headquarters which was being dive-bombed almost nonstop, Killy's little party took refuge in a ditch, where they were joined by a further five, very demoralised German soldiers.

Killy, as he subsequently described it, turned on the propaganda machine and persuaded all the Huns to surrender, and pose as his escort, until they reached the allied lines. After further adventures, which included bluffing an SS officer, stealing a lorry, and ending up with an even larger 'escort' which had swollen to twenty-seven, he finally made contact with the Americans and hitch-hiked his way back to B3 – just nine days late. A valiant effort, part of a long and courageous tour, for which he received a well earned DSO.

Before it finished Killy was appointed to 197 as a flight commander and was then posted to Boscombe Down. Putting one of his temperament on to carbon monoxide testing was not a good idea. Bored to death in his Tempest he beat the living daylights out of the place. Up in front of the commandant, he was threatened with an immediate return to a fighter squadron. Killy treated it as an offer, thanked him, and departed soon afterwards to the Air Fighting Development Unit.

The sortie on which Killy went down was an armed recce with bombs against the rear areas of the Mortain salient on 7 August. Led by Bill Switzer, commanding A Flight, it proved frustrating beyond words. The search area was surprisingly untouched by war. Yet only a few miles to the west, where the ground-attack squadrons had just delivered a decisive blow against the panzers, the countryside was devastated and strewn with the debris of battle.

We tracked back and forth across the gentle rolling wooded contours. But the Hun was lying low after his battering on the previous day and so Bill brought us down and down, trailing his coat, until we were less than 1,000 feet above the ground. Eight Typhoons, in two sections of four, cruising in battle formation – asking for trouble, until Killy was caught by a sudden burst of flak and called out that he was heading home and an imminent forced landing.

For almost half an hour more we sweated it out, hunched in the heat of our cockpits under a cloudless sky, willing Killy to make it, until shortage of fuel brought an end to the fruitless search.

Frustration turned to anger when we were told to bring our bombs home. Yet Bill was probably right. An astute enemy commander might well have pulled his forces back after the disaster at Mortain, in order to reduce the risk of encirclement. And we had seen absolutely nothing to attack. Better to save our bombs for another time.

The defeat of Panzer Group West was decisive in the Battle of Normandy. It was largely attributed to rocket-firing Typhoons. As Von Kluge, who took over when Rommel was wounded, somewhat tersely recorded: 'The armoured operation was completely wrecked – exclusively by the Allied Air Forces'. Yet, in a contemporary trial it had taken eight Typhoons with sixty-four rockets to achieve three hits on a captured German tank and operational research showed that the average Typhoon pilot, firing eight rockets in salvo had roughly a four per cent chance of achieving a direct hit. So why the discrepancy?

In reality the Typhoon was a splendid tank crew morale buster. That has since emerged in many prisoner interrogations and intelligence reports. When an attack developed – even before the first tank brewed up – panic often ensued. Unlike with other lethal weapons you could actually see them aiming at you – at *your* tank! Many crews bailed out as cannon fire set soft-skinned vehicles alight and routes became hopelessly blocked. For the Germans, movement by day had become virtually impossible on the run up to the invasion. After the landings, as the battle developed, it had become worse. In the ensuing weeks it would be infinitely more terrible.

Yet, even in defeat, the enemy fought back with great courage. His flak was ever present, well controlled and very lethal. The Typhoons were suffering too.

A few days after that frustrating sortie I was flying number two to Bill. A dawn show on a lovely summer's morning. The heavy dew had settled the dust for once and we were off in fours. An armed recce – cannon only – and Bill was angry I guess, looking for scalps trailing his coat again, heading low to the south of Caen. Suddenly the tracer came hosing up. He was hit in the starboard nose tank and started to burn. I shouted at him to bale out, swinging above him in a climbing turn but there was no sign of a parachute, and his aircraft dived vertically into the middle of a large wood where it exploded on impact.

Bill was still very much in the land of the living however. He had fallen into the trees, not far from the burning remains of his aircraft, his parachute opening in the nick of time. Concealing himself as best he could, despite a broken leg which he strapped with his dinghy thwart, he survived in the middle of a major battle. He was picked up by the enemy and then hid in a ditch until our forward troops appeared on the scene. By which time Jimmy Simpson had taken over the flight.

As the enemy fought to extricate his forces, after their failure at Mortain, the occupants of the orchard at St Croix sur Mer were involved in a battle of a different sort. The log which straddled the crudely screened toilet trench behind ops was crowded with miserable figures cursing and groaning. Fortunately there was plenty of Kaolin and some lucky chaps seemed to remain immune. As a result we were able to keep going, near enough at full strength, although the same could hardly be said of our physical state.

Pride of place in the story of the Normandy Dog must go to Doc Horn of 197 Squadron who organised a supply of sanitary towels. Stockpiled at B3 they were to be used for a purpose which their designer, even in his wildest dreams, could never have foreseen. It amused us hugely to imagine the enemy reaction had they ever captured and examined a pilot equipped with one of Doc's secret weapons!

Speed was of the essence and they were delivered immediately thanks to the 'beer run', a well established service with origins of a different nature.

Dust on the beachhead landing grounds in the early days had caused a spate of engine failures. Vokes produced a simple carburettor air intake filter and an emergency modification programme was put in hand. Units based in France flew their Typhoons back to England, a few at a time and these were soon returning with two firkins of beer apiece on their bomb racks.

The beer run continued long after its primary purpose had ceased to exist, by the simple expedient of rostering an aircraft on a round trip to Tangmere at regular two-day intervals. Pilots changed over at the far end, giving each the benefit of a short leave in England, and the obligatory barrels were loaded up for the return flight. Doc's sanitary towels travelled by the same route packed into the gun bays of our beer barrel bombers.

The enemy forces trapped in the Falaise Pocket fought desperately to escape and there was a brief resurgence of German fighter activity in an attempt to stem the savage losses which were being inflicted on them from the air.

The wing reacted with a number of fighter sweeps and there were a few encounters with twenty and thirty plus 109s. However our main role continued to be that of ground-attack directed increasingly towards the escape routes back to the Seine.

As the ground battle went mobile 146 Wing's 'Bomphoon' squadrons expected an instruction to change over to rockets. There were two important advantages. Drop tanks could be carried in addition to RPs, which increased the radius of action, and the rockets themselves were considered to be more effective against targets, particularly armour, on the move.

Johnny Button, and Allan Smith of 197 Squadron, fought against the idea, arguing that the wing must be able to respond instantly with bombs – even under the most fluid battlefield conditions. The Luftwaffe's re-appearance was further justification for retaining some Typhoons with bomb racks as they were faster, and more manoeuvrable, than those fitted with rails.

While the two squadron commanders were making and winning their case, I was briefed by the wingco on 19 August to accompany him on an armed recce.

In the cockpit with five minutes to go. Five minutes to run through the familiar drills, deep breathing on oxygen, feeling the tension that stems from the challenge of a compelling and deadly sport, its excitement and its uncertainty – the very essence of operational flying. And this sortie had an extra twist. My number one was the top scoring Typhoon pilot with thirteen and a half kills.

Johnny Baldwin seemed such an unemotional man, so very different from his colourful predecessor, yet his skill and his unruffled confidence was an inspiration to all around him. In the air you sensed an exceptional and considerate leader. A very *parfit gentil knight.*

How, I wondered yet again, had I come to be flying with him alone? Perhaps as a belated comeuppance for an indiscretion on a fighter sweep south of Paris. Sprog of the lot, I had been first to answer his question on the radio. Identifying a bunch of impossibly distant specks with the words: "Mustangs Bigshot," and then having to sweat it out!

Whether that was the real reason was of no importance at all. What mattered most, as Jimmy Simpson put it bluntly: "If you're flying with the wingco on his own you'd better have your finger well and truly out!"

What I never realized at the time was the possibility that this sortie might be my evaluation as one of his regular number twos. Sealing my fate might be a better way to describe it. For the flak inevitably concentrated on the formation leader and, almost as inevitably, under deflected, to the detriment of the chap following closely behind! (They didn't call our great Denys Gillam 'Kill'em Gillam' for nothing. Not that it was his fault at all, but rather the inaccuracy of the German gunners.) As it happened the squadron went to armament practice camp soon afterwards, and the wingco went on rest following our return, so I never flew with him again.

Ground crews swarmed over the surrounding aircraft preparing them for the next sortie. Most of them were stripped to the waist, tanned and fit as never before, thanks to Adolf Hitler – although they might have put it differently. Some were draped with belts of 20mm ammunition, others, working under the wings, were filling drop tanks. Today, again, there would be no bombs.

In the background, where Stan Carr's office and workshops were located in a cluster of camouflaged tents, a Chore Horse[2] chugged softly away, pleasantly soporific in the warm sunshine. Stan and his boys. They never let us down. Highly skilled improvisers and scroungers, they kept our aircraft serviceable under the most daunting conditions. Up to every legitimate demand we put upon them and, as I was to discover in the months ahead, a few more besides.

Senior NCOs like Stan Carr were the backbone of the service. Ex Desert Air Force and still in his early thirties, he had an iron determination, and ran his crew like a veteran. To us he was always relaxed, polite and helpful. Nothing was too much trouble. Stan and Joe Hickey, his right hand man, identified totally with the squadron, and we with them. 6193 Servicing Echelons[3] was 193 Squadron, whatever officialdom might say, and they supported us magnificently.

The muffled crack of a Coffman starter on the far side of the airfield was a reminder of more urgent matters. Careful strokes on the cylinder pump. Press the starter and booster coil buttons. The engine coughs and bursts into life.

The two Typhoons taxied out to meet at the runway threshold, clattered on to the PSP tracking, and took off together in a gathering storm of dust.

We turned east, crossing the twin waterways of the River Orne and the Caen canal, catching a glimpse of Lisieux Abbey in the distance – brilliant white, almost luminous. A dramatic outline far removed from the ugly scenes of devastation which lay ahead. For the enemy had been forced to move in daylight and was paying the price.

The roads leading across the open plain were littered and blocked with wrecked and burning transport. Columns of smoke hung in the summer sky. In the midst of all this carnage more vehicles, of every sort and description, motorised and horsedrawn, continued to straggle out from the hilly countryside to the south east. These were the survivors, who had fought their way out of the trap at Falaise, only to face annihilation from the air on their final dash to the Seine.

But before we turned our attention to the roads there was something else, the wingco's voice sounded in my ears: "Bigshot going down now – enemy gun position."

As I followed, searching the ground ahead, bare earth showed faintly through camouflage netting, revealing the telltale outlines of newly dug weapon pits close to the bottom of a reverse slope. 88s probably, part of some hastily assembled battle group, ready to fight it out to the bitter end defending the flanks of the retreat. A dangerous trap set to catch the advancing Canadians as they topped the crest ahead. But lack of time had prevented adequate concealment and, in revealing their position, the Huns had given us an opportunity to hit them first.

Cannon smoke trailed back suddenly from the wingco's Typhoon and his first burst ripped viciously through one of the crudely camouflaged emplacements.

No time to take in more as I opened fire on another, seeing the flash of exploding shells in its shadowy depths, followed by a burst of flame. Back on the stick, and a gun barrel, long as a telegraph pole, centred in my gunsight. The cannons thumped again. A fleeting impression of crouching, stumbling figures engulfed in a carpet of firecrackers – then up and away.

As we swung hard to port the flak came up, late and inaccurate. Moments later we caught a half track, accompanied by a large lorry, skulking along the edge of a wood and both erupted in flames. There seemed to be ambulances everywhere threading carefully amongst the wreckage on the roads. All were plastered with huge red crosses. Difficult to believe that every one was genuine. But we left them alone. There were plenty of other targets. I spotted two Tiger tanks tucked under cover and went after them. The wingco stood off; probably to watch my shooting! I was hitting them OK – one pass at the cooling louvres, and the second at the tracks. But my shells were bouncing off. My four cannons were like peashooters against their armour.

A couple of days later 193 Squadron went visiting on the ground. Released from ops for 24 hours we scrounged a 15 cwt truck and headed south. The roads were almost empty and we made good time, stopping only to check our way in the middle of a small village.

Or rather it had once been a small village. Now, like so many others, it was just an open cross roads, surrounded by shattered houses and piles of rubble. Here and there an odd balk of burnt timber, a broken picture frame, a dirty remnant of curtain – all that remained of a little community which had been caught in the whirlwind of destruction. Yet not quite all. The sound of drunken song, and before we could locate its source a swaying figure emerged from the ruins and came reeling towards us. This survivor, gently and happily inebriated, produced a bottle and demanded that we toast every conceivable aspect of 'la Liberation'.

As the road climbed towards Mount Pincon we looked back, savouring the warmth of his raw Calvados, and saw him standing there, a lonely scarecrow, waving to us from the desolation of his home.

Mount Pincon was a shambles. In and around the orchards and homesteads, the spiked and shattered guns stood burned and blackened. Abandoned equipment, empty ammunition boxes, the jetsam of battle lay everywhere. The remains of a classic defensive position, where the Germans had fought to the death, until overwhelmed at last by sheer weight of numbers and superior firepower.

Here the dead were already buried, each temporary grave marked by a rough wooden cross, with a few hastily scrawled words, under a steel helmet. Even the aroma of death had begun to fade and the predominant smell was of pulverised buildings with overtones of farmyard manure.

Not so as our truck jolted and rumbled on down the winding roads to the south and east of Falaise. The sickly sweet odour grew steadily worse, until it dominated the senses, and there was no escaping its dreadful embrace. Surrounding us on every side was the reality of what had been happening, down there in the Bocage, inside the ring of steel which had closed and tightened around the German armies in Normandy. It was like a vision of the apocalypse.

From Trun to Vimoutiers ran the awful highways of death where the retreating columns had been cornered, and systematically destroyed, as they tried to escape. Stalled nose to tail they had been devastated by nonstop air attack, on roads swept by torrents of artillery and mortar fire, until hardly a living creature remained.

We climbed down from the truck and walked among them in a valley still as the grave itself, where no birds sang and nothing moved except the flies and maggots. They lay where they had fallen, amongst the debris of their broken weapons and ruined vehicles. Some were hideously torn and disfigured, or charred and blackened until their shrunken corpses were hardly recognisable as those of human beings.

Others lay seemingly untouched, calm and peaceful, handsome in death, their sightless eyes staring forever into space. The horses were the saddest sight of all. Unable to escape they had been mown down where they stood. Their bodies swollen and distended, their noble heads grimacing in rigor mortis, pitiful beyond words.

The scale and the horror of it all was almost too much to take, and it was a thoughtful little party which returned to St Croix sur Mer that night. Yet there was hope too. For we had seen the twisted symbols of Nazism broken in the dust. Entrails of a defeated army. The victory at Falaise had struck a massive blow for freedom.

CHAPTER NINE

SHARPENING THE WEAPON

The defeated remnants of the German armies in Normandy took another severe mauling as they struggled across the Seine. The flak was intense above the ferry crossings, but to no avail, and the Typhoons kept them under continuous attack. The retreat degenerated into a rout. There was no coherent line of defence as the enemy fell back in disorder towards the Pas de Calais and the Belgian frontier. And the squadrons, soon operating at maximum range from their beachhead airfields, harried them from dawn to dusk.

Ranging eastwards, on armed reconnaissance, there was a flak trap near Beauvais, where numerous wrecked vehicles had been arranged as in convoy, surrounded by well sited 20mm and 37mm flak batteries. But word soon got around and we gave it a wide berth.

We were stalking a demoralized opponent, who could still be very dangerous, ready to catch the careless or unwary amidst the uncertainties of mobile warfare. For the Hun was desperate to conceal himself and upset us with unexpected threats. There was a strange, almost ludicrous, feeling of tiptoeing noisily overhead willing the flak to remain silent and the enemy to break cover.

If you were patient, and he made a mistake, then came the moment when you had him at your mercy – in the glowing arc of your reflector sight – yet there was no feeling of hatred, no emotion at all.

It happened to us, in a big way, on thc last day of August. Johnny Button had gone on rest and Guy 'Plum' Plamondon, a French Canadian, had taken over the squadron. He was leading eight aircraft on armed reconnaissance when we caught an enemy convoy out in the open between Arras and Douai. Trapped on one of those poplar-lined roads which run straight as a die across the plains of northern France without a hedge or a scrap of cover in sight.

Plum placed us perfectly. We swung into line abreast and dived towards them, drop tanks tumbling away. A motley collection of military and commandeered civilian vehicles, some horse drawn, they were crawling along in the heat and seemed oblivious to their fate.

When they spotted us at last a few wild bursts of flak came up – but it was all too late. The wagons at the front and rear were knocked out almost simultaneously, and many more were caught on the first pass, trapping the remainder. The flak trucks were swamped. The return fire died.

We came in again, taking out most of the rest and, as we pulled away, nothing moved on the road below except billowing flames and clouds of dirty smoke. We had accounted for twenty-two vehicles and reduced a whole column to ruins in a matter of minutes.

The next sortie on 2 September, another armed recce, further up the Pas de Calais, was briefed to cross the Channel and land at Manston. Approaching the search area our headphones were swamped by radar noise:

"Yoy…ing… Yoy...ing… Yoy…ing…" An incessant pulsing sound, ever more demanding in our headphones. Easy to picture the long gun barrels swinging far below, the high velocity rounds slamming home, a swift succession of muzzle flashes above the emplacements, shell bursts erupting around us. And then we saw a gaggle of Lancasters ahead attacking a heavily wooded position, their giant bomb bursts marching through the trees, marking the hoped for destruction of a V2 launching site.

Further north we shot up a couple of heavy MT[1] a few miles inland from Boulogne. Then a horse-drawn wagon appeared charging along a country lane frantically seeking cover. Caught by a burst of cannon fire it stopped abruptly in the entrance to a large field. I looked back and there tucked in around the perimeter were the wagon lines of an enemy transport unit:

"More targets under the trees Bassett Leader!"

And Jimmy Simpson, encouraging: "Roger Dave, lead us in."

Cannon shells scythed amongst them and there were rearing horses, falling horses, dying and panic stricken horses, absolute chaos. The field was in the bottom of an awkward hollow and I hung on too long with my second burst and almost mushed in. Pulling up rather shaken as Felix Cryderman came through on the radio – loud and very upset:

"You bastards can do what you like – I'm not attacking no more horses today – or any other f****ing day!" And Jimmy, calm and understanding: "OK Black Three – stand off and watch our backs." Moments later we had reduced another enemy unit to absolute ruin. But who could take pride in such a massacre of defenceless animals?

For Felix, the Canadian lumberjack, who had lived and worked with horses all his life it must have been hell. Yet the German army depended on them and it was our job to destroy their transport.

Jimmy's voice again – flat and deliberately unemotional:

"That's enough chaps. Time to go home. Bassett Leader setting course."

All was peaceful as we passed low over the chalk cliffs, keeping well clear of Boulogne, before climbing out over the sea. The late afternoon sun gleamed on our canopies and reflected across the water. Dungeness looked as if you could reach out and touch it.

There was only one salvo, but it was enough. The familiar oily bursts blossomed right across the formation. Several aircraft were damaged and Jimmy's Typhoon began to stream glycol. The heavy batteries at Boulogne must have been tracking us from the moment we settled into the climb and had fired with great accuracy. Jimmy sweated it out, as his coolant slowly drained, and we tucked in beside him, hardly daring to breathe. But his engine kept going and he made it back to Manston and a normal landing.

We were inside the nearest local within minutes of opening time. The beer tasted splendid. Just what was needed to wash away the dust and stink of Normandy and drown the images of those dead and dying horses. It was a lengthy session.

Shortly afterwards long-range tanks, and round trips via Manston, were not enough. We became birds of passage, moving from strip to strip, trying to keep up with the pace of the advance.

On one occasion, ferrying an aircraft from an ALG near Beauvais to our new base at Lille Vendeville, I diverted to the Canadian war memorial on Vimy Ridge, recalling as I did so the story of my Uncle Jack. On those very slopes below he had urged his men forward, by walking ahead of them with a battered umbrella, as if cocking a snook at the enemy bombardment. The attack went in and he survived the war. What courage.

As I dipped in salute, over the towering outline of the memorial, the flat countryside of Flanders lay beyond me to the north – the mining villages, Ypres, the Menin Gate, Passchendaele. Such familiar names from way back, and all of them still in enemy hands. I thought of the chaps in their Camels strafing the trenches – they called it 'Battle Work' – and the casualties were dreadful. How, I wondered, would our war end? We could not, we must not, let them down.

I landed in thoughtful mood at Lille Vendeville, to find an airfield largely demolished by endless allied bombing, where we lived under canvas and took off from much mended runways. Our targets were the German garrisons defending the French channel ports. The squadrons attacked them continuously – hoping to break their morale – and showered them with leaflets inviting surrender. It was boring, thankless work and we were acutely aware of the suffering French inhabitants. In the meantime 197 Squadron had stumbled across a cellar full of champagne and were visibly enjoying their splendid windfall. Mean bastards, they refused to share it with anyone else, and maintained an armed guard until it had all gone.

All, however, was not lost. A forecast of non flying weather led to a spontaneous night on the town. The liberation was very new and everywhere 'les Aviateurs Anglais' were warmly welcomed. Some hours and many drinks later we came across a vast emporium with swing doors reminiscent of a Western saloon. Inside was a large room with a sunken floor covered in sawdust. On the far side, standing with her back to the bar was the most remarkable creation – an Amazon warrior in the flesh – and what flesh! The skin-tight black-leather bra and pants showed off her well endowed shape to perfection and the force of her personality was positively elemental.

She strode across the sawdust towards us, brandishing a whip and sadly, as she came nearer, the image changed. The flesh was just too substantial and the beautiful face was hard and demanding. This harpy took one look at Felix – in build, apart from the obvious differences, they were not dissimilar – and decided that she had found a soul mate, or at least a mate for the night. She threw herself at him with glad cries of "Mon Dieu," "quel magnifique!" and the like. To which Felix responded ungallantly "Christ I'm off".

In the end we persuaded him to stick around as the rest of us were more than curious about the goings on in this very strange establishment. Felix was scared to death. He only recovered his confidence when there was a burst of machine-gun fire out in the street. That was something he understood and could cope with.

Having no wish to become involved with a bunch of trigger-happy Frenchmen, who seemed at one in their determination to eliminate the hated traitors of France, we returned to the jeep and drove back to base.

Charlie Hall and I found a German bomb dump. The 250kg bombs had been fitted with screamers, four to a bomb. The thought occurred to us that we might fit a larger version to our Typhoons. Stan Carr organised several prototypes, and they kept us amused for days. But the idea was quickly forgotten when we moved to APC[2] at Fairwood Common on the Gower peninsular in South Wales.

The APCs provided range facilities, a supply of bombs and RPs[3], aircraft servicing and rearming. The rest was up to the squadrons. For those like myself, who had been forced to learn on the job, it was a golden opportunity.

We flew with eight practice smoke bombs or four RPs and the benefit of continuous practice, with rapid feedback of results, produced a dramatic improvement. The final squadron average, 25 yards low level and 30 yards dive-bombing, seemed a reasonable basis on which to go back to war. But we had certainly hoped for better than 27 yards with RP. While I discovered that individual sortie averages like 7 yards, 10 yards and 6 yards respectively were equally possible.

At low level the lightweight practice bombs virtually stopped where you put them. But 1,000lb bombs with delay-action fuses could go bouncing into the distance. So, bombing for real, there were two alternatives. If the target was solid enough to stop your bombs, and stood well above its surroundings, go in as low as possible, virtually straight and level, and release at the last moment. This required accurate navigation because pulling up 'for a look' on the final run in could be suicidal. Sometimes a fast shallow dive, steep enough to dig them in, was the better option.

Dive-bombing, so far a matter of trial and error, emerged with a very clear message. Get it steep and pressed well home for maximum accuracy. Gravity drop was minimal and the compensation required, by easing the nose upwards through the target, correspondingly less. From then on it became my favourite technique. As for tactics – dive-bombing a well defended target could swing the balance in favour of the attacker. Running in at or about 8,000 feet made it more difficult for the heavy flak, and allowed sufficient height to settle the diving aircraft without

Low level bombing demo. Method suitable for real against a substantial upstanding target....

Top: ....or, failing that, a shallow dive to dig them in.
Bottom: Loading rocket projectiles (RPs). Hard work at 60lbs each for the heads alone.

getting too far down into the light flak barrage. And be warned, the latter, visible as a curtain of white shell bursts, created the dangerous illusion that you were safer once through it and below.

Practice RPs were fitted with 60lb concrete heads. Accurate flying was essential as they were highly sensitive to slip or skid. Range and angle of dive were equally critical in order to correct for gravity drop. To help with the latter the graticule of the standard reflector sight was rotated in azimuth, until the image on the windscreen had been turned through 90°. The inner (top) end of the lower range bar became the RP aiming point and the range bar settings were recalibrated in angles of dive 30°, 45°, 60° etc. Thus providing an adjustable sight line, raising the aircraft nose as the dive became shallower and vice versa.

Bill Tacon, the ace Beaufighter ship-buster, carefully precalibrated his weapons for a very shallow dive. He 'walked' his cannon shells across the water, until they reached the enemy hull at 800 yards range, and immediately rippled his RPs in pairs to hit four below and four above the waterline. Meantime his cannons walked onwards over the superstructure and flak guns. Years later, when I described this briefly to an elderly chum, he looked at me, grinned and said: "Ah!... But our Typhoons were too heavy to walk on water."

The Germans were known to have painted horizon lines on their dive-bomber canopies – as an aid to accuracy. The Royal Navy, on at least one of their ranges, tracked each practice attack, calculated the dive angle and radioed it to the crew. But the RAF in my experience took no part in such matters.

Back in the war at Antwerp we found that we had missed the airborne assault on Arnhem. Not only our squadron – but all nine Typhoon squadrons of 84 Group. It was understandable in a way. We were supporting the Canadian army charged with clearing the Scheldt estuary and the port of Antwerp. This was high priority because the nearest working allied port was at Cherbourg, hundreds of miles to the west.

As for 83 Group the effort requested had been minimal. Wing Commander Kit North-Lewis, leading 124 Wing, flew just two ops supporting the armoured forces moving forward from Eindhoven.

Contrary to suggestions from elsewhere he reckoned that the weather would have allowed a considerably greater effort against the anti-tank guns opposing the advance, which might have made a world of difference.

How come this dreadful failure? It would appear that Airborne Forces headquarters, despite all the experience of army and RAF ops rooms working in close proximity – in the Western Desert, in Italy, and more recently in Normandy – had insisted on staying put in the UK. It had not been good news for close air support.

At Antwerp the enemy was still holding out in the northern suburbs of the city. The docks had been captured almost intact and the fight was on to clear the way for shipping. The Germans, well aware of what was at stake, were doing their utmost to prevent this happening. They hung on doggedly, even on the south bank of the Scheldt, where they were totally cut off.

We took our first casualty on 12 October attacking the coastal batteries at Breskens. It happened with sudden and unexpected violence. Fire and flame mushroomed amongst the diving aircraft, only to be snuffed out in an instant, leaving an ugly pall of smoke hanging in the air. A voice said: "Hap's bought it!" and at the same moment the smoke swirled and faded revealing a few unrecognisable bits of debris. They tumbled lifelessly away, and disappeared for ever as we concentrated on the target.

No one else was touched except the CO, who took the full force of the explosion, as his number two blew up. His ailerons were almost immovable and one undercarriage leg hung down uselessly, wrenched and twisted out of line. Yet he got back to Antwerp, landing last of all. The damaged leg collapsed and he slewed off the runway. His aircraft was a write off.

Some days later I accompanied Jimmy Simpson to ops, sneaking a preview of the target, as he prepared to brief A Flight for a low level show. Neville Thomas climbed down from his van and joined us. He looked decidedly angry and out of sorts, not at all his usual urbane self, and muttered about the unspeakable bastards we were going to attack.

Eventually it all came out. The Canadians had overrun an enemy position, in the immediate vicinity of our target, and found the body of one of their soldiers who had been captured on the previous day. And then, barely able to contain his rage, Tommy looked at us and said: "Those filthy Huns had hung him over a fire and roasted him to death."

For the first and almost the only time, as Jimmy headed the jeep along the peritrack, I felt hatred and loathing for the enemy troops who were shortly to be at the receiving end of our guns. A feeling that would not go away... that got worse as I ran through the familiar drills, swamping all rational thought.

Down below it looked just like the photograph. A pillbox surrounded by a network of trenches – sodden, treeless, and low lying – beside a narrow lake with the river beyond. A bleak and cheerless place to die in agony.

We came in slowly. Eight Typhoons with sixteen one thousand pound bombs. Hell bent on revenge. The pillbox filled our gunsights – smothered in bursting shells. The first section was through. Bombs gone

Top: RP aiming shallow dive. Depressed sightline to offset gravity drop.
Bottom: RP aiming steeper dive. Reduced allowance for gravity drop.

and twenty-five seconds to go. Eight muddy explosions. And another eight. A direct hit. Others cratering the spidery network of diggings. We went back again and again. Ferocious, bloodthirsty, strafing runs, hammering the damaged pillbox. Raking the trenches from end to end. Willing our shells to tear such a monstrous enemy to shreds. Until the ammunition ran out and our cannons clattered into silence.

Jimmy as usual called us to order and we cruised home, through the quiet autumn skies, drained of emotion.

A successful attack on the coastal batteries at Flushing brought the wing three useful recruits; from the Spitfire-equipped naval bombardment unit to which I had been posted before D-Day. It so happened that Geoff Hartley had been controlling a shoot with HMS *Warspite* against the same target. But the guns could not get it right and salvo after salvo pitched uselessly into the floodwaters around the gun emplacements. When the Typhoons appeared, and plastered them with bombs, it was the last straw.

On landing Geoff applied for an immediate transfer and encouraged Bob Gibbings and John Irving to do likewise. There was a continual need for Typhoon pilot replacements and the last attempt to recruit them, from the Spitfire squadrons of 2nd TAF, had not been very successful. So they were warmly welcomed and put through a rapid conversion course with some genuine bombing practice. Geoff and Bob joined 197 and John went to 263 where he learned all about RPs by firing them in action.

There were many sorties to the north of Antwerp. Close support for the troops fighting their way towards the Dutch border. Destructive attacks on tiny hamlets. Picturesque little places, hugging the canals, their gardens bright with marigolds as we swept low overhead. On a fine evening you could still see them from the circuit. Burning houses, angry red in the gathering darkness, and the smoke trails hanging low.

Once, leading a section of four, against a German battalion headquarters in one of those little villages, I nearly bought it. Totally my own fault. At APC I had developed a tendency to go lower and lower in dive-bombing practice – and here was this large and juicy barn in my sights. The result was inevitable and really stupid. A few moments later I found myself enveloped in smoke and flames with shattered timber and shredded thatch sweeping past, and calls on the radio like: "You OK Bassett leader?" Fortunately there was no real damage. Just some singed paintwork, a few dents, mostly to my image, and another lesson learned. Far better than I deserved.

During an evening sortie on 14 October I almost bought it again, climbing out in line astern, close to the airfield. Emerging from the cloud layer high above, a V2 plunged earthwards, striking at the very heart of the formation. No question of any evasive action – barely a moment to register the classic shape as it hurtled past, huge and menacing, shaving my starboard wing.

Not a word on the radio. How could the others have missed it? For me, however, the effect of that near miss was very odd. It created an extraordinary feeling of euphoria, almost of invincibility. The sortie had done its worst. There was nothing more to fear. Then, as if to prove the point, we ran into a bad combination of low cloud and concentrated flak. Almost dark by now and the chaps were tense on the radio, trying to avoid each other and those lethal, glowing, firefly streams. I felt strangely remote and immune from it all.

During our time at Antwerp V1s and V2s arrived at a combined rate of forty to fifty a day. This rose to almost eighty when the offensive was at its height, providing ample opportunity to study their behaviour.

It was said that a V2 never gave any warning of its arrival. True in a sense, but our experience was different. On a clear day the walking stick trails could be seen from the ground at Deurne, soaring upwards above the launching sites, before they vanished into the tropopause. Four minutes later, and you could almost set your watch by them, they arrived in characteristic fashion. An exploding warhead followed by the sonic boom echoing and re-echoing backwards into the empty sky.

Those with a warped sense of humour took a fiendish delight in timing them secretly and then announcing:

"V2 arriving in ten seconds!... three!... two!... one!.... NOW!"

To make matters worse, the wretched missile frequently disintegrated en route.

Once, visiting station headquarters (we were into winter accommodation by now) to collect some cash, I was talking to the accounts officer when I spied a momentary image and suddenly disappeared under his desk. He had time to say: "What the..." before the warhead exploded and we were showered with broken glass. So much for the belief that a V2 gave no warning at all.

The bombardment intensified and there was growing concern about our lack of dispersal. The pilots, in their terraced cottages at Deurne, were said to be living dangerously close together. A single hit might knock out most of the wing. In the end it was agreed that a number of us would be accommodated in town and 193 moved into a block of centrally heated flats.

After unpacking, as we were relaxing on our beds and enjoying the unaccustomed warmth, the building rocked violently. There was a sudden blast of air and the lights went out. Groping around by torchlight it was soon apparent that all the glass had gone, the heating had ceased to work, and the door had been thrown right across the room into the window embrasure.

We were lucky that night. Saved by the reinforced concrete structure, which remained standing when the V2 exploded thirty yards away, and the fact that we were lying down when the massive door flew over our heads. Only Bunny Austin, shaving in the bathroom, was slightly the worse for wear, his face cut by flying splinters. The dispersal scheme was promptly abandoned and 193 returned to base for the winter.

V weapons and winter quarters were evidence that we were into a new phase of the war. Everywhere from Switzerland to the North Sea the advance was slowing down.

The enemy was not on his way back to Berlin, as we had fondly imagined until a few weeks ago, at least not this side of Christmas. In our sector, on the left of the line, he was retreating towards the River Maas. A natural defensive position. Stalemate seemed likely until the spring.

In the cramped cottages we were preparing to dig in as well. The tiny kitchen cum living room, which I shared with Jimmy Simpson, contained our camp beds, a couple of chairs, and a cupboard. Otherwise it was completely bare, down to the stone floor. In cold weather, even with the old stove going full blast, it chilled to the marrow. At night, huddled for warmth in our blankets, we slept fitfully as the flying bombs thundered across the sky. Occasionally, when one cut out too close for comfort, the moment of silence would be broken by an ever hopeful: "Missed again!"

Top left: Christmas 1944. With my father, Douglas Ince, home from Italy.

Top right: In a Harvard, Canada, summer 1943 – blissful days.

Middle left: Wings parade, Calgary August 1943. Morning after the night before!

Bottom: Harvard out of Airdrie. Satellite circuits and bumps away from the madding crowd.

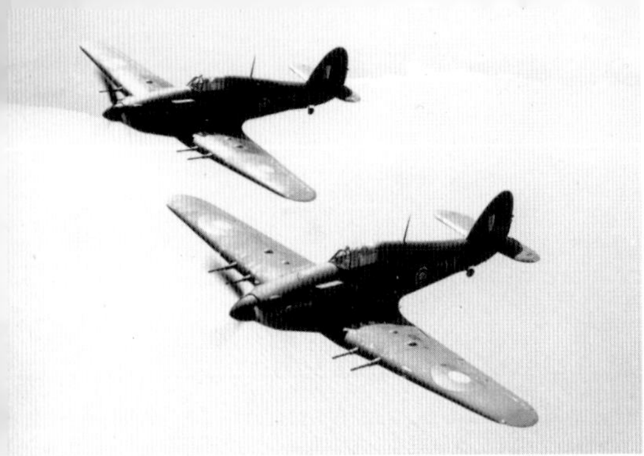

Top left: Hurricane IIc. Hawker breed par excellence. Sadly passing its sell-by date.

Top right: Mustang I. Great engineering, underpowered but surprisingly fast.

Middle: Spitfire Vc. Superb boy's aeroplane, even when clipped, cropped and (somewhat) clapped out.

Bottom: Early Typhoon. Too fast to need a rear view. Rhubarb! Rhubarb!

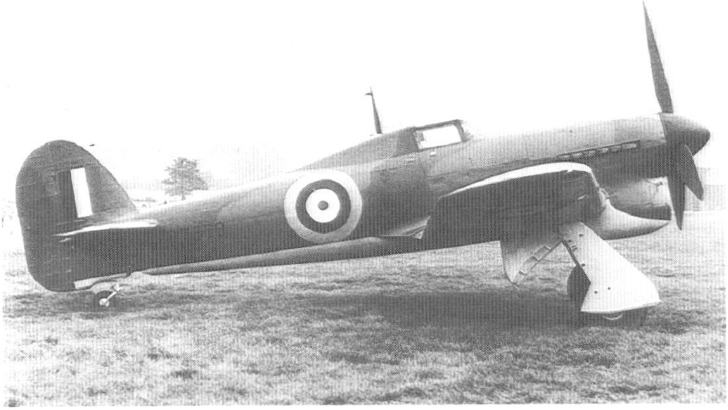

Top left: Thick wing takes loads of ammunition.
Top right: Swanning in Normandy with Pete Langille and Jimmy Simpson.

Bottom: With Killy and Pete on a duff day.

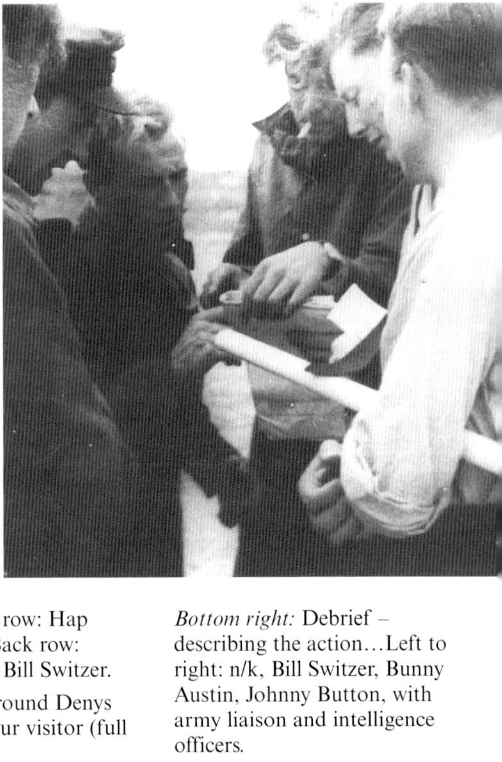

Top: Orchard at B3. Zipp Button and A Flight. Front row: Hap Pratt, Killy Kilpatrick, Johnny Button, Jim Darling. Back row: Jimmy Fishwick, Al Sugden, Jimmy Simpson, author, Bill Switzer.

Bottom left: Churchill visits the wing. In middle foreground Denys Gillam with forage cap. Second and third right from our visitor (full face and in peaked caps) are Rod Davidge and Killy.

Bottom right: Debrief – describing the action…Left to right: n/k, Bill Switzer, Bunny Austin, Johnny Button, with army liaison and intelligence officers.

Top: ...and unwinding. Colin Gilmour tells the tale to Wee Mac McCartney, Sac Bilz and Toddles Pratt. On the right is Bill Hurst.

Bottom: 193 Squadron Normandy.

Back Row left to right
Toddles Pratt, Bill Hurst, Jimmy Fishwick, Ned Statters, "Gilly" Gilmour (Aus), Gus Gough, Sac Bilz (Can), Jim Darling, Mike "109 King" Bulleid, Dave Ince, Hap Pratt.

193 SQUADRON
St Croix Sur Mer, Normandy
1 August 1944

Front row left to right
Jimmy "Simmy" Simpson, Ian "Sox" Ross, Al Sugden (Can), Eddie Richardson, Charlie "Flamer" Hall, Johnnie "Boots" Brown, CO Johnnie "Zipp" Button, Bill Switzer (Can), Adj Louis McBride, Felix Cryderman (Can), Pete Langille (Can), Ben Lenson.

Top: Argentinean artist, Carlos Garcia, catches Ronnie Sheward's Hurricane, in the thick of it, at disastrous Hansweert.

Bottom: The Arado 234 flew a number of high altitude, photo recce, sorties over the Normandy beachhead in August 1944. The first jet aircraft ever to do so.

Top left: Vianen Bridge. An elegantly engineered single span…

Top right: …and a superb bombing performance…

Middle: …by the man who scored two direct hits. Ben Lenson with his crew.

Bottom left: Arthur Todd. Toddy was 257 Squadron's final wartime CO.

Bottom right: Forward oblique of enemy MT repair unit Doetinchem. Some really good pictures at last.

Top: Mustang IV alias P51D. Two-stage Merlin and new canopy made a world of difference.

Middle: Squadron targets in Neustadt bay, 3 May 1945. Shipping strikes and the horrors of Belsen were not a good combination.

Bottom left: Luftwaffe 37mm light flak. Bravely manned and much respected. Shot us down and sometimes saved our lives.

Bottom right: Eddie Richardson, founder member of 193. Two operational tours and the ultimate squadron diarist, a proud record.

Top: Another Balbo to come. The four Typhoon squadrons of 146 Wing lined up on Hildesheim airfield July 1945.

Middle left: Charles Woodcock. 6193 rigger, amateur photographer and man of many parts – especially forward oblique cameras and napalm.

Middle right: Acting CO's aircraft at Hildesheim in full postwar livery.

Bottom: Armourer, Johnny Deall, and napalm for Goslar demonstration.

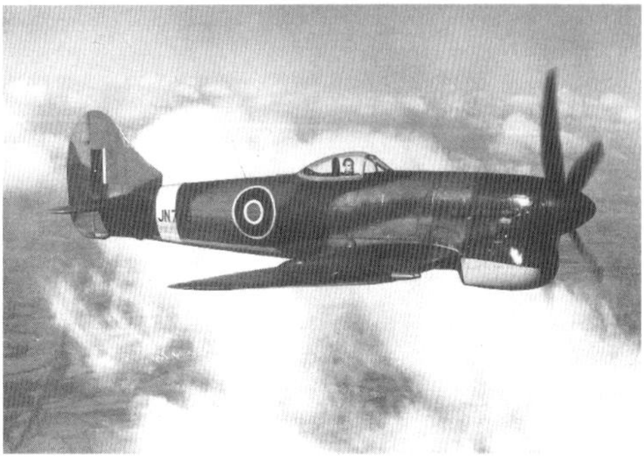

Top left: He 219. Ugly and boxlike but a very formidable night fighter.

Top right: Tempest V. Shades of the Tiffie with better handling and more performance. How we envied their extra range and deep penetration sorties.

Middle left: Dornier Do 335. A development aircraft hidden at Hildesheim. Why the Air Disarmament Wing ignored it remains a mystery.

Middle right: Gloster E1/44. So near and yet so far. Vanished like my test flying career.

Bottom left: Spitfire FR XIVc. No boy's aeroplane this. Gyroscope of an engine and rules which you broke at your peril, but the performance was – wow!

Bottom right: Author with his Spitfire XIV. Peacetime temptation and fun. Just as well that we were both more mature.

No. 4 COURSE, 1946

Sqn.Ldr. W.D.K.Franklin; Sqn.Ldr. K.C.M.Giddings D.F.C.; Flt.Lt. J.G.Haigh; Flt.Lt. P.S.Flight [illegible]; Sqn.Ldr. T.F.Neil D.F.C.; Wg.Cdr. M.E.Blackstone D.F.C.; Gp.Capt. R.C.Hockey D.S.O., D.F.C.; Flt.Lt. N.F.Duke D.S.O., D.F.C.; Sqn.Ldr. D.R.Turley-George D.F.C.; Sqn.Ldr. P.J.Garner; Sqn.Ldr. K.A.Major D.F.C.; Sqn.Ldr. P.G.Evans D.F.C.; Flt.Lt. D.A.C.Hunt

Sqn.Ldr. R.F.Martin D.F.C.; Flt.Lt. P.R.Fowler; Sqn.Ldr. E.F.S.May; Flt.Lt. P.P.C.Barthropp D.F.C.; Lieut. [illegible] Davies D.S.C., R.N.V.R.; Lieut. R.B.Mancus R.N.V.R.; Lieut. H.C.N.Goodhart R.N.; Lieut. P.G.Lawrence M.B.E.; Lieut. [illegible] S.Wilson R.N.; Lieut. K.R.Hickson R.N.; Lieut. J.F.Rankin D.S.C., R.N.; Flt.Lt. D.A.Taylor D.F.C.; Flt.Lt. E.L.Heath; Flt.Lt. H.J.Dodson; Flg.Off. K.A.Butler

Flt.Lt. G.E.C.Genders D.F.M.; Flt.Lt. D.H.G.Ince D.F.C.; Flt.Lt. W.H.Else; Mr. J.R.B.Spink B.Sc.; Flt.Lt. F.R.Arnold; Sqn.Ldr. W.R.Morris A.F.C.; Sqn.Ldr. H.G.Hastings A.F.C. A.F.M.; Wg.Cdr. H.P.Powell A.F.C.; Gp.Capt. H.J.Wilson C.B.E. A.F.C.; Mr. G.M.Humphreys B.Sc., A.I.P. A.F.R.Ae.S.; Flt.Lt. L.H.Tolchard D.F.C.; Flt.Lt. F.E.Clark; W/O. C.Rutter M.B.E.; Mr. S.I.R.Nicol B.Sc.; Flt.Lt. P.R.Cope; Flt.Lt. I.D.Crozier; Flt.Lt. A.E.Marriott

Top: Empire Test Pilots School – No 4 Course, Cranfield 1946.

Bottom left: Horten IX V2. Prototype crashed in February 1945. Exact non-flying replica shown here was built much later in the USA.

Bottom right: Pete Thorne in his Typhoon days. RAF Harrowbeer 1943.

Top left: In the Harz mountains. Author and Ron Howard, colleagues in Elliott Flight Automation, with Karl Doetsch and his family.

Top right: Typhoon and Tempest reunion UK 1987. Author with Mike Bulleid, Pinkie Stark and Ronnie Sheward.

Middle: Gathering of veterans, ASAVN, mayor and local dignitaries at the Typhoon Memorial, Noyers Bocage 2006.

Bottom: With Bob Talalla and George Wood after unveiling the plaque in memory of Bob's uncle, a pilot on 263 Squadron. Normandy 2007.

Top: From left to right Jonathan Simons, author's daughter Ros Ince, Sandy Hunter, with veterans Paddy Byrne, author and Johnny Shellard. Coningsby March 2008.

Middle: Noyers Bocage 2009. Thanking our French hosts after the remembrance ceremony; and exchanging fraternal greetings with the German aircrew association. Left to right author, David Morrow (nephew of Typhoon pilot John Friedlander), Richard Boyce (schoolmaster and committee member ASAVN), Harry Hardy (Canadian Typhoon pilot).

Bottom: Le Manoir 2009. After the unveiling with daughter Ginnie and XI Squadron's Andy King.

Top: Plaque unveiling in memory of F/O Frank Thomas, Le Manoir 2009. British and Canadian veterans with the mayor, members of ASAVN and the XI Squadron detachment from RAF Coningsby.

Bottom left: Sandy Hunter. A tower of strength. Even more so since the welcome day in 2007 when he agreed to become our patron.

Bottom right: The Typhoon today, a quantum leap forward. The Royal Air Force at its very best.

CHAPTER TEN

WINTER IN FLANDERS

There had been an Me109 production unit at Deurne with sub assembly and stores dispersed around the Napoleonic forts close to the airfield. The instrument bay was a treasure trove – its beautiful AC horizons and DC turn and slip indicators, in their sealed packs, a generation ahead of the ungainly suction-driven devices on our blind flying panels. And the gyro compass, known to us only in principle, was fitted as standard to the Gustav[1].

First I had to acquire a selection of instruments, some of which might be useful right away, and others – well just to keep for the moment – and then to explain myself to Charlie Hall who had been watching with interest:

"Those miniature ball-type skid indicators. Might improve our dive-bombing if we mounted them on the gunsights. And a gyro compass would be super for navigation."

Charlie was rather offended by the thought of my gunsight modification. Until he recalled how easy it was to build up a significant sideslip angle in a steep dive. Then he saw the point. But he remained less than enthusiastic about the gyro compass. It needed power and the master unit had to be mounted in the rear fuselage which could be difficult. And then, as if reading my thoughts:

"There's enough material in those forts to assemble several brand new 109s, what about one for the squadron?"

The CO and Jimmy supported the idea. Stan Carr, without whom it would have been impossible, was delighted to take charge. A team of volunteers was soon recruited to help collect all the parts. Operation Gustav was under way.

Once we strapped a complete fuselage to the back of an open truck and towed it tail first, on its undercarriage, through a maze of greasy cobbled streets. The last leg of that hazardous trip passed close to 35 Wing which occupied the far side of the airfield. We drove gingerly past and they looked at us as if we were mad. Perhaps we were, or maybe it was just a passion for things aeronautical.

For the prototype skid indicator, I stripped down one of the miniature turn and slip indicators, removed the ball-type unit and attached it to the gunsight body with a lump of plasticine. It was easy to use and certainly seemed to help. So I called Stan to look at it. Very soon we had a batch of aircraft fitted with them. Attached by proper, if rather large, Jubilee clips. A sort of head up display.

One of our pilots, Bill Hurst, an ex Brat[2], thought bigger and better. He acquired a gyro compass, master unit and cockpit repeater, wired them up with an inverter and battery and proved that they worked. He then spent every spare moment buried in the rear fuselage of his Typhoon. Until the great day when he connected it all up and flew an operational sortie.

It was an unauthorised modification to the electrical system and the EO[3] was livid. Especially when every pilot who flew with it wanted one for himself. But Bill would not oblige. He was in far too much trouble already.

In the centre of Antwerp the heady post liberation days had gone forever. The New Century, a hotel which had seen its share of wild and spontaneous parties, was virtually out of bounds. Crowded with base wallahs who seemed to be taking over all the best places in town. But not, let it be said, before the wing had made its mark. 197 Squadron, aggravated by the hotel orchestra's failure to create the right sort of music, had already distinguished themselves by decorating its members with a selection of potted plants.

By the time we felt able to go there again the base wallahs had arrived in strength and were occupying most of the upper floors, including those above the ballroom where our parties usually started. All went well until the backwoodsman in Felix Cryderman suddenly reasserted itself. Out came his revolver and his soft laughter, always a sign of danger, was lost in a fusillade of shots as he tried to destroy the chandeliers over our heads.

We shouted at him to put the bloody thing away, which he did with surprising speed, and not a moment too soon, as a bunch of indignant brass hats stormed into the room. Felix looked up at them from the depths of his armchair, wreathed in gunsmoke, oblivious to the atmosphere of menace.

"Some fat drunken Canadian pilot," he said quietly. "He went that way." And then, more audibly to us: "Serve the buggers right – most of them look shit scared."

After that we took our custom elsewhere. To 'Scabby Gabby's', the noisy saloon bar near the airfield, or to other more discrete if dubious spots away from the city centre. Places where there was safety in numbers, if only to support those who might yield to temptation.

One evening these precautions were of no avail. The setting itself was innocent enough. Half a dozen of us sitting round the bar, in conversation with Madame, whilst her assistant hovered in the background. No hint of the unexpected until it suddenly registered that one of our party had been missing for some time. Madame pulled back the heavy curtains. And there, like the male lead in some erotic play, was our missing colleague in *flagrante delicto* with Girl Friday. We stood transfixed, trying to find words to express our... who knows? – and then gave up, closing the curtains gently and leaving them to their pleasures.

We were dedicated party goers. It was part and parcel of squadron life. A way of unwinding at the end of the day. Celebrating a successful show, trying to forget, or when we had just lost a friend. Like the night after Pete Langille bought it attacking an enemy column, caught by flak, too low to bail out. Pete, loyal and dependable, never seeking the limelight. His courage had been an inspiration. We would miss him like hell.

Charlie's voice broke in on my thoughts: "Another snort old man?"

And the ever watchful Jimmy, like some demonic conductor, urging us on:

"Cats! Sister's Cat's! My Sister's Cat's! Up My Sisters Cat's!

Pudding Up My Sister's Cats! Black Pudding Up....!"

We bellowed it out again and again through all its lewd permutations. Helpless with laughter as the drink took hold and the mistakes became more and more frequent. Laughter which relieved and relaxed. Wonderfully therapeutic. And we knew that wherever he was Pete would understand.

That night was long ago and the memories grow dim. Was it just about Pete alone? Or all of them? The ones who never came back.

About that time up on an air test, braving a miserable wet afternoon, I had just completed a tidy slow roll over the middle of the airfield and was feeling rather pleased with myself. Suddenly there was a sort of commotion ahead and this angular shape passed below me going like the clappers with a Typhoon (Gus Gough as it subsequently turned out) following closely behind trailing a great plume of smoke – cannon or exhaust or probably both.

In fact Gus was just too late for, as I pulled round hard to observe them, the V1 went down into the docks. The explosion shorted out the whole overhead power line network of the Antwerp tramway system and, for a few brief moments, the gloom of that November afternoon was lit up by a magnificent lightning display reflecting off the wet tramcars and streets.

Back in the dispersal Gus, and Eddie Richardson who had been flying as his number two, were convinced that they had scored a victory. But I doubt that the good burghers of Antwerp would have seen it that way.

When Johnny Baldwin went on rest, 'Bomber' Wells took over as wing leader. His arrival coincided with a series of new developments, phosphorous incendiaries, blind bombing, underground radar control and target photography.

Our camera-equipped Typhoons, survivors of the ones which I had helped deliver to Odiham in the previous June, were acquired by Denys Gillam from 35 Wing as they were about to depart for Gilze-Rijen. He could claim that he was doing them a favour, taking over their unpopular Tiffies as they started re-equipping with Spitfire XIVs. In point of fact his wing would now be able to fly its own photographic sorties and he would get the results quicker than before.

Sadly the conversion of 2 Squadron to Spit XIVs led to the death of Pat Garland, famous from our ITW days and the episode of the sheep. Pat bounced on landing – applied a bit of power which came on late, so he applied a bit more which came on with a rush and he ended up inverted.

Jerry Eaton, a flight commander on 257, and I were to be Denys Gillam's guinea pigs. Loaned from our squadrons, as and when required, to fly unescorted missions. Our FR[4] Typhoons carried three F24 cameras, one oblique and two vertical, in the port inboard gun bay. We planned to use the vertical pair only, making our target runs at about 4,000 feet.

My first sortie on 26 November, flown several hours after the attack on 15th Army headquarters at Dordrecht, was abandoned due to weather; 35 Wing got in first the following day.

The German army commander, von Busch, was lucky to be away at the time as the target was well and truly pranged. The Dutch Resistance responded quickly with a list of casualties, and the date and place of the military funeral, and asked whether the wing would please oblige with another attack to finish off those who had escaped!

Going in immediately after an attack on a heavily defended target, which soon became standard practice, was character forming to say the least. Better to be part of a squadron, bombs and cannon in hot blood, than sweating it out alone waiting to plunge into a hornet's nest. Or was it?

Photo reconnaissance offered a unique challenge. That of bringing back the first real evidence of success or failure and simultaneously, not to say unavoidably, providing a measure by which the quality of your own sortie might be judged. Not surprisingly it exerted a powerful attraction.

Thoughts to encourage the loner in photo 'M', sitting high above Rotterdam, looking down on the perfection of a late autumn day on 29 November. The outlines of the city shimmering softly through the haze.

Black shell bursts stained the sky. The squadrons moved into echelon and plummeted earthwards. Light flak veiled the target merging into a carpet of destruction, and the diving aircraft became vague shadows darting through layers of murk and smoke.

Brief words of command, leaders reforming their squadrons, and then silence on the radio. The storm of flak died away. A pall of dust hung over the target area. My time had come.

The 88s opened up immediately, a muffled thud shook the aircraft, and oil began to smear the screen; it spread rapidly, still thin, but enough to obscure the view. The cockpit filled with fumes and the curtain of oil grew darker.

On instruments now. Fear caught at me and I strove to fight it down... Hold the dive!... Hold it!... You must hold it!... Level out and switch the cameras on!... By now I was down to about 2,500 feet – rocketing blind across the centre of the city – at least the flak was invisible.

The return trip was agonizing. Trying to spare the engine resulted in a suicidally slow passage across the docks and I expected a direct hit at any moment. Winding the canopy open was no help at all. An alarming close up of the Dordrecht bridges, heavily guarded by flak guns, frightened me out of my skin, and I was deluged with hot oil. After what seemed an age I reached friendly territory and called 'Longbow'[5] to alert the nearest airfield, Gilze-Rijen, to my predicament.

The wingco came on the radio – something about relaxing, taking it easy, which made me angry and he got rather a blunt reply. Oil continued to flood over the windscreen obscuring my goggles and, when I raised them, stinging my eyes. Time to start the approach, staying high in case the engine failed, and slightly offset to provide a view of sorts until the last possible moment. The temperatures were almost off the clock and the oil pressure falling rapidly... Undercarriage... Flaps... Into the final turn... Two Spits taxiing frantically out of my path....

It was a surprisingly good landing which came to a shuddering halt alongside a group of airmen and a Coles crane. Difficult to know who was the more taken aback. But reaction was beginning to set in and I shouted across to them, "You can take it away!" The effect was rather spoilt when I slipped on the oily wing root, and ended up in a heap on the runway, fortunately without further damage.

Photo 'M' had been hit in the spinner, which was like a colander, and the constant-speed mechanism had been badly damaged. The fuselage looked as if it had been painted glossy black. It was a miracle that the engine had kept going.

In the mess after a late lunch, still red eyed and stinking of oil, David Hurford, Nobby Clarke and others dropped by to take coffee. It was good to be amongst the BFs again. Even if there was more than the usual leg pulling, about usurping their role, that it served me right for fiddling my way onto Typhoons, and so on.

By now I was getting anxious about the dance that night but the wingco must have forgiven me because he sent one of our air liaison officers to collect me in an Auster. On the final approach to Deurne a V1 came rolling past to starboard, so close that you could almost reach out and touch it, and dived into the abandoned 35 Wing dispersals. I must have done something to upset the enemy that day!

The dance was a great success, thanks to Jimmy Simpson. A set of Glen Miller records, which he had purloined from heaven knows where, had been turned into musical scores by the Belgian orchestra. So we drank and danced the night away to the best of Big Band sounds. Jimmy had also, perhaps unwisely, offered to find some partners for 'Plamondon's Playboys'. Organised, as he admitted later, through a local seminary, complete with chaperone. He assured us that there were no nuns.

Perhaps the squadron diarist was thinking of the latter as he commented unkindly that: *when they appeared, there was speculation that Flight Lieutenant Simpson's eyesight might not be up to the standard which the Service required of its fighter bomber pilots.*

Far be it for me to criticize Jimmy's selection, for the dance was perfectly timed, after the events of a highly charged day. I slept like a log – never heard a single V weapon that night, ate a hearty breakfast the next morning and felt ready to face the world once more.

I had reckoned without Derek Erasmus, Rhodesian and a flight commander from 266 Squadron, who had just been promoted to take us over. For 'Plum' had now gone on rest. 'Rastus' was able and demanding, a determined leader, yet sensitive and understanding towards those he led, and his impact was immediate and very positive. We could not have wished for a better commanding officer.

He called me aside before briefing to say that he had asked Jimmy to stand down, so that I could take the second section of four, on the sortie which he himself would be leading. Perhaps he wanted to see how I was coping. Much more likely, as I came to know him better, was his awareness that extra challenges are one way of moving on after a hairy do. Like you cannot do LMF when you are responsible for others. In the end however it resulted in rather more than he had expected.

For we were caught running close to a narrow gap in the overcast, providing the German gunners with excellent tracking data, and our new CO's aircraft was badly damaged. There was outrage in his voice as he handed over the lead, and turned back with his number 2, while I took over the rest and started a long let down for our low level attack.

By now I was afraid. Not so much of the enemy but the weather, which was atrocious, and for the chaps who were with me. Afraid that I might fail to find the target or bring them safely home.

Below cloud base, skirting a violent storm, reflector sights glowed ruby red against a receding wall of mist. Rain curtained the railway line, lower still, catching the outlines of a level crossing ahead – dim original of our photograph at briefing. In the final moments we spotted a repair gang at work and raked their truck with our cannons in a single flying pass. A burst of tracer reached up to bar the way and vanished in the surrounding downpour. More rain obliterated the scene before the first bombs went off. I pulled up into a turn: "Bassett White Leader orbiting port three miles south of the target."

And back came an anxious: "Black Four – there's no one ahead of me!"

That was the last man to attack. What on earth did he mean? Had all the others bought it? Then reason prevailed and a quick glance confirmed that four Typhoons, and a distant fifth just visible through the murk, were closing up rapidly from behind.

"It's OK Black Four. I have you in sight. We're all here. Come on up and join us."

Van C was the man who needed nursing that day. On his first tour he had suffered engine failure on take-off from Manston and had crashed in a nearby railway yard. Lucky to escape with his life he carried the marks of very bad facial burns. He was now on his second tour. A truly brave man he should never have been allowed back on ops. Fortunately his condition was spotted in time – and soon afterwards he was sent on rest – otherwise he would probably have killed himself and possibly others as well.

This was the beginning of a most difficult time and we were fortunate indeed to have Rastus in command. For the dreary and seemingly endless task of interdiction – depriving the enemy of his V2 supply routes – had just became top priority.

The command had gone out. London had taken enough. The deadly flow of V2s to the launching sites must be cut down to size or, better still, stopped completely. The enemy thought otherwise. This was his ultimate terror weapon, shortly to change the whole course of the war, and nothing must stand in its way.

He strengthened his flak defences and, when the lines were cut, drove his repair gangs with utter ruthlessness. So we went out and cut them again and again.

Other targets came in every conceivable form – embankments, goods yards, signal boxes, junctions and bridges, especially bridges. Dreary, yes, but there was one consolation. The V2 offensive, against Antwerp also, would have been far worse without it.

That was the theory. The practice was more difficult. Day after day after day the clouds hung low over the sodden polders. Fog and rain made navigation more difficult. There were losses due to weather. Attempts to get through to our targets were frustrated time and again. Worst of all were the periods when no flying was possible; and that nasty syndrome, 'The less you fly – The less you want to' began to rear its ugly head.

Combined with the urgent need to stall the V2 offensive, which seemed to create a lot of pressure, this proved too much for two of our pilots. The saddest case had flown over eighty sorties. A figure which, in many circumstances, could be considered tour expired. We certainly thought so; with the poor chap showing marked signs of twitch. That sort of thing could be contagious so he was posted. We expected that he would go on rest. But no, it was to another Typhoon squadron in 83 Group, to continue operational flying. It was a dreadful mistake, made worse when he was killed shortly afterwards, following engine failure on take-off.

The other was strange rather than sad. He was a Yank in the RAF, had flown one operational tour already, and was posted to the squadron at Antwerp as a supernumerary flight lieutenant. Rather an exhibitionist, he wore his service revolver in low slung cowboy fashion, and edited the squadron diary in an amusing and light hearted way. He amazed us all one day, by posing for a photograph in the cockpit of his aircraft, wearing an American Fortress gunner's anti-flak helmet.

When asked where he had got it he said that, as an American, he had friends in the 8th Air Force. Then he announced that he would be wearing it on ops from now on, as the flak was becoming extremely dangerous. So our CO decided that enough was enough and confiscated his treasured headgear.

As can be imagined, his behaviour had provoked a certain amount of amusement. Perhaps teasing might be a better word. This came to a head one morning at breakfast when someone was unwise enough to mock his usual combination of dried eggs, tinned bacon, soya link and *marmalade*! Our friend drew his revolver, pointed it at the culprit, and threatened to blow off his head. Until then, apart from a few minor idiosyncrasies, he had seemed fairly normal. But this threatened assault was clearly for real and soon afterwards he departed from us, with a robust medical escort, immobilised in a strait jacket.

There seems to be such a fine balance between courage and fear. If you can forget the hairy episodes you're winning – if you can't you're losing the plot. A modicum of fear stimulates – well controlled it may actually improve your performance. A load of it is an absolute disaster.

A lack of it is worst of all, immensely dangerous to yourself and those around you.

Sometimes an easy show produces unexpected hazards. As happened on 10 December when I took a section of four to destroy a set of lock gates east of Nijmegen. An ideal target for a low level attack, no flak, and our bombing seemed to be spot on. Except that I almost collided with the target, mushing violently through the plumes of spray thrown up by my own cannon shells.

As we reformed after the attack Ben Lenson warned me that I had a double hang up[6], which explained a great deal. He was closing in for a look.

"Bassett Leader your aircraft looks OK. Your bombs too. But the fins are badly damaged."

So what about those two little propellers, safety elements in the fusing system, had they gone too? Ben wasn't sure. I checked the selector switches, operated the bomb push continuously, and pumphandled the control column. All in vain. The bombs stayed put.

I called Craven A[7] for assistance and there was an armourer waiting at the end of the runway. He came forward, as I slowed carefully to a stop, and disappeared under the wings. Moments later he emerged grinning broadly and giving me the thumbs up. Panic over! The fins

Adjusting the bomb crutches. Critical and vital skills.

looked horrible. Battered and twisted, the propellers torn off, so that the detonator pistols were floating free. The slightest jar would have blown my aircraft to pieces.

Hang ups were all about the crutches which steadied the bombs. Getting them right, with no torque spanners, was an armourer's nightmare. Too loose and the bombs wobbled – too tight and they would not release, and this quite apart from any effect of temperature changes and humidity. It says a lot for our chaps that they rarely got it wrong.

With the first snows the polder countryside surrounding the Zuider Zee, which contained many of our interdiction targets, became even more bleak and secretive. Dyke and canal, villages and farms, stood out against a covering of white.

The landscape looked flatter, more vulnerable than ever to the whims of the enemy, who might inundate it again at any time. Snow storms stalked the leaden skies creating worlds of dazzling blindness.

This seasonal weather brought with it other, more significant, changes. The Luftwaffe began to appear again in increasing numbers. And suddenly, incredibly, the Hun was on the offensive, pushing forward with armour into the Ardennes. On Tommy's map in ops the enemy spearheads, and the bulge in the bomb line towards the Meuse, began to look distinctly ominous and there was even talk of a breakthrough from Liège towards Antwerp.

For the present General Winter seemed firmly on von Rundstedt's side, and the Allied Air Forces were grounded for days on end, allowing the German columns to move forward unimpeded. Our new wing leader, encouraged by the way in which the weather often seemed to improve after dark, began to consider night intrusion. When a Ju88 over Deurne illuminated an American convoy, and shot it up, his enthusiasm knew no bounds.

The idea was hardly new, but the thought of ranging around those dreaded polders, in the darkness and the dead of winter, did not appeal. It became even less attractive when I found myself in pole position on the wingco's short list. Then came the German paratroop rumour and night intrusion seemed like the lesser of two evils.

It started with a 266 show against Deelen airfield to the north of Arnhem. The place was said to be full of troop transports preparing for an airdrop on Deurne. Strategically, as part of a concerted plan to link up with the armoured drive westwards from Liège, and assuming that the Germans still had the resources, it made good sense.

266 returned from Deelen empty handed. But the rumours intensified. The Ju52s were definitely there, too well camouflaged to be seen, and the woods around were swarming with troops. These veterans

of Eban Emael, and Crete, fanatical battle-hardened troops who had fought in the snows of Russia and hung on for months in the ruins of Monte Cassino, would be dropping in to beat up the pilots tonight, and if not tonight, maybe tomorrow night, or the night after.

We set up every conceivable kind of booby trap and retired to bed, fully dressed, pistols at the ready. Visions of coal-scuttle-helmeted giants, armed to the teeth with machine pistols and potato masher grenades, disturbed our sleep. Came the dawn, and Goss the batman trying to revive us with his mugs of hot sweet tea, but we were flaked out and exhausted.

We never slept in our clothes again but there were other nights of alarm before the German advance was finally halted. As for the night intruder project, it never got off the ground.

By day we continued to be thwarted by the weather. A fighter sweep towards Aachen on 23 December, conducted above an impenetrable layer of mist and low cloud, was notable only for the number of engines which began to run rough after more than a week on the ground. The Luftwaffe had disappeared. And the enemy's armoured spearheads were hidden in the murk below, totally out of reach.

Stuck between that blanket of white and the cloudless vault above was to feel totally naked and frustrated. My engine vibrated horribly. Drop tanks drained. Eyes searched unceasingly for enemy fighters, or a gap in the murk below through which we could find something, almost anything, to attack. We came home empty handed and thoroughly fed up.

193 tangled with the Luftwaffe on Christmas Eve, and on Christmas Day as well. The first occasion was a fighter sweep in the Osnabrück area, and I was airborne as spare, determined not to miss the fun after the fiasco over Aachen. The bomb line came and went. No one turned back, I hung on, hoping against hope. The Rhine came into view, and the CO was not amused: "Spare go home NOW!"

I was furious. But there was much worse to follow. Four aircraft turned back, with engine and other problems, minutes after my departure. The remaining four soldiered on and were bounced by fifty plus 109s and 190s, near Enschede. One Typhoon was never seen again, and another was damaged, with no claims against the enemy. 197 in the same area fared even worse, losing two and one damaged, to twelve 190s which suffered no losses in return.

On Christmas Day B Flight, caught by a mixed force of about sixty enemy fighters whilst attacking a train, helped to redress the balance. The locomotive blew up in a cloud of steam. Mike Bulleid destroyed a 190, another was badly damaged, and the Typhoons returned without loss.

In the evening Johnny Baldwin attended Christmas dinner as our guest. He had just been awarded a bar to his DSO. There were speeches, and toasts, but most of us went to bed early.

Derek Erasmus's skill as a leader was well demonstrated in the destruction of an MT repair unit west of Arnhem. It was our last op of the year, with twelve aircraft, and the squadron was carrying a mixed load of high explosive and incendiaries. The aiming point was unmistakable, a massive rectangular roof in the middle of a heavily wooded site, and his dive was beautifully positioned and uncompromisingly steep. The bombs went off in a single rolling salvo, and the whole building disappeared in a sea of smoke and flame. Incredibly there were no near misses amongst the surrounding trees for the whole bomb-load had fallen inside the four walls of the target.

We came home in a state of high elation ready to sign off with a storming squadron break. And that December afternoon, with Derek's exhortation, "Make it a good one chaps!" ringing in our ears as we let down towards the airfield – we excelled ourselves. Tight across the threshold, pulling up one by one with controlled violence and metronome precision like guardsmen on parade, undercarriage selection from an inverted position and the tightest steepest curved approach into a closely sequenced stream landing.

A splendid team manoeuvre. Like the Typhoon it had become part of our lives – signing off each sortie and showing the world that we were the best.

The mood changed abruptly with the news that 197's popular CO, Allan Smith, had been shot down leading a low level attack against a bridge over the Waal. It was a great loss for, by any standard, he was an outstanding squadron commander. His pilots reported that he had put down OK, and had run from his aircraft, so there was good reason to believe that he was alive. Even so they were devastated and attempted to mount a revenge sortie. Which was not a good idea. All in all New Year's Eve became a pretty subdued affair.

CHAPTER ELEVEN

CHALLENGE AND CHANGE

New Year's Day dawned cloudless with scarcely a breath of wind and a hard frost. Perfect flying weather. But the squadrons, briefed and ready to go for almost an hour, were stuck on the ground. The runway was still being de-iced. Such a delay was unprecedented. The RAF Regiment, whose responsibility it was, had been caught out by Hogmanay and when the air raid warning sounded they were decidedly unpopular.

A train had stopped on the line beside the airfield and, when the sirens sounded, the engine driver started reducing his boiler pressure. The effect was prodigious. Great billowing clouds of white, brilliant in the low sun, which must have been visible for miles. I raced Jimmy Simpson to the top of the embankment and we confronted the culprit in his cab.

"Arrêtez vous tout de suite!" had no effect – apart from a mumbled *"Non il est necessaire."* So we drew our pistols and threatened him with instant death.

At this, much to our relief, he cut off the offending blast of steam. Simultaneously a Bofors opened fire from the opposite side of the airfield, sending a clip of shells low overhead. The driver looked very upset. But we were unrepentant: "Serves him bloody well right! Creating a beacon like that!"

The sound of diving aircraft came almost as we saw them, a loose gaggle of Me109s, swarming towards us above the rooftops of Antwerp. Bofors thumped, cannon and machine guns responded abruptly, and the snarl of engines rose to crescendo as they flashed across the airfield, all mottled camouflage and splashes of yellow.

In their gunsights were eighty plus Typhoons. Out in the open, most of them fully armed and fuelled. The target of a lifetime. Yet only the first eight carried out any sort of attack. In a single pass they destroyed just one aircraft and caused minor damage to eight others. Two further enemy formations appeared in the circuit. Flying aimlessly around at low level, they made no attempt to avoid the defensive fire, and departed to a cynical chorus of "Weave, you buggers, weave!"

Long afterwards it emerged that JG 77 had put up about 100 aircraft for the attack on Deurne. Trained essentially as fighter pilots by a Luftwaffe under intense pressure, and with negligible navigation skills, their Ju88 pathfinder vanished all too soon. As a result only one gruppe of about thirty found the target while the rest searched in vain to the north. On the way home they blundered across the V1 routes to Antwerp, where the massed ack ack took a dreadful toll. JG 77 never flew again in geschwader strength.

Within the hour we were on our way to attack a suspension bridge over the Waal. Almost next door to the one which had been Allan Smith's downfall, it was to remain standing for another three days, before we finally took it out. Ben Lenson, who was flying number two to Jimmy Simpson on the second attack, scored the two vital hits. His thousand pounders exploded on the roadway in the middle of the main span, after which – so he said – my near misses had caused the whole structure to roll slowly sideways before sagging into the water. But it was his scalp without a doubt. A superb piece of bombing.

The day had begun with enemy fighters. For 193 it ended with intense flak, one pilot shot down in flames, and a remarkable escape. The survivor was Charlie Hall. A 20mm shell exploded inside his starboard main tank and the fuel failed to ignite. Lucky Charlie.

Charlie joined me shortly afterwards with two other pilots, on a trip by road to Chièvres south east of Brussels. There we were due to pick up four new Typhoons, part of a larger batch, being flown in by the ATA on their first continental delivery. Chièvres, until recently a USAAF base, had become the temporary home of 123 Typhoon Wing which been had moved there in an essentially political gesture, to support the Yanks and confront the German armoured thrust in the Ardennes.

Our Typhoons arrived at last light, just before the snow started to come down in earnest, and we were grounded. Billeted out in a country house which even then managed to boast huge log fires, clean sheets and feather duvets. Much appreciated as the blizzard swirled outside. But it began to look as if we might be stuck there for ages.

Field Marshal von Rundstedt's spearheads continued to move westwards and the air was full of rumours, fact and fiction, like the paratroopers of Deelen. This time they included the legendary figure of Otto Skorzeny, famous for rescuing Mussolini in 1943, and now said to be leading a special force, in American uniforms, creating havoc behind the lines.

Elsewhere, so the stories went, allied fuel and ammunition dumps had been overrun and blown up. An American forward airfield had been captured by tanks, the Mustangs destroyed, and most of the personnel killed or captured. It was difficult to know what to believe.

In the end we got airborne, late on the fourth day, splashing down the runway concentrating hard to keep straight between the banks of bulldozed snow and ice. For our host's wing leader, 'Farmer' Dring, had just lost his life skidding into those lethal obstructions at the end of a spirited aerobatic display. It was a tragic waste.

As the others settled around me in battle formation the air was crystal clear and an occasional dying cumulus, pale in the evening light, drifted slowly across our track. On our journey home the snowfields thinned and faded, giving way to plough and pasture, until the landscape below took on its familiar sodden look.

Deurne lay shadowed under a huge cumulonimbus, which extended northwards as far as the eye could see, trailing low across the Scheldt, extinguishing the gleaming tracery of waterways and flooded fields. To starboard the dark wall of turbulent cloud reared upwards and the towering thunderheads far above were touched with crimson by the last rays of the setting sun. The awesome power, and the unearthly beauty, was breathtaking beyond words. All the fears and frustrations of the last few days were lost and gone forever, and I became convinced that Hitler's last offensive was already over.

During our enforced absence the Gustav had acquired RAF livery, with yellow undersurfaces, and the prototype letter P to identify it as a captured enemy aircraft. Almost ready to fly, it was strapped down on a set of jacks, just clear of the ground. The DB 605 fired first time, and in less than ten minutes Stan had run through the checks, operated the undercarriage and flaps, exercised the propeller, and taken the engine up to maximum boost and RPM. No problems at all. He gave his audience a delighted grin and shut down.

We had a goer, or so we thought, Charlie and I. A briefing from Chiefy, permission from our CO and the wing leader, a couple of Typhoons for close escort, a word to flying control, and we would soon be learning all about the Gustav. Sadly authority decreed otherwise and it was sent back to England, to the Central Fighter Establishment, where 'Plum' our previous CO was the only member of 193 to get his hands on it.

Johnny Wells took advantage of a brief improvement in the weather to conduct the first blind bombing trials, whilst I flew attendance with a photo-recce Typhoon. On the run in, flying straight and level, MRCP[1] gave corrections port or starboard and a countdown to the precalculated bomb release point on their radar screens. It seemed dreary in the extreme. As the bombs fell away I switched on the two vertical cameras half hoping, if the truth were told, that they would reveal a substantial bombing error.

At the end of the photographic run I went into a long dive towards

Schouwen Island where the wing had recently carried out an attack in force. A low pass and a steep turn round the target would be sufficient to collect a series of pictures on the oblique camera. It was a different approach to obtain more detail and make things easier for pilots who had not been photo-recce trained. When the prints came through the low obliques were excellent. The blind bombing, as expected showed an error in hundreds of yards. But 84 Group still insisted that it should go ahead.

The enemy offensive, which had started so well before Christmas, ground to a halt. The deep salient south of Liège slowly collapsed and we were grounded once more. Cloud and mist shrouded the airfield. Snow fell, froze, turned to slush, and fell again. Some hardy souls located an indoor pool which had no heating and went swimming. B Flight found an abandoned American ambulance, brought it back to Deurne, gutted the interior and built in a set of wooden lockers for our flying clobber and parachutes. It was a great success.

My own activities centred around a Fortress which had crash landed close to the runway. With New Year's Day still fresh in our minds I persuaded Stan Carr to remove one of the twin 0.5in calibre turrets, and we helped ourselves to several spare guns and every round of ammunition on board.

The turret fitted nicely into an old German flak position close to the squadron dispersal. If the Luftwaffe ever returned we would have our own means of defence.

While we were adding the finishing touches a V2 fell apart, directly overhead. Pumps, turbines and twisted shards of metal came showering down around the sandbagged emplacement, accompanied by the familiar receding thunder of a sonic boom.

That experience led to an interesting evening with Neville Thomas. I had called at his trailer for what was intended to be a brief chat. In the end we talked far into the night, keeping the cold at bay with the help of a whisky bottle. We talked about the enemy offensive in the Ardennes – their jet and rocket aircraft, and weapons to come – even frightening ourselves with the thought of V2s carrying poison gas and atomic warheads.

One for the road – and the moment had come to try out my latest idea, a forward-facing camera installation for our photo-recce Typhoons. I explained that the technique would be very similar to low level bombing. It would require no special training and should give us really close up target pictures. Tommy looked at me owlishly – we had been at the whisky for a long time:

"If you can do it Dave, and it works, Denys Gillam and Johnny Wells would be delighted."

He paused, obviously dying to say more, and then the drink getting the better of his natural caution:

"You'll have the opportunity soon enough, Jerry Eaton is going on rest and you'll be responsible for photo recce."

Urging me to keep quiet about our conversation, he went on to talk about 257 Squadron and their recent losses. Arthur Todd was about to become the new CO and I would be joining him as a flight commander.

No hang ups about that. I felt ready for a flight, 257 were as good a bunch as one could hope to meet and Toddy was fine. Given his understanding and confident hand at the helm we should go from strength to strength.

Toddy had joined 193 in the autumn, on what was probably his fourth tour. In the weeks that followed, after he moved in with us, Jimmy and I learned a little about his background. He had flown Hurricanes in the defence of Malta and subsequently against the Vichy French in Sierra Leone. Posted home to 164 Squadron, pioneers in RP ground-attack, he had continued flying Hurricanes and then Typhoons, adding to his score of enemy aircraft. Sent on rest, soon after D-Day, he had spent the following months engine testing for Napiers at Luton.

His descriptions may have sounded flippant. But he was not a happy bunny. "They wanted us to forget all about engine handling – or so it seemed, and run the poor old Sabres at full chat until they blew up. When that happened the boffins took over, closeting themselves like a bunch of cardinals until the white smoke went up, and you started all over again." For Toddy it all came to an end when engine failure left him with an emergency landing, wheels down short of the substantial boundary fence, or wheels up on the airfield. He chose the latter and applied for the posting which brought him to us at Deurne.

Keen to get the forward-facing camera installation under way, I sought out the ever-willing Stan Carr yet again, whilst there was still time. We set up an F24 with a 14″ lens, as far forward as possible inside the gun bay, pointing towards the leading edge. It was no good. The cannon aperture was too small and cut off much of the picture. Enlarging it was quite out of the question. So we scrounged a 20″ lens and it might have been made for the job. I left the detailed engineering to Stan and turned my attention to other matters.

When the weather improved the V2 supply routes had again become high priority. The Hun had used our enforced absence to improve his supply position. Antwerp and London were suffering badly again.

Much of the effort was now being directed at a variety of smaller rail bridges across the polders. Difficult enough targets at best, the enemy had made them even more so. Those sections spanning the water were rolled back, along the permanent way, so that nothing was visible from above. A number of bridge-bombing sorties were diverted, as a result of this subterfuge, before we got wise to it. From then on, if the structure had disappeared, we concentrated on the bridge approaches.

Just before my departure from 193, Rastus and Jimmy Simpson rostered me to lead an eight-aircraft show, on which they would both be flying. Typical of them to set this up, so that their trainee flight commander would join his new squadron with the advantage of having done it at least once before.

This was learning on the job with a vengeance. A process which had started from the day you joined the squadron. A combination of being watched, evaluated and supported by the other guys – quite informally – they might even deny that it happened at all. And being super aware of everything, absorbing it like a sponge. Knowing that your life could well depend on it. Your first sortie or more would be flown as number two to the CO. Then for weeks, maybe months, you would be flying as number two to all and sundry – until you found yourself being rostered for the odd sortie, with your own number two, as a very junior leader.

More variations on the theme. Ops where you led a whole section of four. Like the one which Rastus had sprung on me, for a different reason, on the day after my photo-recce trip over Rotterdam in December. I thought of it again as I prepared to take my first squadron briefing. The pace had certainly quickened since he had taken over 193. But that had been a most realistic and understanding decision. He was a great guy our Rhodesian squadron commander.

Jimmy's voice softly in my ear: "Remember the cigarettes Dave?" Yes, I did remember. The leader should always pass his cigarettes round at the start of briefing – excellent psychology and with Jimmy's example I had been fully converted to the idea. Now, as he gave me a conspiratorial smile, and helped himself from my open case, the awful truth suddenly dawned. Briefings in future were going to be a major drain on my duty free supplies. Such were the unexpected burdens of command.

Whether that leadership thing happened to you or not, there was a strong sense that you were continually improving, becoming a more effective member of the squadron – really pulling your weight. Like Rod Davidge one of our Canadians who became a flight commander and insisted on the aircraft letter C. With the squadron letters it became DP-C – Damned Proud Canadian! I guess we were all Damned Proud. Damned Proud Typhoon pilots! Damned Proud of our squadrons.

That desire to be better, to be the best, showed itself in all sorts of ways. Accurate briefing, with positive thinking, as every pilot identifies the target. In the air, tactical flexibility, fast in and out, an endless striving for accuracy and attacks pressed home with determination.

These were the names of the game. They contributed to the damage and reduced the risk to ourselves. We used them to the full. Wing shows provided an opportunity to exploit and develop this further. Low level with bombs at the start – steep dive attacks as the surprise was lost and anti-flak support as the attack progressed.

Despite the enemy skills in camouflage and concealment, despite his flak defences, despite our crude weapon aiming systems, we were hitting and hurting him. The grateful signals from army commanders at every level confirmed that the Typhoon force had become extremely effective at supporting troops on the ground. Soon, although our diversion to combat the V2 menace would continue for a while, we hoped to get back to that primary role.

On my first sortie with 257, 2 February 1945, the weather clamped at base and the squadron diverted to Woensdrecht. The night turned bitterly cold and the black painted ex Luftwaffe huts, amongst the pine woods, provided little comfort. In the morning, when Toddy briefed us for the next op, the thought of returning afterwards to our tenements at Deurne was very welcome.

Minutes later I was standing beside him when we heard the sound of a diving aircraft and caught sight of a Spitfire, plunging vertically, high against the blue. Suddenly, and with quite appalling violence it began to recover. Both wings folded upwards and broke away. The fuselage pitched nose down again and fell headlong, throttle wide open, to crash less than a mile from the airfield.

In the silence which followed we watched the wings fluttering downwards, above the mushroom of smoke, and a voice said softly:

"Poor sod, what the hell was he up to?"

And another, as if in reply:

"It would never have happened to a Tiffie."

Had anyone spoken, or was it all in the imagination? I looked round, hoping to find the answer, as Toddy called us to order:

"Right chaps, let's get a move on, press tits in ten minutes."

A favoured explanation was lack of oxygen, an uncontrolled dive, and a violent out of trim recovery. More likely, with hindsight, that critical Mach number effects had led to coarse application of nose up trim with the inevitable tragic consequences.

The move to B89, at Mill, south of Nijmegen on 8 February coincided with the opening of the assault on the Siegfried Line. We were up early. Valises and kitbags stuffed to bursting with the accumulated bits and pieces of four winter months. A last quick breakfast in the terminal building and the wing was on its way, squadron by squadron, back to the work of close support and the start line of the first spring offensive.

The day was unseasonably mild with difficult flying weather. On the first op our target was obscured by cloud. As the squadron orbited I spotted two Spitfire XIVs beating up an adjacent enemy position and Toddy chose to attack it instead. The result was impressive and quite unexpected. A massive explosion surrounded by ever expanding concussion rings as the pressure waves tore at the moist air.

Approaching Mill and a layer of stratus was already spreading rapidly across the unfamiliar airfield. The circuit was full of aircraft, trying to get down as fast as possible, and the last few unfortunates were reduced to groping around at less than 300 feet before it clamped completely.

By midday the conditions had improved sufficiently for an attempt at blind bombing, creeping up though a gap in the overcast and setting course to the north east. In tight formation – sections in finger four – dangerously silhouetted against the clouds below as we responded to the controller's instructions:

> "This is Cosycot, steer zero six zero... port five degrees... steady... thirty seconds to go... twenty seconds... ten seconds... five... four... three... two... one... zero!"

Bombs gone, and nothing to see. No cannon fire, no flak, no explosions down below. Just a solid layer of cloud. To a man we disliked it intensely and doubted its value. But group and the army seemed happy enough. Who, we wondered, was kidding who?

Late on the same afternoon the sky cleared completely and we were briefed for a wing show against the northern hinge of the enemy line. Overlooking two great rivers, with the Reichswald screening its southern flank, the Matterborn feature looked almost impregnable. A fortress guarding the heart of Germany.

Now it was under siege. The red-roofed hamlets and dark patches of woodland were being subjected to a massive artillery bombardment. Fire and flame wreathed the landscape. The smoke of battle rose high in the air and the approach roads were crowded with advancing allied columns as we had not seen them since the heady days of Falaise. As we dived on the camouflaged positions, and the defences responded with a violent barrage of light flak, it was evident that the winter stalemate on the northern sector was over at last.

That night, long after we turned in, I caught the pulse jet resonance of an approaching V1 and wakened to utter silence. A memory of Antwerp which would haunt me, on and off, for years. In reality there was little enough to disturb our sleep. Just a faint rumble of guns, when the wind was in the east, and the familiar dawn chorus of Sabre engines.

The huts in which we slept might have been worse, and they had stoves to keep us warm when the nights were chilly. But the wooden prefab buildings, at the back of each dispersal, were more like field shelters of the sort that are used for animals. Mill, like all ALGs, was pretty basic and had been completed in some haste. The PSP runways and perimeter track were surrounded by lethal acres of soft peaty soil and drainage ditches. High ridges of earth had been thrown up by the levelling operations and then abandoned. Our jeeps could barely cope. But help was at hand. The squadrons were about to be issued with Bren carriers!

The Luftwaffe only appeared twice during that early spring offensive. On 14 February an Me109, flying straight and level over the airfield, was caught by a section from B Flight. They lined up one at a time, drilling it with cannon shells, until it responded by diving into the ground. Less impressive still was the Me262, in fighter bomber guise, which made a hit and run attack on the next door airfield and appeared to run out of height as it headed for home.

I have to admit that something of my army background caught up with me about this time and, with Toddy's agreement I started briefing our ground crews on the battlefield situation and our own sorties. Although the field shelters were cold, draughty and almost unlit, these occasions, supported by maps and reconnaissance photographs, became rather popular.

As our troops worked slowly south they came up against stubborn resistance in the German frontier towns and villages. In reality these formed important sections of the Siegfried Line and many were 'liberated' in attacks, which involved successive waves of Typhoons, battering them for hours on end.

On 21 February in one set piece attack the wing destroyed an ancient Dutch castle, which formed the core of a strong enemy position, on the east bank of the Maas. Bijen Beek looked magnificent. But the occupants refused to surrender and there were allied lives at stake. We took it out in a combined effort, three squadrons with thousand pounders, followed by one with RPs.

The classic outline, standing four square inside its rectangular moat, made a splendid aiming point and 257 released as low as possible with instantaneous fusing. As we pulled away, and 263's rockets rained down behind us, the place was in ruins – massive walls breached, roof fallen in, barns and stables razed to the ground, burning from end to end.

The destruction of Castel Bijen Beek provided me with a dramatic subject for the close up – steep turn – photo recce which followed. Even better when Tommy told me that the results had found their way to the prime minister's private entrance to the Air Ministry as a 'Classic attack of the week'. Good show 146 Wing.

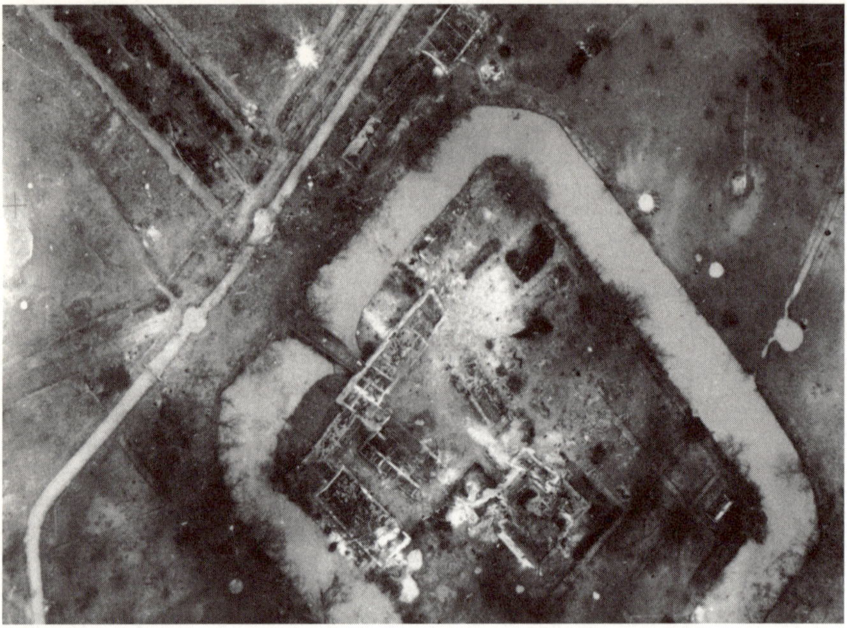

Top: Castel Bijen Beek. Target photography stage one. Steep turn oblique as displayed in Churchill's viewing room.
Bottom: Stage two – forward oblique camera. Wing leading edge enclosure. They made robust picture frames in Antwerp!

Fighter-recce Typhoon. Removing the port inboard cannon created a camera bay and the vital forward oblique opening.

About forty years on my cousin Alastair (he of our 1939 Glasgow rugger team), an ex wartime infantry captain and later TA major, was leafing through some of my old photographs. He stopped abruptly and looked up in astonishment:

"Good heavens its Bijen Beek!"

"It is indeed." I agreed: "Believe it was late February 1945 and we pretty well destroyed it."

"And saved our lives into the bargain."

He looked at me quizzically, poured out a couple of large whiskies, and brought one over.

> "We had a hell of a time with that place. Sent in a fighting patrol and they wiped it out. Every time we probed they hit us back hard. When the order came to attack we thought we were goners. But air support had been promised and, after your attack, we just walked in. They surrendered without a fight. Here, and belatedly, is a heartfelt toast to you lot in your splendid Typhoons."

What a story! If only my old mates could have heard it as well.

Photo-recce sorties, using the steep turn technique, were producing some excellent results. Bill Hurst in particular had proved an apt pupil.

But it was just as well that the forward-facing camera would soon be available. His low obliques of a bridge near Emmerich were an example of sheer perfectionism and considerable hazard. The flak guns could be clearly seen, following him round as he circled his objective three times with the camera running.

Bill's superb photographs of a church and seminary south of Goch, which had been used by the Wehrmacht for more secular purposes until destroyed in another attack, were also given VIP treatment. Displayed, like my less elegant effort of Bijen Beek for the PM's private viewing. Another example of 'Classic attacks of the week'.

Target photography was flown unescorted and, whenever possible, immediately after an attack. A reflection on the weakened state of the Luftwaffe; and the dubious belief that some protection might be provided by the last attacking aircraft. Although there was no brief, as such, to support the photo singleton.

In relation to any flak defences it was not good news, although we accepted it at the time, recognizing the need to assess the results with minimum delay. In fact some of my best, and least uncomfortable, pictures were obtained when the flak was no longer ready and waiting, and the fires and smoke had subsided. Target photography was a dangerous business. In crude terms it accounted for some ten per cent of my operational sorties and about ninety per cent of my battle damage.

One day Toddy and I were watching B Flight about to set course on a late afternoon show. Suddenly one of the aircraft dropped out, with its engine cutting, and swung into the circuit. We could see that he was going to undershoot and ran for the Bren carrier. Below 500 feet and he had forgotten his bombs. Without a wireless it was impossible to warn him. Then he realised, jettisoning them live in his haste, and they exploded on impact. Moments later he dropped out of sight, wheels and flaps down, into a thick plantation short of the runway.

The carrier got there, in a flurry of mud and spinning tracks, and we were looking at the Typhoon flown by Jock Ewans. Inverted, where it had come to rest, after cutting a swathe through the saplings. And we were afraid for him because of what might happen before we could get him out. The ground was soft, the inevitable sand and peat, and access to the site was obstructed by ditches, so that the only possible route for the crane was a long way round. In the meantime the canopy had gone, the top of the fuselage, windscreen, armour plate and pilot's head were buried in the topsoil. The hot engine creaked and sizzled gently as liquid seeped from inverted tanks and broken pipes.

We dug at the soft earth around the cockpit walls, with our bare hands, and then remembered the shovels in the Bren carrier and managed rather better: "Jock, are you there?" Of course he was, but it seemed wrong to ask a man in his position if he was still alive. There came an answer too, through a mouthful of mud, full of apologies. For bending the aircraft. For being so much trouble. We dug some more until the trim moustache became visible, and it was possible to switch off the ignition, turn off the fuel, and get the mud out of his mouth. We told him not to release his harness, that we would get him out soon, and to stop apologising.

After that it was a matter of waiting for the crane, the fire tender, and blood wagon. We lay in the damp earth on each side of the upturned cockpit and Jock was passing calm, but nothing would stop the flow of apologies.

It was almost dark by the time he was out and on a stretcher. Only then did he admit to any injuries. How bad we never discovered, for the doctors were noncommittal when we visited him in hospital. Then he was gone. Evacuated to England.

Jock was the squadron's last casualty. For 257 was about to be disbanded. Less than a week later, before that happened on 24 February, I experienced the most irritating op of my whole flying career. We caught a troop train, in broad daylight, on a loop line which emerged briefly on the south side of Amsterdam before turning back into the built-up area. Our attack had to be quick in and out, to avoid civilian casualties, and catch the flak off guard.

But our bombs were not fused for low level attack and the need for rapid engagement required a dive angle, at right angles to the target, which was far too shallow for accurate aiming. By some extraordinary fluke two bombs hit the train and two more fell on the track just ahead of the locomotive. We followed this up with a strafing attack, as troops poured into the surrounding fields, and the flak came up thick and fast. Then it was down on the deck – the tracer chasing us to the south – lucky to escape untouched.

I argued endlessly with Toddy during those final days about how we might have done it better, and there was some comfort when B Flight caught a convoy of thirty trucks and destroyed the lot. At least the squadron had gone out with a bang! When the AOC[2] visited us, he unwisely suggested that the decision had been taken due to a shortage of trained Typhoon pilots. Other squadrons he assured us were being similarly affected. 257 had a proud record and would live again. We thought of the unwillingness of the Spitfire boys to volunteer for Typhoons and his comments went down like a lead balloon.

Some of the pilots went on rest, others were posted round the four remaining squadrons. Toddy went back to the UK on Mustang IVs and the wingco sent me up to the front as a VCP[3] controller.

I set off, greatly displeased by the turn of events. Yet this was an opportunity to broaden my knowledge of close support and I made a determined effort to approach it in a positive frame of mind. So much for good intentions. Stuck at divisional level, on permanent standby, it seemed as if my services would never be required. Even a request to visit the forward areas, with the idea of drumming up some unofficial trade, was turned down.

After almost three weeks of enforced idleness my little team was suddenly ordered to move up, close to the Rhine, opposite Wesel. The brigade headquarters to which we had been directed was just moving into the local bank where they discovered a vast cache of wine. The slim bottles, packed in straw-filled wooden cases, made a mouth-watering sight.

Soon after dark we began sampling them, sitting on our camp beds amongst a jumble of signal wires and the intermittent ringing of telephone handsets, until our hosts rather wisely closed the bar.

In the morning I woke, to the sound of mortar fire, convinced that our moment of glory was at hand. But nothing happened except a signal from group calling the whole thing off. The operation to clear the west bank of the Rhine was now in its final stages. There would be little need for VCP in the immediate future.

When I got back to Mill the story of Ronnie Sheward's trip to the battle area was still going the rounds. Ronnie's war, so far, had been tough enough. An Anglo-Argentinean, he had volunteered for the RAF in 1940 and argued, fought and bamboozled his way to pilot training even though he was way over age. Pointed inevitably at bombers, he threatened to return home, won the argument and ended up on fighters.

Having survived his first tour breaking new ground on RP Hurricanes, a lethal activity, which included the disastrous attack on the Hansweert canal described on page 201, Ronnie went on rest as a ground-attack instructor. He joined us at Antwerp, for his second tour, as a flight commander on 263 Squadron which had strong Argentine connections. Promoted to lead 266 Squadron, as its last CO, he found the high spirited Rhodesian pilots very similar to his Anglo-Argentine friends and much to his liking.

Battlefield visits were quite in vogue – most of us went 'swanning' from time to time – but rarely with the enthusiasm of Ronnie and his pilots. Pushing forward, as far as possible, and driving through a German village it all became very noisy. An infantry officer waved them down urgently and suddenly they were under fire. They dived into the nearest shop. It was full of top hats! Almost before the firefight died down they emerged, sporting a quick change of headgear, and the surrounding troops were highly amused.

You might think it foolhardy and dangerous. But they were young and adventurous, with just that important touch of bravado, so who could really blame them? Besides which the old man of the wing was out in front and egging them on. No doubt only too well aware that 'Top Hats into Battle' is the sort of legend that grows and inspires.

During my absence much had been happening at Mill. Word had come through that Allan Smith was a prisoner of war. Denys Gillam had been posted to group headquarters. Partly, it was said, to prevent him from flying on ops. Not that it did much good because he continued to visit us as often as possible, borrowing an aircraft and a number two, and quietly disappearing to war. We had seen it all before while he was commanding the wing.

Gillam was a legend – flying Spitfires in the Battle of Britain, bringing the Hurribomber into action, first Typhoon wing leader, commandant of the Specialised Low Attack Instructors School. The most highly decorated British fighter pilot and undisputed master of ground-attack with more than 2000 operational sorties to his name. He had nothing to prove. Yet Mike Bulleid remembers flying with him less than a fortnight from the end of the war. No wonder that we were proud to have served under his command.

Johnny Wells, now a group captain, was commanding the wing and the CO of 266 Squadron; Johnny Deal had become wing leader in his place, hence Ronnie Sheward's recent promotion.

The really bad news was that Derek Erasmus, whose leadership had done so much for 193 Squadron, had been lost on a low level attack against the main V weapon railhead at Raalte in Holland. There was a lot of cloud in the target area and hardly anything had been seen. No obvious flak or power lines. Just an aircraft, diving into the ground, after releasing its bombs. Perhaps he had been caught by an exploding tanker, hit by his shells on the run in. But even that is conjecture. His death will always remain a mystery.

193's new CO was plump, ebullient, and prematurely balding, with a nose which must have been well and truly broken earlier in his career. 'Butch' Taylor, and the nickname matched his looks, had joined up, in the late thirties, on a short service commission and had been given command of his first Typhoon squadron back in 1942. He was posted, without a break from ops, to lead 197 Squadron and only went on rest after D-Day flying Ansons with 84 Group Communications Squadron. One way and another he had been around for a long time. When he joined us at Mill his main preoccupation seemed to be that of playing himself into a postwar permanent commission. The contrast with Derek could hardly have been greater.

Sadness at Derek's death turned swiftly to regret that 193 had not been entrusted to Jimmy Simpson. Maybe he was almost tour expired. But the war in Europe could not go on forever. His behaviour, almost his every action, revealed what the squadron meant to him, not only as a unit but in human terms as well. He knew what made us tick. Able and trusted, popular with air and ground crews alike, he was the obvious choice. But Jimmy, still commanding A Flight, was on leave and I was about to become his successor. Felix Cryderman was on a fighter leader's course with the AFDU[4] at Tangmere and B Flight had passed into the capable hands of 'Snowy' Harrison, an Australian from 266.

CHAPTER TWELVE

DYING REICH

My return to ops on 22 March coincided with a spell of anticyclonic spring weather. The Americans were already across the Rhine at Remagen. Along our own front, north of the Ruhr, the British and Canadian armies were poised to cross this last major barrier to the heartland of Germany. After the mistakes at Arnhem, things were to be very different this time. The scale and the numbers involved were awe inspiring, with an Anglo-American air armada exceeding 1,500 transports and glider tugs and 1,200 gliders, escorted by almost 900 fighters. And the Typhoons were to be fully committed in support – mainly in an anti-flak role.

Two days to go to the Rhine crossing. Leading eight aircraft on interdiction – cutting rail lines vital to the German defences – the Rhine from 8,000 feet was only a faint glimmer through the haze. Running in on our target near Hengelo, a number of Lancasters were clearly visible in the middle distance. They were bombing one of the German border towns. On the way home I led the formation towards the bomber stream in the hope of finding some German fighters. But there were none, except for a couple of Me163s, strange tailless shapes darting like gadflies from high above the heavies and then zooming vertically upwards – totally out of reach – and seemingly doing no damage at all.

We hung around climbing gently, just in case any of them happened to come within range or run out of fuel. Meanwhile the Lancs stoked up a lethal firestorm. Flames roared through the doomed town, drawing air inwards from all around, and throwing a tornado of debris and red hot ash thousands of feet upwards. The core pushed straight through the inversion to produce a towering cumulus, brilliant against the unbroken blue.

One day to go. My twenty-fourth birthday. It was shirt sleeve weather as we drove across the muddy airfield in our Bren carriers after briefing, and the sun shone out of a brazen sky as if summer had come too soon. There was a wing show in the morning against an ammunition dump near Emmerich and I found myself flying with Butch for the first time, leading the second section. The target was well marked by fires and explosions from the squadrons ahead and we came down through the murk adding to the conflagration with our incendiaries. A few days later, when I took a low oblique, it had been razed to the ground.

That afternoon I took a section of four against enemy troops in the area of the airborne landings planned for the following day. The smoke-filled haze was worse than ever and, as we climbed towards the inversion, its smell invaded our oxygen masks. Brick dust and burning, drifting in from the heart of the Ruhr, mixed together with more of the same from the battlefields down below. The smell of Hitler's dying Reich.

It was a satisfactory little show. The target was easy to find in spite of the poor visibility and the bombing was accurate. The flak was ferocious, as so often seemed to be the case on the eve of an Allied offensive, but we returned to base unscathed. Tomorrow we might not be so lucky. However Jimmy was back from leave and selfishly perhaps, for he was so nearly on rest, we were happy to know that he would be flying with us again.

After dark Bomber Command directed a concentrated raid on Wesel. Target indicators lit the sky, prelude to a display which belied the sixty miles from Mill. We stood in unaccustomed silence outside the officers mess, watching the distant fireworks, our thoughts on that vital strip of land across the Rhine. More particularly about the guns around it on the outskirts of Wesel. Perhaps some of them would be destroyed in this attack. Or they might run short of ammunition. One could always hope.

Gun crews in open emplacements were best dealt with using anti-personnel weapons. So the Typhoons of 193 and 197 had already been armed with cluster bombs. Whilst those of 263 and 266 were carrying thin-walled RPs for maximum shrapnel effect. 193 headed the roster, with sections of four taking off every thirteen minutes. We were in for a busy day. Out on the patrol line it was a glorious spring morning. All was peaceful. The smoke and haze of yesterday had gone, and the dropping zone lay bathed in sunshine. At first the sky was empty, and then we saw them in the distance – a vast armada reaching back beyond the horizon, Operation Varsity on its way. Soon the leading formations were clearly visible. Dakotas and Hadrians sporting white USAAF stars, Dakotas with roundels, Halifaxes, Hamilcars and Horsas, an endless stream of glider combinations.

They moved like a flood tide, rolling on remorselessly to break above the gentle wooded slopes beyond the Rhine. Parachutes blossomed in their hundreds and gliders, with barn door flaps extended, stooped like birds of prey. An elite force, trained to perfection, at the high noon of its endeavour.

And in that moment, explain it how you will, the flak totally lost its threat and was replaced by a determination to neutralize it utterly – to wipe it out at whatever cost and so to protect this splendidly courageous airborne army.

Near the limit of our search area a heavy flak battery opened fire. The pattern of trenches and gun emplacements was clearly visible, hastily camouflaged, in the middle of an open field. We went in fast with our clusters, strafing for good measure. A burst of flame and smoke shrouded the site – and I could hardly hide my satisfaction:

"Well done White Section! That should keep the buggers quiet!"

For the rest of that sortie it was rough close quarter stuff with our cannon, weaving and diving, dodging flashes of perspex and alarming close ups of Yankee stars.

"Tally Ho White Leader – Tracer 5 o'clock one mile. Down sun of wood."

"Roger Ben. White Leader diving starboard. Lead us in."

Trying to keep our four Typhoons clear of the plunging gliders as the battle haze and the smoke grew and thickened was a nightmare. As we pulled g, searching and sweating in our cockpits, a Hamilcar slanted past on the way down and, unbelievably, the front loading doors flew open and a tank burst out plunging steeply earthwards into the murk.

"Oh the poor bastards!"

It was my number two. I knew how he felt. And then, with almost perfect timing, Snowy on the radio.

"Bassett Blue Section running in. How's trade Dave?"

"Good show Blue Leader. Targets twitchy – trailing our coats – give 'em hell. White Leader going home... port two eight zero... go... Battle formation starboard... go!"

On the way we passed a Dakota, dragging along on one engine, with occasional bursts of flame from the other. He was losing height rapidly and eventually crashed in a field near Xanten, on the west side of the Rhine, where the crew abandoned ship with commendable rapidity. We reported his position and pressed on back to base.

Time for a quick bite, whilst our aircraft were refuelled and rearmed, and then off again. To another afternoon of brilliant sunshine, above that grimy inversion, cooking gently under our canopies. The pace had slowed by now, and the haze was thicker, but the flak gunners were still active. So we worked in pairs, flying one low down to draw the flak and the other higher to observe. Once again my brilliant Ben Lenson spotted two more sites which we left the worse for wear.

It had been a game of cat and mouse with the German gunners. Encouraging them to have a go, but mostly they lay doggo until our backs were turned. Then streams of tracer came chasing up from behind, and with luck you spotted the muzzle flashes – and came down on them like a ton of bricks. It was hairy exciting stuff. As the squadron diary, tongue in cheek, recorded the day: "*We were not really scared of the flak – just highly strung.*"

Back at Mill the sections of four came and went. For a long time no losses occurred. Then a section from B Flight, led by Snowy Harrison, returned without him, he had baled out amongst the gliders.

At the final count the wing had flown a total of eighty-eight sorties. Two Typhoons were missing, with one pilot safe and the other, Snowy, still outstanding.

Varsity had been lucky with the weather, which broke immediately afterwards, and it was possible to catch up on other things. Stan Carr had just completed the prototype forward-facing camera installation and the first test flight proved that it worked.

For the operational trial Tommy suggested an SS battalion headquarters, in a small group of houses, which we had recently destroyed. It was ideal because 35 Wing had already taken a vertical pinpoint and this would provide a conventional target photograph for comparison.

The approach in a shallow dive was exactly like a low level attack. Even the bomb/RP push started the camera running. The results were spectacular, showing a degree of detail which was not apparent in the previous pictures. An unexpected feature, created by the relationship between the leading edge aperture and the lens, was the way in which the centre of the shot was highlighted as if by a very powerful flash.

Examples of these first 'forward obliques' were forwarded to group headquarters. They requested 100 copies which were circulated widely. Rumour had it that 35 Wing, in the person of their CO, were not amused. We were stealing their thunder.

A week or two later Tommy invited me into his office. A set of prints was lying on his desk. 35 Wing had fitted a forward-facing camera in the slipper tank[1] of a Spitfire XIV and they too had circulated their first results. 'Death of a Hun – by Group Captain Anderson' featured a human figure caught on top of a set of lock gates and being mown down by cannon fire as it tried to escape. Tommy smiled at me benignly:

"Now look what you've done! You shouldn't go around stirring up group captains like that."

Snowy returned, long after we had given him up for lost, looking scruffy beyond words and utterly clapped out. We thrust a large drink at him and listened enthralled.

> "I was badly hit and had to bale out fast. To find myself floating down in the middle of a pitched battle – with all sorts

of nasties being thrown up at me. Fortunately they missed. Abandoned my chute and found myself surrounded by American paratroopers. So far so good, I thought to myself. But no such luck. Being tall, fair haired, wearing a 'Gott mit Uns' belt and a Luger which I had half inched from somewhere, they refused to accept that I was an Australian!

"'Go to the wrecked jeep on the top of that hill' they said 'and start unloading supplies. If they hit you, you're dead. If they miss you're a German!' So I set to work and – when the jeep was empty – they put me onto the gliders. Never felt so exposed in my life. Eventually managed to convince an American officer that I was what I claimed to be.

'"Right", he said, 'get over there buddy – draw yourself a rifle, ammunition and armband. And now it's your turn. You can start taking out those lousy German snipers.'

"What a rotten job! I'd had no training and sure as hell they'd pick me off first. How I longed for my Typhoon. If only to improve the odds. So I dug myself the biggest foxhole that you could ever imagine and tried to obey orders. When the British armour broke through I hitched my way back to base – and now I'm famous – at least for today."

We told him that he looked and stank worse than any tramp and pushed him into a huge hot bath. As he fell asleep over supper, his voice slurring with exhaustion, we caught these final words: "They were very hostile days." He slept the clock round twice.

A USAF P51D – Mustang IV in the RAF – made an emergency landing at Mill and required an engine change. Keen to fly anything new, I let it be known that Mustangs already featured in my log book, and that I would be happy to do the air test.

As I climbed aboard the memories came rolling back – the well engineered cockpit, toe brakes and tailwheel lock, pistol grip control column and electric propeller controls. For a moment I feared a re-run of my negative feelings about the Mustang I. But absolutely not. The Merlin 61 sounded reassuringly like a Spit IX as it crackled into life, and the big teardrop hood made a world of difference. One seemed to sit higher, more in command. I ran up the engine and waved the chocks away.

The Merlin had more power. I applied too much of it, too quickly, and maybe the trim was wrong. I certainly lifted the tail too soon. The big paddle-bladed prop swung the aircraft to port. Maximum starboard rudder was not enough and more power would only make the situation worse. For what seemed an age I hung on grimly, as the Mustang veered across the runway, until by some miracle it lifted into the air, within seconds of mud and disaster.

After putting the replacement engine through its paces, I concentrated on the approach and landing. It was in the groove, the touchdown sheer perfection. But I felt a real Prune after that squalid take-off. Tempting to have another go. Much better to leave well alone. I taxied in and returned the Mustang to its ground crew.

An impressive aircraft. In a totally different league to the Allison-engined version. But the old problem, whether or not to use the flaps for manoeuvring was still there. Almost as important, something which I had noted at OTU, was the need to adjust to its greater inherent stability. Given time to know it better, nothing would have been more satisfying than a chance to fly a Mustang IV on one of its deep penetration missions.

By the time the weather improved our troops were across the Rhine in force and moving fast. One thrust had swung southwards to cut off the Ruhr and another was driving towards the north German plain, threatening to trap the enemy forces in Holland.

Time to find out what the Huns were up to. Perhaps we might even catch them on the roads again. On 31 March B Flight went first. Jimmy Simpson and I, each with a number two, followed soon afterwards.

Near Hengelo, accompanied by Bob Waldron, I caught a long convoy struggling eastward and we started several fires amongst the trucks. Back at base comparing notes with Jimmy, whilst our aircraft were being rearmed and refuelled, it seemed a good idea to have another go at them before dark. Ideally we would have carried phosphorous incendiaries on all four aircraft, but there was no time for that, and only Waldron's was bombed up.

Airborne again I found myself prey to conflicting emotions. Satisfaction at catching the enemy out in the open again. Concern in the knowledge that we had never before cut it so fine in terms of daylight. And an uneasy feeling that I had encouraged Jimmy, one of the few among us who was married, to fly an extra sortie at the very end of his tour.

The light was going fast when we got to the scene and the convoy, marked here and there by fires still burning from the previous attack, was nearly invisible. Our cannon shells sparkled brilliantly in the gloom, and Bob Waldron's incendiaries spread themselves across the road in a scintillating carpet, but it was too dark to see anything else.

On the way home we headed into the setting sun. Down below the land had grown indistinct. Not a light to be seen. Farms and villages lost in the purple darkness. Yet we flew on in sunshine, aircraft burnished with light, each propeller a disc of shimmering gold. Up here was warmth and life. We could go on forever. A few spans away the rugged shape of Jimmy's Typhoon hung motionless in the sky, his head hunched forward in familiar silhouette, and I experienced a sharp sense of loss. For this would be our last op together.

The demand for forward obliques came thick and fast. Catching up on some of the recent wing shows was high priority. One, which included a general's house and signals centre, came the day after Jimmy's farewell party. Fortunately it was a peaceful trip, and for other reasons as well, because several runs were needed to capture the individual targets on film.

Napalm, that controversial weapon of future wars, came to us in preview as a converted drop tank, nearly eight foot long, and two foot in diameter, like a beer barrel with a spherical nose and straight tapered tail. Painted all over in red dope.

Another pilot was given the doubtful privilege of dropping the first pair on the s'Hertogenbosch range, and I accompanied him on 9 April in one of the photo-recce aircraft. The results were disappointing, a series of nice clear photographs of a low flying Typhoon but nothing else. The igniters had been reversed, and failed to work, and the target was drenched with 180 gallons of useless petroleum jelly. Immediately afterwards the napalm pilot was sent on rest and the groupie, with encouraging words like "You know all about it Dave!" instructed me to take over.

Some days later I watched as the armourers went through the laborious process of filling the bombs by Jerrican, through a large funnel. Twenty x 4½ gallons per bomb, at 2½ minutes each, almost an hour.

A & AEE[2] Boscombe Down had carried out trials with the ninety-gallon version, and a smaller one as well, back in December. But no information had reached us and I had to work out my own dropping technique. Despite their streamlined shape, the bombs had no fins, and they were certain to tumble. I decided to drop them from the lowest possible altitude.

The effect was most impressive. The fiery mass sprayed forward and upwards, in a cascade of incandescent reds and yellows which threatened to engulf my tail. Seen many years later, the Boscombe Down report recommended a minimum dropping height of 100 feet, at speeds not in excess of 290mph. However their cine pictures suggested that I was probably quite safe.

The upshot of that demonstration was a napalm strike against a strongpoint near Arnhem which led to my first clash with Butch. Totally ignoring the non ballistic properties of our new weapon, he briefed us for a dive-bombing attack. I could hardly believe my ears. Driving over to the aircraft we had a stormy discussion as I tried to persuade him to

Napalm versus Arnhem strongpoint, April 1945. Mostly near misses. But the Germans surrendered without a fight.

rebrief for a low level delivery.

Just to make matters worse the target was partly obscured by artificial smoke and Butch revealed his indecision with a shallow dive, releasing above 2,000 feet. The bombs tumbled all over the place. But my request to lead the second section low level was sternly refused,

Butch had an opportunity to retrieve the situation later that day, going back with twelve aircraft, and a mixed bomb load. After the napalm fiasco we wanted to hit the enemy hard. This time we went in on the deck, and the artificial smoke hung about us, rolling downwind like dirty fog banks on either side pointing the way.

When the Canadians overran the position they found the house at its centre razed to the ground. Our phosphorous incendiaries and anti-personnel clusters had wreaked havoc amongst the surrounding trenches and dugouts, and the survivors were totally demoralised. Even the earlier, inaccurate, napalm bursts had played a significant part due to their unexpected and frightening nature.

That was the first and last time we flew operationally with napalm, inconclusive but obviously potent, and possibly the only time it was used by the RAF in World War II. USAF Lightnings had dropped napalm in Italy during 1945, although where, and how often, is not clear, and the bombs used on the Boscombe Down trials had attachment lugs for British and American racks.

As I wrestled with the problems of napalm, Bob Gibbings, one of those who had joined 197 Squadron from the Naval Bombardment Pool the previous autumn, was having his troubles elsewhere. On an armed recce led by Geoff Hartley he was strafing an airfield when the target blew up in his face, in his graphic description:

> "I found myself flying through a red hell, convinced that my last moments had come. The engine stopped, presumably from oxygen starvation, only to restart immediately as I emerged from the holocaust. To my utter amazement I was still flying, and I climbed gingerly away. The windscreen and canopy slowly cleared revealing an aircraft that was almost a total write off, leaking fuel, oil and glycol, the leading edges burst open, everything scorched and burnt."

Incredibly Bob flew on for twenty minutes climbing to 7,000 feet in the process. A few miles short of the lines he decided that there was no hope of getting home, and prepared to bunt out, jettisoning the canopy and releasing the straps. Just a little trial to make sure the system worked. He pushed the stick tentatively forward, and in a trice was half out of the cockpit, trying desperately to hang on to the spade grip.

Another minute and his battered Typhoon would have been safely back over friendly territory. Instead he was dangling on the end of a parachute being shot at by the enemy. He landed unhurt only to fall into the hands of a one-eyed madman, a major from the Russian front, who threatened him with a firing squad. Hostilities ended before he reached a prison camp and he eventually found his way back to the wing.

As the ground troops swept on, towards Emden and Bremen, the enemy garrisons in the Netherlands were cut off from their homeland, and the Dutch were facing starvation. In a sense ours had become a war on two fronts. With the demands of the drive across the north German plain to meet the Russian spearheads, and bring them to a halt, set against the need to continue hitting the Germans in Holland so that they collapsed quickly.

In the event the major effort was to be eastwards against the surviving enemy forces – supported by their remaining elements of aircraft and flak. Challenging enough in itself and unpredictable to a degree.

Over the familiar landscape west and north of Arnhem our secondary task, and its purpose was pretty clear. As ever to harass the Germans, to deprive them of any movement by day, and hopefully to make them abandon arms. And, by doing so, to save lives, Dutch lives.

So we scoured the roads with a renewed sense of urgency, evading the occasional bursts of flak, hitting and burning the lorries and half-tracks as they tried to move from cover to cover under the trees. For this was the full flush of our last wartime spring and the plight of the gallant Dutch was ever with us. So strongly indeed that even stalking a motorcycle combination, and seeing it erupt in a violence of cannon shells, flame and death, left me quite unmoved.

We moved onto German soil wondering what to expect. But the satisfaction was real enough on 16 April as the wing formed up and set course for Drope north west of Osnabrück. Sixty or more Typhoons cruising low, over the homeland of a broken enemy, on a route surrounded by landmarks familiar from months of fighting. Now all was peaceful. The Wehrmacht and the flak guns had gone but the war was not over yet. So we flew in battle formation searching the skies for danger.

In my battledress pocket was a piece of paper newly issued to every pilot. A Union Jack in full colour and a message to our Russian allies, which started with the words – *Ya Englichanin*, obviously intended to increase the chances of surviving a forced landing in Russian-occupied territory. It underlined the unpleasant fact that they were already besieging Berlin. For there was almost total distrust of Stalin and his evil regime.

We never talked about the end of the war. To do so might raise images of survival and these could be counter-productive. Better by far to soldier on as if the odds were unchanged. Otherwise you might be tempted not to press home your attacks. It was not so much a matter of courage as a form of self protection.

At another level the end of hostilities would mean the loss of a way of life that, incredible as it may seem, many of us had come to cherish. The wonderful camaraderie of a front-line squadron in which possessions and class played no part and what mattered were basic human values – skill, integrity and trust. The challenge and uncertainty of operational flying and a modern, heavily armed, fighter aircraft at your fingertips. Small wonder if we continued living for the present.

As for the Germans, fanatical in defeat, we might well be faced with a period of final redoubts, of Luftwaffe remnants carrying out suicide missions. Who could tell how and when it might all end?

Allan Wyse, our last recruit, joined the squadron just after we got to Drope. A first class sportsman and a natural pilot he had reached a Bomber OTU, flying Halifaxes, before they decided that he was too short to cope. Transferred to fighters, he had suffered the trauma of hearing that the rest of his crew had been shot down and killed on their very first op. Allan seemed to feel that he had let them down. But it was no fault of his and I was very pleased to have him on my flight.

His first show with us was particularly satisfying – destroying a train which had been reported south of Hamburg, We found it exactly as described at briefing, sitting in a little country station, the engine billowing smoke, Butch set up a copybook attack and we blew the whole thing to bits.

Once again Butch had shown that he could lead a very effective operation in straightforward circumstances. Yet that show was followed immediately by another on 24 April, which was an utter shambles, and resulted in my last and most violent clash with him.

It was low level against an SS battalion headquarters, directed by B Flight's Bunny Austin, who was doing a spell as a VCP controller. Bunny drew our attention to the Y-shaped drive leading to the target and it was clearly visible as Butch led the way with his section of four. As I prepared to follow, their cannon shells exploded around an adjacent farmhouse, and it was obvious that they were not going for the right place.

I aborted my own attack, and another argument ensued, with Bunny supporting me strongly. Butch insisted that he had bombed the correct target and that my section must attack it as well. In the end, as with the napalm at Arnhem, he left me with no alternative except to obey his orders.

This time it was too much, I organised an air test and came back with a set of photographs. These showed that we had attacked the wrong target and the undamaged house, with its Y-shaped drive, was unmistakable. Butch knew that he had no control of my photo-recce activities, for which I was directly responsible to the wingco, and that I would do the same again if the need arose. After that he left me to lead my own shows. And he never held it against me. It was one of the nice things about him.

Two other episodes marred my time at Drope. The first happened, landing back, after Ben Lenson had been hit in the radiator and forced to bail out in the battle area. I was worrying about him as we returned to base and failed to register a warning that there was an aircraft stuck on the grass runway. After touchdown, rolling fast, the wingtips of a Spitfire suddenly appeared very close on each side of the nose. Too late to do anything except brake hard and cut the switches. The Typhoon ran on, propeller chewing up the Spitfire's rear fuselage, pitching slowly up on its nose until I was looking down the engine cowling into the other cockpit.

Difficult to know what to say in such a situation. I shouted in the sudden silence: "I'm awfully sorry old chap!"

He never replied, just leapt out and ran, as if pursued by the fiends of hell. The markings on his Spitfire were Free French, the Cross of Lorraine. Perhaps I had spoken in the wrong language.

The engine was shock tested, a new radiator and propeller fitted, and my aircraft was airborne again in a matter of days. The Spitfire was a write off. *Vive le Typhoon!*

Around the same time, flying photo-recce on a wing show near Emden, the attack ended quicker than expected. Badly positioned, and trying to follow the last aircraft in before the ground defences had time to draw breath, my approach was too steep with insufficient nose down trim. Holding the dive to get the usual close-up photograph I was forced to make a violent recovery, pulled far too much g and passed out completely.

As consciousness returned I could hear the engine, feel the spade grip in my hand, and see nothing. Vision cleared, and the aircraft was in a gentle climbing turn to port, the target far below. Sunshine flooded the cockpit like a reprieve. And then I looked at the wings. On each side, inboard of the cannons, there was a massive chordwise wrinkle and there were missing rivets all over the outer panels.

I flew gingerly home reflecting that, even in the circumstances, the amount of g had been quite phenomenal. Extra care was always needed to pull off a smooth landing in the photo-recce Typhoons, although the elevator felt perfectly normal on the ground. There was undoubtedly something different about them. I determined to find out what.

Stan Carr inspected the mainplanes in silence and consulted the squadron engineer officer who had been a stressman at Hawker's before joining the RAF. In the end they decided that the spars were undamaged – the wrinkles on the inboard wing section which was not stressed skin, were of no consequence and new rivets would take care of the rest. After that had been done, and the wrinkles hammered flat in an effort to recover the original aerodynamic shape, photo 'C' was returned to service.

The Typhoon's rugged structure had probably saved my life. But any investigation of its unusual flying characteristics would have to wait. For much to my relief we were moving on once more. I had seen more than enough of Drope.

Alhorn, B111 as it had now become, was an ex Luftwaffe night-fighter station south east of Bremen. The runways, except for one which had been hastily repaired, were cratered and useless. The hangars no longer existed and the dispersals, on the edge of a pine forest, were crowded with burned-out wrecks. A few buildings, surprisingly including an excellent officers mess, were virtually untouched.

There was little time to enjoy any of that. As the fronts, east and west, converged on the Elbe it was reported that a major German force was moving northwards to make a last stand in Norway. It would travel by sea, and embarkation was already under way, an ideal target for the

Typhoons. We were up before dawn on 3 May, to a forecast of perfect flying weather, and the news that 2nd TAF had ordered maximum effort against shipping in the Lübeck/Neustadt area. This was out of range from Alhorn, so the squadrons were to operate from B150 Hustedt, north of Celle, alongside 121 Wing under 83 Group control.

I well remember those last hectic days of the war. Not least because Hustedt was close to Belsen and 121's wingco had just visited it himself. Between sorties he attempted to describe what he had seen and could still barely believe. And we, for the first time, became aware of the horrors of the concentration camps.

I led two shows that day and the second, with eleven aircraft remains as clear as yesterday; it was a beautiful afternoon. Visibility must have been upwards of forty miles, and a line of cumulus shadowed the Schleswig peninsular to port. Lübeck Bay was shrouded in smoke from earlier shipping strikes. Further up the coast, beyond Neustadt, flames suddenly erupted from an enemy airfield. The fire grew and spread, feeding a huge column of smoke which drifted away inland.

Immediately ahead in the lee of Fehmarn Island, a modern passenger vessel lay at anchor, uncamouflaged, dirty white in the sunshine, with a freighter nearby. We went down on them almost vertically, hanging in our straps, through a salvo of rocket flak and the familiar curtain of shells, the hulls expanding in our sights. Both ships were engulfed in bomb bursts, flame and smoke from direct hits, and near misses cascading them with water.

Climbing away there was an excited call on the radio, someone had spotted a flying boat low over the sea. Mike Bulleid as always was quick off the mark. At full throttle, overtaking fast, it was an impossible deflection shot but he hit it fair and square with his first burst. By the time the rest of us got there the BV 138 was already doomed. We were supposed to be credited with an eleventh share apiece but, without question, it was another for Mike's bag of enemy aircraft. Fantastic shooting.

As we left the wreckage, and headed for home, an MTB appeared zigzagging flat out. Perhaps it was on an air sea rescue mission, but the thought never crossed our minds as our cannons tore it to shreds. The wingco's story about those poor devils at Belsen was there to spur us on. There was no mercy for the enemy that day.

Fuel was running low so I reduced speed for maximum range, and opened up the formation. The final part of the flight crossed an area of flat and featureless countryside dotted with hundreds of small woods. Difficult to know your exact position. There was a certain amount of twitch on the wireless and we came straight in to Hustedt without a circuit.

On the way home that evening we cruised into the setting sun, the air was calm and still, the last of the cumulus fading away overhead. It had been epic stuff. The chaps had done the squadron proud. Almost as if they realised that it might be the last time. As if they intended to safeguard its reputation right to the end.

Around me was the very essence of 193. Ben Lenson, safely back from his recent parachute descent. Jimmy Fishwick, his commission just through after many months, and Bob Waldron. From B Flight there was Snowy Harrison supported by a formidable quartet, all of them nudging the 200-sortie mark – Charlie Hall, Mike Bulleid, Eddie Richardson, sometime keeper of the squadron diary, and Bunny Austin recently returned from his spell as VCP controller. And there were the new boys too. Mike Thexton, who had joined the squadron when 257 was disbanded, and Allan Wyse flying like a veteran as my number two.

A few words on the radio and they moved into tight line astern, preparing for the let down and break. As they did so I caught a fleeting glimpse of propeller discs, golden in the sunset, and was possessed once more by that wonderful feeling. Flying on forever above a fading, dying, landscape.

Less than twenty hours later, after more shipping strikes around Lübeck Bay and Fehmarn Island, we had fired our last shots in anger.

CHAPTER THIRTEEN

BALBOS AND BOOZE

The end of the fighting in Europe came with a spell of magnificent weather which seemed set to go on and on. Like the celebrations at Alhorn. The party to end all parties. Each morning after the latest possible breakfast, or no breakfast at all, we took ourselves off into the surrounding countryside seeking the spoils of war. In the evenings, surrounded by a growing collection of motor vehicles, the party rekindled itself with renewed vigour. We moved indoors as darkness fell, pausing briefly for solid refreshment and thundered on into the small hours.

On the third day I went back to work. Group wanted photographs of the final shipping strikes and Charlie Hall had volunteered to come along as my number two. There was a ceasefire in force. But hostilities were not due to terminate officially for another twenty-four hours and Tommy, briefing us beforehand, stressed that we should take nothing for granted. Our aircraft were fitted with drop tanks, in order to make the round trip from Alhorn, and the cannons were fully armed.

We cruised low down across the rich farmland of Niedersachsen and Schleswig Holstein, past the sprawling ruins of Hamburg and the burnt-out shell of Lübeck until Travemünde lay ahead. Skirting the white beaches we dropped down towards the *Deutschland* and the *Cap Arcona*, lying close together, on their beam ends in the shallow water. The vast hulls loomed large against my gunsight and I switched the camera on.

The whole of that forward-oblique pass between Lübeck Bay and Fehmarn Island was a graveyard of sunken, burnt-out and capsized ships. Charlie and I returned to base, well satisfied with what we had seen, happy that the Typhoons had played a major part in frustrating plans for that final Nazi stand in Norway. On our subsequent reckoning 146 Wing alone had sunk more than 40,000 tons of enemy shipping.

Shortly afterwards we learned that some were prison ships, whose wretched inmates had been removed from their concentration camps in the last weeks and days of the war. Whether they were hostages for the safe conduct of their unspeakable jailers, or about to be sunk in an effort to destroy the evidence of atrocity, had yet to be ascertained. Whatever the truth our attacks had unwittingly added to their sufferings. It was to be a long time before the full story came out.

Back at Alhorn it began to sink in that the war had really ended. We had lived by the Tannoy calls to briefing – endured those long stressful moments in our cockpits, waiting for the leader to start up. And then, as the air was filled with the crack of Coffman starters and ejector exhausts spewed oily smoke, that never-to-be-forgotten mix of tension and rising excitement. The familiar prelude to battle. It had become our way of life. Perhaps, though we didn't think of it much, even a way of death. Something which had always happened to the other chap.

And now it was over. There were no more calls to briefing. Our very purpose had been taken away. It came as a bit of a shock, I must say.

Snowy had departed for home, immediately the fighting ended, and Felix Cryderman had become my fellow flight commander. With equal speed he had grounded himself, confronting Butch, and refusing to fly a Typhoon again; claiming that it was no longer necessary and much too dangerous. From then on he ribbed us unmercifully for risking our lives, until they sent him home to Canada, which was just what he wanted. Ironically he was to be killed, bush flying in British Columbia, before many years had passed.

When the AOC visited us to present the squadron badge, Butch was in his element, determined as ever to secure that elusive permanent commission. You could see it in his face as the band fell in and he took command of the parade. Air Vice-Marshal Hudleston's words were complimentary. But there was a dreadful sense of anticlimax. Had he really been talking about us? Our future, and that of the squadron was obscure to say the least. In a month or two we might be scattered to the four winds. We celebrated the occasion with mixed feelings.

The wing was at Alhorn for barely a month, the beginning of a long period of painful adjustment, coming to terms with the concept of peace and thinking about the future. Some were attracted to the idea of a career in the RAF. Others kept their heads down and soldiered on hoping for the earliest possible release. For me at that time the way ahead was clear – test flying if I could make it or failing that a career in the RAF.

My name had already come up on the postwar list of permanent commissions, as a substantive flight lieutenant with backdated seniority. It seemed a good omen. So, I sat down and wrote a letter to Frank McKenna at Glosters.

Charlie Hall and I explored the Alhorn base together. Starting with the mess basement, which was knee deep in Nazi photographs and magazines, with a few swastika arm bands and ceremonial daggers abandoned in haste by their owners. The rest of the airfield was a dead loss. Everything had been destroyed. But a train of flat cars, on an adjacent railway line, was loaded with damaged aircraft which yielded a few more instruments for my bottom drawer. Most were Ju188s and amongst them an almost undamaged Tempest V.

That railway line ran through the depth of a pine forest, where we tried our hands at deer stalking, lethally armed with German machine pistols. We never actually hit anything and this highly dangerous sport came to an abrupt end when two stalking parties opened fire on each other as the quarry fled between them!

Fortunately there was plenty of flying, practising for the Victory Air Parade, and there were extra flights for the leaders too as they learned accurate station keeping between squadrons. This was a new skill and the range bars on our reflector sights proved invaluable until it became second nature. Then came the Balbos[1] proper, sweating to hold station in the turbulent air, with 193's Typhoons proudly sporting their new scarlet insignia. Butch was on leave and I was happy to be leading the squadron again.

After the Victory Air Parade there were others. Until life seemed to become one long round of formation flying and parties. Photographic sorties continued, mainly to obtain information on ex Luftwaffe airfields. We followed the system which we had developed in the latter stages of the war, to assist in planning and layout, before the wing moved to a new location.

On one such sortie over Oldenburg airfield I saw a couple of coxed fours practising on the Weser. The slim hulls and the swinging oars brought back memories of prewar bumping races on the Severn at Tewkesbury. It seemed like another world.

The target for my photographic sortie on 31 May was a grass airfield south of Hanover. Shortly afterwards in early June, following yet another Victory Air Parade over Nijmegen this time for Princess Juliana of the Netherlands, the wing moved to its last home at R16 Hildesheim. Although the town itself had been heavily bombed the airfield was virtually untouched. There were hangars for our aircraft and all personnel were accommodated in modern quarters.

Doug Borland, a flight commander on 266, leading an attack on a German airfield in those last weeks of fighting, had the dreadful experience of seeing his twin brother Noel shot down and killed. It almost unhinged him and he was temporarily grounded in case he attempted a suicide mission. It says a lot for Doug that he was soon airborne again and that he could write such a calm and balanced statement about his early postwar experiences.

> "At first we were expected to behave like victors, not conquerors, but winners. A non fraternisation rule was introduced; we were to have no social contact with the Germans. In a demonstration of our superiority the local mayor was ordered to appear before the commanding officer and instructed to provide the station with fresh vegetables and waitresses for the officers mess. In fact the Germans were only too willing to oblige. Because we paid them, for their subjugation, in new 'occupation' marks.
>
> "There was a canal running beside the airfield and the local Hildesheimers liked to stroll along the grassy banks. We hadn't much to occupy our restless minds, so we joined them, and the non fraternisation rule somehow never worked. They were remarkably friendly and the girls very pretty. I suppose that if the Germans had won the war they would have been better at being victors than we were!"

Hildesheim was an interesting place. It had been the last base for a staffel of the Luftwaffe's clandestine special purposes unit – KG200[2]. From here they had operated a variety of aircraft, including captured Fortresses and Liberators. In the aircraft graveyard, apart from these, were examples of many German types, including the outstanding Daimler Benz-engined Fw190D. Typhoons from 146 Wing had tangled with a couple of them briefly, shortly after the Luftwaffe's last fling on New Year's Day, and found themselves totally outclassed.

From Hildesheim it was only a short distance into the Harz mountains, driving up the railway track when the road became impassable, to reach the summit of Broken. Here, almost 4,000 feet above sea level, standing amongst the ruins of a hotel and the distorted aerials of a burned-out radar station one could look out across the plains towards Magdeburg and Berlin.

Only the core of the hotel remained. A massive, ugly, hall and staircase. An overblown mural covered the walls, towering above its surroundings, three witches flying in line astern. Innocent enough you might think. But the Nazi artist obviously intended otherwise for the way in which they sat astride their broomsticks was powerfully erotic to say the least.

On the same trip we went further into the mountains, searching for an underground V weapons factory in a salt mine near Nordhausen. There was nothing to identify it from outside. Just a single-track railway leading into a narrow tunnel. A miserable place where V1 and V2 assembly was carried out, far below the surface, in the most primitive conditions. Inside, even on a hot summer's day, the air was cold and clammy.

Shortly after our visit a large area of the Harz, which included Broken and this unique plant, was due to be handed over to the Russians. However it was obvious that they were not going to get their hands on the contents. The whole place was a hive of activity, brilliantly lit, its production lines being stripped down and removed before our eyes.

The Americans in charge of the operation were extremely cagey, but they opened up when we asked them about the previous workforce. It was like the horrors of Belsen all over again. A nearby concentration camp, created for the express purpose, had supplied the forced labour. Many of the prisoners had lived and died underground. There were regular transports to an extermination camp for those who were no longer able to work.

Due to the allied bombing campaign much of the German aircraft industry had been moved to the east, particularly, so we understood, around Leipzig. The temptation to see something of it was too great, and one hot and hazy afternoon I went airfield touring near Halle.

At one several Fw190Ds were parked in the open and at another, Burg, a number of Mistels, those remarkable pickaback arrangements with a piloted Me109 or Fw190 mounted on top of a Ju88 or He111. They were brave men who took them into battle, surviving the most dangerous of take-offs, and facing all the normal hazards of ground-attack and a few more besides. For each unmanned bomber, a great blunderbuss of a missile was released at point-blank range by firing a set of explosive bolts.

Burg, although I did not know it at the time, had been another KG200 base. Here a force of some fifty Mistels had been concentrated to carry out last-ditch missions against the Oder and Vistula bridges which had fallen intact to the Soviet armies. I wanted to land at Burg and take a closer look. But this was Russian airspace and it was unwise to hang around.

One of our chaps, who inadvertently did, a flight sergeant, got lost and landed in the Russian Sector. His 'Ya Englichanin' form and its message was a waste of time, as none of his captors could read, and he was treated like a prisoner of war – locked up overnight with a bare minimum to eat and drink. In the morning an officer appeared and he was grilled at length. He returned a shaken man, much relieved that they had let him go, and grateful that his engine had started on its first cartridge.

It was becoming daily more obvious that our Russian allies would be very difficult bedfellows in future years, and many of us inclined to the view that we should deal with this problem now, whilst the Western military machine was still mobilised and ready to go. It was a view undoubtedly shared by some of the top brass for we found ourselves briefed to take part in bomber interception exercises. A most unlikely role for the Typhoon; but a first indication of the cold war to come.

With such thoughts in mind it was dreadful to stand idly by whilst a whole wing of Czech Spitfires refuelled at Hildesheim on its way home. We were forbidden to speak to them. Perhaps to avoid a confrontation; or the risk that they might be persuaded to turn back at the eleventh hour. We watched uneasily as they took off for Prague and wondered what fate, or the Russians, might have in store for them at the other end.

About this time 266 Squadron flew back to England and was disbanded. Doug Borland and another pilot were stranded with unserviceable aircraft. They had also been left with a huge stock of cigarettes – Cape to Cairo, known more rudely as Camel to Consumer, the remains of regular supplies from Southern Rhodesia throughout the war. So, without any permission or authority, they loaded up a jeep with Jerry cans of petrol and set off eastwards on the autobahn from Hanover – to do business in Berlin.

The autobahn was almost empty and there was little activity to be seen until they ran into a crowd of Russian soldiers near the Brandenburg Gate. These clouted the bonnet in drunken gestures of solidarity, and were very friendly, until a women soldier appeared amongst them "with breasts, like a child's drawing of mountains, festooned with medals". This caused such amusement that the Russians became most offended and threatening, and our two Rhodesians had to beat a hasty retreat. Later, in a quiet street, they were surrounded by Berliners. These local people, who were obviously desperately afraid of the Russians, insisted on shaking hands. Quite extraordinary in a heavily bombed city, where Doug and his colleague had appeared in uniform with pilot's wings, and might well have been treated as *terror fliegers*.

In the end business turned to cigarettes, in penny numbers, in exchange for cash in handfuls. This paid for their hotel accommodation in Berlin, and all their recently departed squadron's debts, when they returned to Hildesheim. Looking back on that visit to Berlin, Doug reckoned that they had been extremely foolhardy, and were very lucky to have returned safely.

A trip which I made with Neville Thomas to headquarters 7th Armoured Division at Cuxhaven, where his brother was CRE[3], led to a splendid evening in the mess. Something that frequently happened to those who went swanning with Tommy. Nearby Cuxhaven airfield, with its treasure trove of Luftwaffe hardware, was an unexpected benefit.

Most of the aircraft were radar-carrying night fighters, Me110s and 410s and, seen in real life for the first time, a Heinkel He219. High and boxlike on its stilted tricycle undercarriage, this particular aircraft carried an armament of four 30mm and two 20mm forward-firing cannon. They were supplemented by two more 30mm cannon mounted in the centre section, which were tilted to fire forwards and upwards, the lethal *Schrage Musik* (literally 'slant music') for stalking an enemy bomber from below.

Both occupants were provided with ejection seats, the first we had ever seen, and the crew compartment was heavily armoured. The straight control column, seen on earlier German designs, had given way to one which was more like the split stick on our own fighters, except that it was topped by a two-horned yoke instead of a spade grip. The instruments were well up to the standard of our Gustav at Antwerp with additional features such as an autopilot and radio altimeter. The He219 may have been ugly but it was a formidable beast.

Tucked away in a corner, amongst all the radar-antennaed night fighters, I found two gliders, a Grunau Baby and a Meise. In no time at all Stan Carr sent a Queen Mary up to Cuxhaven and the gliders were derigged and brought back to base. A local gliding site, which was marked on the map, had obviously been used for bungey launching and yielded nothing except an empty barn. We needed a winch, a Tiger Moth, or a Jungmeister. As we cast around for one or other of these, 84 Group Gliding School at Salzgitter heard about our gliders and they were 'officially' removed. We never saw them again.

Another sad blow, the result of a clamp down on ex enemy transport, was the loss of our treasured BMW sports roadster. We got wind of this when someone flying near Bremen spotted a check point, with a long queue of vehicles leading up to it, and a field alongside into which almost every one was being diverted and parked. In the weeks that followed they became a major hazard and any German car or truck not carrying an official permit was confiscated on the spot. The unfortunate occupants were returned to unit, regardless of rank, in the back of a 30cwt or 3 tonner. For transport around Germany, from then on, it was back to the ubiquitous jeep.

Hildesheim had one fascinating relic. A rare, and until then unknown to us, Dornier 335 single-seat fighter. Tucked safely away in a small building under cover and out of sight, it seemed virtually complete. The usual bunch of enthusiasts looked it over, noted the push-pull configuration, trying to visualise ground angles and rear propeller clearances. We thought that it must be a prototype and wisely decided that it was not for us. Although it was a decision which we took with some regret.

Apart from its unusual layout the Do335 was an aircraft with many advanced features. Like the He219 it had an ejection seat, very necessary with the rear propeller, an autopilot and radio navigation equipment. It had powered ailerons, and the front propeller had a reverse pitch position for braking. The armament once again was formidable, three 30mm and two 20mm cannon. The new two-horned yoke control column was also in evidence, the horns in this case being even more festooned with well positioned controls, bomb release, cannon and gun buttons, auto pilot and radio press to transmit.

Surprisingly the Do335 remained undisturbed throughout our stay at Hildesheim. Scientific officialdom never came to collect it or even inspect it. Yet reports, published later, suggested that RAE Farnborough, with only a two-seat Do335 to fly and evaluate, were unable to lay their hands on a single-seater.

This absence of interest seems even more remarkable in view of developments at Volkenrode, an aeronautical research establishment, less than twenty miles away on the Hanover-Braunschweig autobahn. Here, under the auspices of the Ministry of Aircraft Production, a special unit was being set up, with senior scientists from the UK, supported by RAF personnel, and an air commodore in charge[4].

Their task was to scour Germany for prototype aircraft and the key personnel associated with them, to bring them to Volkenrode, and to finish the construction of those which were still incomplete. In part at least they should have been out and about, round the airfields of 2nd TAF, asking the units what they had seen and enlisting their aid in the search. In practice it was just the reverse. There was no publicity and visiting them was strictly forbidden.

A number of prototypes were out of reach in the Russian zone. Those in the American and French zones were almost equally inaccessible. In the end, largely through lack of trust between the Western allies, there was no will to continue and the whole project collapsed. It was a tragedy. After the end of the war there was so much in Germany available for the taking and so much was lost.

One place which we were encouraged to visit was the 84 Group Rest Centre in the Harz mountains. On arrival at Bad Harzburg our little party debussed in a cobbled square surrounded by timber and stucco houses. It was like being transported to a different moment in time. The streets were clean and tidy, with masses of flowers in tubs and hanging baskets, even the inhabitants looked well turned out in a threadbare sort of way. The little town, overlooked by wooded hills, felt peaceful and secure. Bad Harzburg appeared virtually untouched by war.

The small hotel was airy and comfortable, with a balcony outside each bedroom, where we could relax and watch the world go by. The bar offered plenty of choice, and in the galleried dining area there was a small orchestra which played to our bidding. As the evening wore on, and candlelight gleamed softly on the long stemmed glasses, we took a great fancy to the Radetzky March. It was rousing, blood-tingling stuff. We would adopt it for the squadron and put words to it. The unfortunate orchestra was urged to play it again and again – and the wine flowed like water – until we were almost incapable of putting words to anything.

In the morning we woke to the sound of bells and a multitude of hurrying footsteps down below in the square. The locals were out in force on their way to church. Churchgoing on this scale no longer happened in the UK. How could we even begin to reconcile it with the Germany we had known as our enemy? The arrogant brutality of the Nazis and the horrors of the concentration camps were still too close. In the future perhaps we might come to terms with the idea that behind these outward evils there had been something else. A despairing silent majority, decent citizens for the most part, dragged down into the abyss, fearful for themselves and their Fatherland.

The shattered towns of north Germany seen from the air, or close at hand on the ground, were in unbelievable contrast to Bad Harzburg. For those who have no personal experience of the destruction wrought by Bomber Command it is almost impossible to describe the appalling devastation, the endless acres of rubble, the total absence of shops and public services of all kinds. And everywhere was just dust, more dust, and the ever present smell of burning and death.

To have seen the urban and industrial wreckage of Germany, in the summer of 1945, was proof enough of the extent to which the bomber offensive must have affected the course of the war. Those who still argue to the contrary claim, as of course they would, that the substantial growth in enemy arms production from 1942 onwards, was clear evidence of its failure.

But, and this seems to be the fundamental weakness in their case, there has been little effort to assess the further increases in output and the acceleration in new weapon programmes which would have occurred if there had been no strategic bombing campaign. The scenario might have been very different if that extra capability, and fuel, together with the resources tied down for home defence, had been available to the enemy on the Russian and Western fronts.

At Hildesheim my photo Typhoon investigation got underway at last. Comparison flying soon revealed that there was a marked difference in the handling compared with other aircraft. You could pull g much too easily, accurate slow flying was difficult, and on landing there was a definite tendency to pump handle and overcontrol in pitch. Stan Carr went right through the elevator circuit. Nothing wrong there. Friction, mass balance and elevator profile were quite normal.

What else was different on these aircraft? A camera installation replacing the port inboard cannon? Extra armour around the engine and radiator? And then it clicked. The forward armour had been removed at some stage. But the extra tail ballast was still in place. The three photo-recce Typhoons were weighed. We had been flying them for months, and on ops, with the centre of gravity behind the aft limit! It was a sobering thought. The offending tail ballast was removed and, for the last two months of their lives, they handled like normal Typhoons.

CHAPTER FOURTEEN

IN A QUANDARY

As the photo Typhoon exercise ended 146 Wing acquired an Anson XIX. On the strength of his time with 84 Group Communications Squadron this aircraft became Butch's responsibility and, to my surprise, after all our disagreements, he converted me onto it before anyone else.

It so happened that I had worked out a forward-facing camera installation for the Tempest V – based on an otherwise unoccupied section of the leading edge near wing root. If we could make up a sample I would have a ready-made excuse, or so I thought, to deliver it by Anson to the Central Fighter Establishment at Tangmere. Once there I could slip across to Glosters, to see Frank McKenna, who had responded positively to my letter.

The upshot of that particular idea was a quick trip back to the railway line near Alhorn. The train of flat cars and its Tempest was still there. We removed a section of wing, and brought it back to Hildesheim, where Stan Carr worked his usual magic. In the end I flew the Anson to Tangmere via Brussels. On board was our Tempest sample, an accompanying set of photographs, and seven passengers on UK leave.

Frank McKenna asked me to spend the night at his home on the outskirts of Cheltenham. He seemed little changed, just slightly more rotund and ruddy faced, and we picked up almost where we had left off more than six years earlier.

After his family had retired to bed he told me that there was a test flying opportunity coming up at Glosters. Phil Stanbury, who was responsible for development flying on the Meteor, wished to retire in the near future. A new single-engine jet fighter prototype, the E1/44, was on the stocks and a development test pilot would be needed to take this on. Glosters would be happy to offer me the job, provided that I could organise myself a test pilot's course before leaving the RAF, and there was one due to start in January 1946.

Returning to Hildesheim I put in an immediate application to ETPS[1], hoping that it might produce the desired result, and then got on with the job in hand. There was still plenty of flying to be done, maintaining operational standards, and the squadrons were targeted at 450 hours a month.

Leading a formation low level, on a visit to the Möhne and Eider dams, the urge to divert briefly and beat up a nearby USAF base proved irresistible. Their Mustangs returned the compliment in much larger numbers, and with immaculate timing, catching us all at tea in the mess a few days later. Johnny Wells was highly suspicious but nobody said a word.

Soon afterwards tea time and tragedy coincided. A visiting flight commander from 33 Squadron had just taken leave of us in the mess. He made his departure fast and low and attempted to sign off with a slow roll. Moments later we were looking at a mass of smoke and flames, rising from the far side of the airfield, where his Tempest had gone straight in.

Our first and last officers mess dance was held at Hildesheim. The dining hall was almost unrecognisable with an imported band on the balcony and the tables decorated and candlelit. Even the garden was a mass of fairy lights, as if Christmas had arrived early, and we were all in our best blue.

Sadly, apart from some slight evidence of returning civilised behaviour, it became just another thrash. Perhaps it was still too soon for most of us to behave otherwise. There was more activity around the downstairs bar, and skittle alley, than on the dance floor. Even those remarkable Luftwaffe creations, with their head-operated flushing pads for the seriously inebriated, may well have been back in use.

"Herr Hauptmann! es ist verboten in der Weinstube. Ausgehen sie schnell nach der Krankenschale. Jawohl Herr Oberst!"

This was to be remembered, and perhaps best forgotten as the ultimate party in a four-month long wake to mark the passing of 146 Wing.

Came the moment of truth when we were visited by Air Chief Marshal Tedder on a whistle-stop tour of BAFO[2] . He arrived by air and gathered us round him, out on the field. The occasion was difficult, for he had come to thank us and, at the same time, to explain that our time as comrades in arms was almost over. Yet he knew exactly how to handle it. His words were sincere and his touch was sure. To all who heard him then he came across as the most understanding of senior RAF commanders.

The day after Tedder's visit there was a summons from the group captain. My encounter with the Free French Spitfire at Drope had caught up with me at last and there was a black endorsement to record it. In time honoured fashion the form was inserted, on the first blank page of my logbook, where the evidence could be removed forever by means of a sharp razor blade!

As he signed the endorsement Johnny Wells looked tired, and almost bald, his alopecia worse than ever. Without a doubt his war had cost him dear. He gave me an encouraging smile, which belied his words, for I seemed to be in even more trouble. When group had heard about my trip to CFE[3] with the Tempest forward-facing camera mock-up, they didn't like it at all. He handed me a typewritten note. It was my copy of a letter addressed to the officer commanding 146 Wing. I glanced at it hurriedly.

...appreciated that Flt Lt Ince unwittingly short circuited the proper channels... requested that you will inform this officer the work he is doing is very much appreciated by this headquarters.... The signature was that of the SASO[4], Freddie Rosier.

The subject changed. 146 Wing would be disbanded in a matter of days, and 193 Squadron within the month, it was time for the usual assessments. The form was already there – lying on my open logbook. As an *F.B. Pilot.... Exceptional....* Endorsements were suddenly of no consequence at all. At the bottom of the page there was an official looking stamp – *Fliegerhorst-Kommandantur Hildesheim*, just that, nothing else, no swastika or eagles. It seemed rather a nice touch.

Early August, 266 Squadron and its Rhodesians had already gone. Only Ronnie Sheward was still around. He had returned briefly to take over 197 as its last CO. Butch had been posted, and I found myself in charge of 193 for the few brief weeks remaining.

In that time we were called upon to give two demonstrations. The first, supply dropping by a section of four Typhoons, took place on the airfield and went off rather well. The second, organised with group headquarters, was to be a combination of low level bombing and napalm. Practice bombs – as many as we chose to drop – and a single live napalm delivery provided that we could find a suitable site.

South of Hildesheim was one of those last-ditch Luftwaffe airfields. We went there by road and it was almost perfect. On open ground, sloping gently up towards a sheer escarpment, not far from Goslar, without a building in sight. Around the perimeter were a number of substantially complete aircraft, mostly Savoia Marchetti Sm79s and 85s, together with a few Ju52s. We selected a viewing area for the audience, chose a suitable target, planned the run in and breakaway for maximum safety, and got down to serious practice.

If nothing else we could use the occasion to secure some good pictures of napalm. So a cameraman was laid on – probably Charles Woodcock – a long serving rigger on our servicing echelon. A keen, and highly skilled, amateur photographer Charles Woodcock was a man of parts. I believe that he had been much involved in the forward oblique camera installation, and in the hazardous ground handling of napalm, even though he was not an armourer.

The proceedings opened with individual aircraft, dropping practice bombs, followed by a section attack. The great bulk of the target, an Sm85, made it absurdly easy and the smoke vortices from a succession of direct hits were duly and well recorded on film.

Back at base I changed aircraft and took off again with two ninety-gallon containers of petroleum jelly. They burst all over the Savoia Marchetti, erupting into a great ball of fire, which went down rather well with the troops. As for those splendid pictures of napalm in action – our photographer had not been properly briefed on the number of attacks involved and had used up the whole of his film on our practice bombs. Of napalm we had nothing at all.

On 7 September 1945 I led the squadron back to England, landing to refuel at Courtrai. Sad and elusive memories. Waving the chocks away and saluting Stan Carr and the boys of 6193 Servicing Echelon for the last time. A low pass across the airfield in tight formation and Craven A's valediction on the wireless as we climbed into the distance.

Pulling up into the circuit, for a final stream landing at Lasham, and the bonds that had held us together seemed to be slipping away forever. We had been comrades in arms – a real band of brothers, inordinately proud of our squadron. Like obsessive sportsmen it had been the most important thing in our lives. At the end of the war we had lost a way of life which we had come to cherish, and now this.

Just time to wish each other luck with promises to keep in touch. Then they were gone, off on leave, posted elsewhere, never to return. 193 Squadron with its motto, 'To Rule the Earth and the Sky', had ceased to exist. I felt gutted.

What was once 84 GSU had suffered a sea change and become the Group Disbandment Centre. In the dispersals they were doing dreadful things to an earlier batch of Typhoons. Wings and fuselages, stripped to bare shells, were being lined up in closely packed rows and bulldozed together, for all the world like a giant scrap bailing press. Tomorrow, or the day after, our aircraft would be under the hammer.

For my Typhoon there was a brief reprieve – back to Germany – and another napalm demonstration on Battle of Britain Day. More urgent, from a personal point of view, was the lack of any response to my application for a test pilot's course. It was essential to see Frank McKenna immediately. I phoned him to make an appointment and obtained a landing clearance at Brockworth for the following day.

The familiar airfield, which had been such a hive of activity just before the war – with Gladiators, Henleys and the glamorous F5/34 monoplane fighter – was almost deserted as I taxied in and parked outside the flight shed. Only a few remaining Typhoons, from the last production batch, would fly from here. All Meteor testing had been moved to Morton Valence some miles to the west.

Frank's comfortable, if spartan, office was dominated by a large-scale Meteor IV. A beautiful example of the model-maker's art, with its long nacelles and silver finish, a replica of the aircraft in which Group Captain Wilson would soon be attacking the World Air Speed Record. Willie Wilson was the commandant of ETPS and we decided that I should get in touch with him in an attempt to break the impasse.

There was only time for a telephone call to Boscombe Down before I left for Wunstorf. It was hard going, and I had the distinct impression that he didn't want to see me, however I managed to fix a date which fitted in with my next visit to the Typhoon breakers yard.

Back in Germany 123 Wing was down to two squadrons, and these would shortly be disbanded, but at least I was among friends. Johnny Baldwin was the CO and Johnny Button his wing leader – and for the first time I met Pinkie Stark who was commanding 609. Short and balding, even in those days, the vigour of his personality was well complemented by a handlebar moustache, piercing eyes which missed nothing at all, and a voice which was deep bass, cultivated and warm. A sterling character.

Back in 1943 when Reggie Baker, at that time CO of 263, went on leave, Pinkie was left holding the fort. Came a ring on the phone and Pinkie, emulating his master, barked "Stark here!" to which came back the classic response: "Put on the bloody light then!" Only a man of Pinkie's character could live with a story like that, which he did with the greatest enjoyment.

Before we flew to Volkel, the temporary base for our contribution to the air display at Ypenburg on 15 September, Johnny Baldwin arranged a highly unofficial discussion group. It revolved around the presence of an ex Luftwaffe major who had turned up at Wunstorf demanding to see the commanding officer. When confronted by Pinkie, who had been told to deal with him, he announced that he was a qualified pilot on Fw190s – and he wanted to fly a Typhoon. The sheer effrontery. But he was an aviator and an enthusiast – and Pinkie likewise. Only it wasn't Pinkie's decision, even if his comment said it all: "If we ever did agree – I would escort you. My cannons would be loaded. The slightest sign of any nonsense and I would shoot you down!"

In the end he worked at Wunstorf as a labourer. His world was aviation and he could not bring himself to give it up. Besides which he needed a meal ticket. To invite him in, to sit and talk amongst us, was of course forbidden by the leaky no fraternising rule. Johnny Baldwin looked at it from a different angle. It was an opportunity not to be missed. To get an enemy view on our operations and tactics at first hand; while memories were still fresh.

The results were instructive. The German pilot had a fixation about our failure, in his opinion, to operate in much larger formations. The fact that they might have been forced into this themselves – once the Luftwaffe had lost overall air superiority – was something that had not occurred to him. And he seemed unwilling to accept the idea that large formations were essentially inflexible.

Against ground targets there was no disagreement. Speed and surprise were all important. Attacks which were pressed home, before the enemy had time to take cover or retaliate, were the most effective and suffered the lowest casualties. Our Luftwaffe major had seen it again and again. As he had also seen the opposite.

They had thought our ground troops arrogant in their neglect of camouflage. The anti-aircraft fire generally ineffective – and believed that the Luftwaffe could have caused enormous damage, given more fuel and better trained replacements.

As for the Typhoons, in the ground-attack role they were greatly feared by the Wehrmacht, but the Luftwaffe considered that we were often easy to bounce. However, as soon as they mixed it with us, the less experienced German pilots were usually outclassed.

In the final stages of the war this had become a vicious circle with high pilot attrition rates and replacements, who had done their primary training on gliders, frequently going on ops with no more than 100 hours of power flying. As for information from the RAE[5] that the Fw190 could outclimb a Typhoon, it may have happened on 130 octane at Farnborough, but their fuel was a long way down on octane rating. In practice he claimed that they could not do so.

He was a forceful, confident, character even as he faced us – having lost everything except his enthusiasm for flying and war. I rather hope that he got back into the new Bundesluftwaffe.

Before returning to England it seemed a wise move to make my number with the CO of 35 Wing. For my army background had caught up with me, and I was about to go back on fighter-recce, posted to 2 Squadron as a flight commander.

My first and only formal meeting with Group Captain Anderson was a disaster in every sense. For a start I had good reason to be apprehensive about his reactions to my forward-facing camera activities with 146 Wing. I tried to dismiss such forebodings and keep an open mind. Here was a man who had led a squadron of Hawker Hectors in 1940, whose feats, in these obsolescent biplanes, had included dive bombing the German forces at Dunkirk. And he was still flying operationally in the last months of the war. Perhaps he would be more tolerant and understanding than I had been led to believe.

But he wasn't. He greeted me coldly and gave me a week to return my Typhoon to Lasham, put my affairs in order and report to Celle. And God help me if I was not there in time. For my part it was pray God for that posting to ETPS. Back at Lasham they wanted my Typhoon for scrap, but Denys Gillam was the CO of 84 Group Disbandment Centre, and I was able to borrow his Tempest V for the trip to see Willie Wilson at Boscombe Down.

There had been just seven squadrons of Tempests operational during the war. We had envied them for their deeper penetration role; and the air combat opportunities which this had given them in the final months. But above all we had coveted their new aircraft. They were such obvious successors to our splendid Typhoons.

The Tempest retained all the Typhoon's best features, allied to a thin, laminar flow, elliptical wing. With the maximum thickness at almost forty per cent chord, the four 20mm cannon had been tucked neatly away inside the wing, and the whole aircraft was painted in a smooth low drag camouflage finish. Denys Gillam's Tempest, with his personal 'ZZ' on the fuselage, looked a thoroughbred as I walked out to it that morning. The cockpit was Typhoon, almost to the last nut and bolt, and I felt immediately at home. The take-off was very similar and required plenty of rudder.

Thereafter everything was that much better, a noticeably higher rate of climb, some twenty miles an hour faster on the cruise. The spring tab ailerons felt lighter, giving a higher rate of roll, which made the whole aircraft feel more agile. There was much less vibration, probably because the engine had been moved forward to accommodate a fuselage fuel tank. Yet, in spite of these major changes and improvements, there was still that marvellous feeling of rugged security, so reminiscent of the Typhoon.

It was impossible to resist a few aerobatics en route. These were further evidence of the improved handling qualities, compared with its predecessor, and the way in which you could throw the aircraft around. Then it was time to join the crowded traffic pattern at Boscombe Down, which required a long, straight, powered approach all the way to touch down. It had been a brief and happy introduction to the Tempest.

Not so my meeting with Willie Wilson. Perhaps he was being bombarded with applications for places on the next course, or under pressure from MAP[6] to keep the numbers down. Maybe ETPS was suffering serious staff losses from demobilisation. Whatever the reason, although he was willing to listen, he showed little enthusiasm for my case. Eventually he put the situation to me quite bluntly. My application for ETPS had been received. But the RAF would not nominate me for the course. If Glosters wanted me that badly they must do it themselves.

Were MAP trying to get Glosters to make some financial contribution? If so it was difficult to believe they would agree. I flew back to Lasham rather depressed, attempted a steep curved approach and ran out of elevator, making a rather untidy wheel landing.

Fortunately the Tempest's owner was not around and I went up and did some stalls, and another circuit, to sort out the situation. The elevator was less effective at low speeds, power off, than the Typhoon. Or perhaps there was a greater rearward movement of the centre of pressure, at high angles of attack, with the laminar flow wing. At all events it required a slightly different technique to the Typhoon, but one which was not particularly difficult to master.

A quick letter to Frank McKenna gave him the details of my meeting with Willie Wilson. He replied within days. Glosters had asked MAP to accept me as their nominee for the next ETPS course, starting 1 January 1946, and this had been agreed. A career with Glosters was on.

Celle, when I got there as instructed soon afterwards, was a depressing place. My ex army friends, the original Broon Fockerrs, had long since disappeared. Demobilisation was in full swing and there was little evidence of any positive activity. For the moment at least 35 Wing seemed to have lost its way. It was a sad commentary on the times.

The officers mess was still the scene of an occasional impromptu party. But there was none of the light-hearted warmth and spontaneity which had illuminated our gatherings in my Typhoon days. When the group captain, supported by Bill Malins, began his song and dance routine with the words: "How're we gonna keep 'em down on the farm now that they've seen Paree?" – we knew that he would soon be leaving us for the night, then we could relax and enjoy ourselves. For Andy at those little gatherings, and on other occasions as well, managed to convey the impression that most of us were on the wrong side of the footlights. Bill Malins, the wingco flying, was an easier and friendlier character altogether but it was not his show.

George Thornton, my fellow flight commander on 2 Squadron, had been around for some time and knew the form. He was a great ally in an uncertain situation. We played it carefully, exchanging any information that came our way, and concentrated on running our flights. No easy task – for there was a distinct lack of enthusiasm amongst some of the pilots impatient for civilian life. Few reconnaissance sorties were actually needed and there was little attempt to define any training requirements. A fighter reconnaissance unit, with its individualistic approach, was particularly difficult to keep going in the face of such constraints and our efforts suffered accordingly. Aircraft serviceability remained surprisingly good, in spite of ground crew losses from demobilisation, but our flying programmes were always hand to mouth.

Without George, whose worldly manner concealed a warm and generous nature, life at Celle would have been a deal worse. We were only together a couple of months, but I shall always remain grateful for his support and the way in which he helped to enliven a dreary interlude. Almost twenty years were to go by before we ran into each other again at the Farnborough Air Show. By then he was looking a little plumper, and more worldly wise, but underneath was still the same old George. He had left the RAF and seemed happy enough, based at Hatfield, demonstrating business jets for de Havilland.

I always enjoyed flying the Spitfire XIV although it had lost the evocative charm of its Merlin-engined forebears. The delightfully simple, almost Tiger Moth-like, feel and handling had been sacrificed, and successfully, for better performance. The Spitfire nose had always been obtrusive. But this one was enormous and the cylinder banks of the massive two-stage Griffon engine seemed to be bursting out of their cowlings.

The rest of the aircraft looked deceptively unchanged, apart from the larger fin and rudder, but the wing loading was much higher and an additional tank had been squeezed in, behind the cockpit, to compensate for the increased fuel consumption. The Griffon sounded rough and raucous, even at cruising power, as if it was running on nails. But its handling had been simplified by a more advanced propeller mechanism. This optimised the RPM so that you could use the throttle effectively as a single lever control.

2 Squadron had the latest clipped-wing FR Mk XIVBs, fitted with full rear view canopies and the new gyro gunsight. The latter was a superb device. You tracked an enemy aircraft by holding it inside a pattern of diamond-shaped spots which was projected on to the windscreen or optical flat. A twist grip on the throttle adjusted the size of the pattern, shrinking it round the target to generate a range input, and gyro precession did the rest. In a quarter attack the whole pattern moved, as you pulled g, automatically setting up the correct lead for deflection shooting.

It was so easy and natural to use that most pilots felt completely at home with it from the start. Lefty Packwood, one of the Broon Fockerrs, was flying a Spit XIV when he shot down his Me109 over Gilze-Rijen on New Year's Day. As the first and only one of us to destroy an enemy fighter in the air I envied him his GGS[7].

As might be expected, in such a stretched version of the original

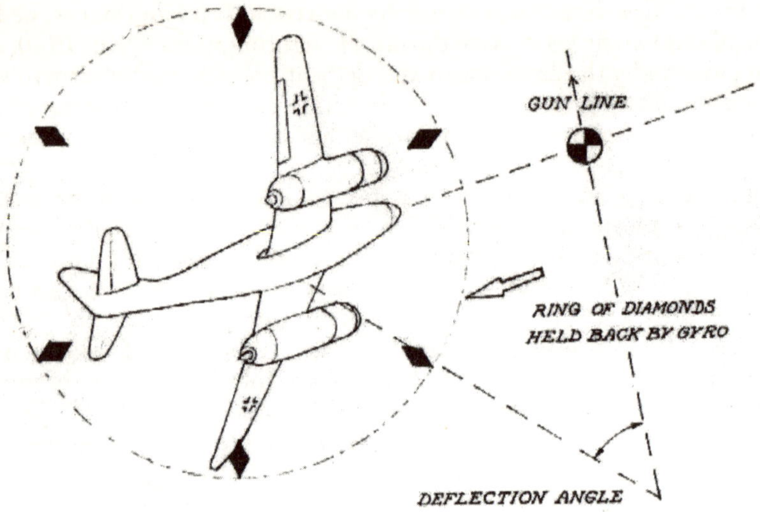

Gyro gunsight. Air combat and pilot's eye view.

design, the Spit XIV had some rather odd characteristics. Plus 12lb/in boost was the maximum permissible for take-off, otherwise you were in grave danger of wiping off the undercarriage. Even so it leant over like a toy aeroplane and you had an impression of moving crabwise. Once airborne the power restriction no longer applied; with +18 available for max climb and +25 for combat emergency.

The torque and gyroscopic effects of the outsize engine, with its five-bladed propeller, were impressive. Pitching the aircraft nose up or down induced noticeable yaw and vice versa. My first attempt at a slow roll was an untidy excursion all over sky. Eventually one got better, but it was always a difficult performance. The two-position flaps, controlled by a lever like an old-fashioned gas tap, had seemed quite in keeping with the Merlin-engined versions. On the Griffon Spitfire they felt strangely out of place. As for the rear-fuselage fuel tank, not to be used on take-off, failure to empty it first pushed the centre of gravity beyond the aft limits.

Despite its idiosyncrasies, the Spitfire XIV was an attractive aircraft with an excellent high altitude performance. But at typical Tac-R levels it was impossible not to compare it unfavourably with the Tempest V, which had none of these problems, was faster low down and an infinitely better gun platform.

A summons from Group Captain Rosier resulted in an offer which caused me to think again about my intended move to Glosters. Meeting him for the first time I was struck by his visible scars and burns, he had been shot down at least twice during the fighting in France in 1940, and even more so by the enthusiasm and dedication of a regular airman who believed in his calling. As I listened to him, extolling the importance and the benefits of a service career, I knew that he spoke with total sincerity and conviction.

His message was simple. My permanent commission had come through at a rank and seniority which was ideal in relation to age and experience. If I decided to stay in the RAF there would be an immediate posting, as a substantive squadron leader with two years seniority, to the new BAFO School of Army Co-operation.

I was in an absolute quandary. In prewar days the RAF had been the height of my ambition – and here it was on offer, with the added inducement of instant promotion. On the other hand I had a strong commitment to Frank McKenna who had done so much to get me on to the next course at ETPS. Freddie Rosier was sympathetic, but adamant about the advantages of an RAF career, and insisted that it was not too late to change my mind. Eventually he sent me back to Celle with instructions to think it over carefully.

I started to create a possible syllabus and, with growing enthusiasm, realised that it was another great opportunity. The result of all my reading, my army experience – and with the ever-impressive Typhoon at war – had given me a wealth of material to digest and pass on. I was hugely tempted. But my late arrival via the army meant that there was still a lot of pent-up flying in my system. I tried that one too with Freddie Rosier. What about the command of a Tempest squadron? He remained adamant. That, he said, would come soon enough, but not now. For the benefit of my career, and the School of Army Co-operation, it had to be his way. I was deeply disappointed, closed my notebooks and prepared to file them away forever.

But somehow that never happened. Slowly, and over many years, I gathered even more material and became fascinated by the history of army support, fighter-recce and ground-attack, the achievements and the failures, the heroics and the lessons learned.

So testing won, but it was a very close thing. If Freddie Rosier had got in first, or offered me a flying job, it would almost certainly have gone his way. Although I had felt totally committed and happy in the RAF at war, peacetime might be different, and my experience with 35 Wing so far had not been encouraging. A service career could so easily be blighted by politically inspired cuts and changes. There had been evidence enough of that between the wars and the behaviour of the newly elected Labour government was hardly encouraging.

At Glosters the situation could hardly be more different. With the

Germans out of the race, they were the leading company in jet aircraft development, with the promise of strong sales at home and abroad for years to come. There would be all the engineering-related attractions of development flying, the challenge of the E1/44, and the exciting new world of transonics.

Now the die was cast and I must concentrate my efforts on 2 Squadron until my ETPS posting came through. The low lying north German plain, divided up by three great rivers, was never more at risk from flooding than in the winter of 1945/46. Earthworks and retaining walls, damaged or suffering from lack of maintenance during the war years, could fail at any time. 35 Wing was given the task of recording the state of the flood defences.

The forward-facing camera in the slipper tank of our Spitfire XIVs was aligned some 15° below the horizontal, allowing a continuous series of forward oblique photographs to be taken in level flight, almost ideal for the job.

I covered many miles of the Weser, and the Maas too, for the risk of flooding was also a Dutch problem as well. The straight sections were easy and small changes of direction could be photographed in a flat skidding manoeuvre. Sharp bends could only be followed in a steeply banked turn which threw the camera wide. The solution was to tackle these in a series of straight and level runs – angled to each other – and

Spitfire XIV. Andy's forward oblique camera.

subsequently linking the pictures together. Awkward but quite effective.

On the last of those river sorties I felt the onset of a cold. At the time I thought nothing of it, never even realising the implications. For in rather less than a year the career, on which I had set my heart, would collapse with devastating suddenness. That common cold turned into acute sinusitis, which subsequently became chronic, but I believed it to be cured after a month of treatment in the RAF hospital at Halton. The deep ray therapy had seemed to work and I was discharged in time for my posting to Cranfield where ETPS had just moved from Boscombe Down.

CHAPTER FIFTEEN

LEARN TO TEST AND...

We were a vintage crew on ETPS No 4 Course, the first in peacetime. Amongst us were two other Old Cheltonians. Jim Haigh, who had spent most of his war with Coastal Command, had been a fellow bandsman with me in the OTC, and Dickie Martin. Dickie had achieved fame in early 1940 as the prisoner of Luxembourg. Flying Hurricanes, with 1 Squadron in France, he had made a forced landing and been interned. Allowed out for exercise, he paraded back and forward watched by an idle and unsuspecting guard. Each day he extended the length of his walk until he got far enough away to make a successful break for freedom. 'Officer Martin' was back with his squadron in time to take part in the Battle of France.

There were thirty-three of us in all. Ron Hockey, the only group captain, with an illustrious record in special forces, was the most decorated apart from Neville Duke. Others stood out too. The hell-raising Paddy Barthropp, and after three and a half years as a prisoner of war who wouldn't be slightly mad, a warm hearted larger than life character. Pete Garner who was to lose his life flight testing the Westland Wyvern and a number of naval officers.

One eclipsed the rest. Forceful, brilliant and ambitious, with a single mindedness which would take him to the top unless he upset too many people on the way. For Nick Goodhart was one of those infuriating individuals who knew he was right and, on the rare occasions when he was wrong, could still drive his opponents into the ground with the force of his arguments and his personality.

Amongst his naval colleagues were others of a different stamp. Ken Hickson, urbane and relaxed, whose appearance, even in his twenties, was vaguely reminiscent of a bishop. In later years, as commandant of ETPS, his looks and manner were almost identical to the genuine article. A charming and gentle rogue – in his element knocking the arrogant off their perches.

There were two other Dickies, Mancus and Turley-George, navy and RAF respectively, ex CAM Ship Hurricane pilots. The similarity between them was quite remarkable. Differing only in degree, they were tall, thin as rakes, and solemn to the point of lugubriousness. The outward impression was totally misleading. Each possessed an unexpected and delightful sense of fun.

We had Cranfield to ourselves and there was a pleasant air of ordered permanence about the whole place. Quite different from the days of my hurried Spitfire conversion. In the hangars an interesting fleet of aircraft, ranging from Lancaster to Tiger Moth, with a Grunau Baby thrown in for good measure, was waiting to provide us with a sample of 'representative landplane types'. And, for the first time at close quarters, there was the exciting and unfamiliar sound of a jet engine.

Ground school could have been tough, after years away from any formal education, and I was grateful for my short spell at Glasgow University immediately before joining up. As the only aircraft industry nominee on the course I chose to sit at the back. This landed me next to Ron Hockey, where there was much to be gained by following his relaxed example.

As for Nick Goodhart he was out in front, fast on theory, faster still on the draw with his slide rule, and sometimes it even seemed as if he was trying to push the lecturer. You couldn't help admiring him. But it was hard on us lesser mortals. And in our youthful, less tolerant days, we were secretly pleased when 'Humph' didn't let him get away with it.

Humph – G. McLaren Humphries – was the chief ground instructor and co-founder of ETPS who had been largely responsible for the syllabus which we were following. A small and deceptively mild mannered man, he saw through the slothful in an instant, yet he could be infinitely painstaking and tolerant with the most mathematically illiterate. Under his guidance we gradually came to grips with the theory of performance and handling, and the mysteries of data reduction. To the trainee test pilot, Humph was beyond price and we held him in the highest regard.

Each morning started with lectures. After Humph the rest of the day was taken over by Sandy Powell, chief test flying instructor, and his flying tutors – with time for a sortie before lunch and more in the afternoon. Sandy, of the dark moustache and swept back hair, had a habit of disappearing by Mosquito on Friday afternoons; allegedly to spend the weekend with his friend Bruin Purvis at Boscombe Down.

We would watch out for his return, almost perfectly timed for the first lecture on Monday morning, and observe the quality of his landing. In that way we could make a guess at the scale of his lost weekend, and hence how to treat him for the rest of the day. It was pretty infallible.

Exposure to a variety of aircraft was a wholly new experience and the ability to switch rapidly from one type to another became essential.

Limited conversion training was provided. But pilot's notes, and a short spell sitting in the cockpit, was the norm. If you couldn't cope on that basis it was too bad. Forget about test flying. In practice the whole thing soon became second nature and flying skills sharpened up no end.

Increasingly, you became aware of the different features, the strengths and weaknesses of each design. This awakening of a more critical and questioning approach was vitally important. The very reverse of squadron practice, where each pilot subconsciously adjusts his technique to the characteristics of his aircraft, and familiarity blinds him to its deficiencies.

Moving from aircraft to aircraft, combined with the introduction of various exercises, soon demonstrated the demands which test flying could impose. You were expected to fly a new type, on a very short acquaintance, with sufficient ease and accuracy to carry out any required programme. And, as if that were not enough, to observe and record, and subsequently to report your findings verbally and in writing. No auto observers or voice recorders either at this stage in the game.

You soon discovered that the value of a test pilot, however brilliant his performance in the air, was almost akin to his ability to communicate the results of his work in concise and lucid fashion. Consequently, report writing became a vital and major chore. Many an evening was spent working away after dinner, sometimes far into the night, extracting data from the ubiquitous knee pad with its stop watch and grubby roll of paper. Reports followed a standard format, which became second nature, until your mind conjured up the headings as you fell asleep each night. The same headlines appeared on your knee pad too – as an aide memoire for your training.

From that time onwards I never approached a new type without that same mental check list – and never walked away from it without at least some notes under each heading. If only for my own benefit I had to record my thoughts on its salient features. In a few short weeks I had acquired the habit of a lifetime.

The policy on type conversion, where for the most part we had to cope on our own, meant that we saw relatively little of Sandy Powell and his team, although they were probably watching us carefully. This was confirmed in later years, after I came to know Sandy much better, and discovered that he had got his former students pretty well taped.

Soon after the start of the course I paid a visit to the Gloster flight test department at Moreton Valence. Llewellyn Moss gave me a warm welcome and a quick tour of inspection: "Everyone calls me Mossie," he said. A countryman at heart, he had been a huntsman before the war, but flying had become his life. Now in his fifties he was chief production test pilot. With full order books, and a steady flow of Meteors to keep him busy, he was a happy man.

"So, you'll be taking over from Phil Stanbury. That's good I've been wondering what was going to happen on the development side."

He wasn't sure about progress on the E1/44.

"I hear the men from the ministry keep changing their minds. But you ought to get your hands on it sometime next year."

Had I got anywhere to live?

"Can recommend my own place, out in the country, quiet and very comfortable. Understanding landlady... that is if you...?"

I assured him I would be very interested.

Later, just before I left, we walked out to the Meteor which he was about to fly, and he told me about his occasional double life. Dr Jekyll was the unruly pilot beating the living daylights out of some inoffensive corner of the Cotswolds. Mr Hyde was the firm and understanding airfield manager, dealing with irate telephone complaints, who promised severe retribution as soon as the pilot returned. Mossie wasn't sure which part gave him greater pleasure.

He climbed into the cockpit and looked down at me.

"Let me know when you want that accommodation. See you again soon."

Back at Cranfield there were more types to get under my belt and some of them stand out still after more than sixty years. The Lancaster was a pleasant surprise. Lightly loaded it leapt off the ground in sprightly fashion and felt right from the word go. On the cruise it burbled along happily, at an indicated 250mph low down, to the satisfying sound of its four Merlins. The handling was pleasant, the controls well harmonised, and the manoeuvrability remarkably good.

The Mosquito, on balance delightful, was another aircraft in which I felt very much at home but in a different, more careful way. Perhaps it was the memory of John Slatter, or the awareness of its high single-engine safety speed, although they were really one and the same thing. I had never forgotten that letter received almost two years previously, which told me the sad news about John, or my distress that we would never see each other again.

More than any other design of its day, the Mosquito seemed to have two quite different personalities. The clean aircraft – fast and lively – and the other with massive drag from its undercarriage and flaps. Throttled right back, with the engines crackling and banging, the approach was steep and the speed well controlled. Similar to the Typhoon and most satisfying.

For all that I liked the Mosquito my first love, as ever, was the single-seat fighter and of these ETPS had a fair selection. The Tempest II was slightly faster than Mk V which I had flown from Lasham but I missed the Sabre up front. There was a similar loss of elevator control at low speeds, only more so, and a trickle of power was needed to three point it neatly. When it came into regular squadron service the pilots were advised to wheel it on because of its tendency to swing. But, as far as I recall, none of us had that problem.

I had a couple of unfortunate experiences with the Tempest. The first, when a complete starboard fuselage panel – from the engine firewall aft to the seat bulkhead – pulled off in a dive. It went with quite a bang and there was a brief dust storm in the cockpit which became very cold and draughty. Fortunately there was no further damage. After I landed, and the remains of the panel had been recovered, the reason was obvious. The Dzus fasteners had been rotated into the locking position but a number of them had not been pushed fully home.

Another time I never even got airborne. The Centaurus died as I lined up for take-off. A fuel line, designed to self seal in the event of battle damage, had sealed itself internally cutting off the fuel supply. Had it happened a few seconds later I would have been in dead trouble.

More spectacular was Jumbo Genders' first Meteor landing after his aircraft had turned itself into a glider. He had suffered compressor surge and a double flame out at altitude, and had been unable to relight its engines. He came in high, fishtailing the Meteor through a series of impossible sideslip angles, and got down safely on the runway. Considering that he had never flown a jet aircraft before, had no propeller braking and little idea of its gliding angle, it was a good effort.

We itched to get our hands on the Meteor and Vampire. Not only were they very different to anything we had flown before but, in a very real sense, they were a glimpse into the future. In my case the Meteor came first. The cockpit felt unfamiliar, with its rather upright seating position and long travel throttles, but the automatic sequencing system made engine starting easy. The rising whine of the turbines was an urgent reminder that they were burning fuel at a vast rate. There was no time to waste. I taxied gingerly, then faster, adjusting easily to the tricycle undercarriage – aware that the Meteor's wheel and air brakes, not to mention its four 20mm cannon, depended for their operation on the contents of a single compressed air bottle. For it was still early days and there was no thrust to spare for engine-driven compressors.

Sitting astride the runway centreline I listened to the turbines winding up against the brakes, watching the twin temperature gauges. Jet pipe temperature was critical on take-off and harsh throttle movements were to be avoided at all costs. Failure to do so was to risk flooding the combustion chambers with fuel and wrecking the hot section.

Although the Meteor was easy to fly it was a disappointment. To be fair the main problem was shortage of thrust, and this was already in hand on the new Mark IVs which I had seen at Moreton Valence. But ours were Mark IIIs. The acceleration on take-off was poor and the climb sluggish. The ailerons were heavy and the stick force per g fairly high. Even a short session of aerobatics was hard work.

The approach and landing was quite straightforward, although the response to changes in throttle setting was much slower than a piston engine. On the first occasion, misled by the splendid forward view, I touched down with the nose too high and continued to hold the stick hard back, until the aircraft pitched smartly onto its nosewheel. The tail bumper had to be replaced and there was much leg pulling.

The Vampire I also suffered from lack of thrust. But it was much more my idea of a jet fighter. The cockpit was simple and functional, with a gunsight reflecting straight onto the armoured windscreen like the Typhoon and Tempest. The throttle lever was much better positioned, with the high pressure cock conveniently close by and the three vital direct-reading fuel-content gauges unmistakably visible immediately below the standard blind-flying panel.

I remember on 23 April 1946 taking the Vampire out over Woburn, where the carcases of heavy bombers, which had been flown there to be broken up, were scattered around the Duke of Bedford's estate like stranded whales. I went higher as the sunshine weakened under the cirrus of an approaching warm front. Enjoying the smooth vibrationless ride, and near silence, which had been such an attractive feature of the Meteor. Just the gentle hiss of air sweeping past the canopy and cockpit sides.

But there was another dimension to the Vampire. It was a thoroughbred with delightful handling and light, well harmonised, controls. I ran through a sequence of aerobatics and found myself over a vast complex of earthworks and concrete runways which was the new London Airport.

The three fuel gauges stared at me accusingly. It was high time to go home. I leaned the nose down in a long shallow dive back to Cranfield, aware of the slippery feel, as the speed built up and the airflow sounds became louder and more urgent. Apart from the delightful absence of torque and vibration, this greater awareness of the surrounding air was one of the intense pleasures of jet flying.

Back in the circuit, low on fuel, and the nosewheel refused to lock down. I went through the usual motions, made a pass close to the watch tower, and they said it looked OK. Still no green light and the tanks were almost dry. This time I held the nosewheel off deliberately for as long as possible and all was well – although there was barely enough fuel to taxi in.

The turbine faded into silence and I climbed out savouring the heat and smell of kerosene. As Gloster's man on the course it was embarrassing to realise that I preferred the competition. In their different ways all the de Havilland aircraft which I had flown seemed to have admirable handling characteristics – Moth, Mosquito, Vampire, and the Dove too later on.

At the other extreme we tried our hands at a couple of very different gliders. Thanks to Ron Hockey, and his special forces contacts, a Halifax and Hamilcar came to Cranfield for several days of intensive flying. The Hamilcar was huge, its tandem cockpits far above the ground and, on tow, the controls were heavy. My two flights were early in the day, when the air was calm and there was no difficulty in holding station just above the slipstream. So I began to ease my way out of position in order to see what the recovery was like, in terms of control loads and response, but the army glider pilot instructor would have none of it. Even when I explained to him what I was trying to do.

The approach and landing was quite dramatic. Having watched some of my fellow students I flew a confident circuit, positioning high above the runway threshold, lowered the vast flaps and pushed the nose down into a steep dive. There was an immediate and disapproving reaction from the back seat:

"You'll undershoot from here! Raise the flaps and go round again."

Go round again – what the hell was he talking about? Yet, once the flaps were up, it all seemed to work with surprisingly little loss of height. The landing was a joke. A headlong diving approach followed by a very determined roundout. Hard back with both hands, the speed decaying rapidly, and a creaking far below as the undercarriage took the strain.

This uncouth manoeuvre had to be initiated at just the right height. Too soon and she would drop out of the sky. Too late and you would hit the ground still going downhill at a rate of knots. Ballooning and floating didn't come in to it at all, and we were flying an empty glider. What it must have been like, landing with a tank on board I hate to think.

We towed the Grunau Baby with the ETPS Tiger Moth and re-discovered aileron drag. A reminder that rudders still had a use apart from countering torque and coping with asymmetric power. As the thermals began to stir, there were brief opportunities to try our hands at soaring. Brief unfortunately they had to be, because we were evaluating the Grunau as another aircraft and not in its operational role.

As if to encourage us further Kit Nicholson, a leading prewar architect and glider pilot who had served in the Fleet Air Arm, dropped in at Cranfield. He was flying a German Meise similar to the one which

I had 'liberated' at Cuxhaven the previous summer. The Meise, or Olympia, was Hans Jacobs' winning design for the Olympic Games, and our visitor had flown it from Bramcote some forty miles away. We were most impressed.

Soon afterwards Robert Kronfeld came to ETPS. At that time a squadron leader in the RAF, he gave a talk about the Airborne Forces Experimental Establishment, where he had been working as a test pilot. His lecture was illustrated with slides showing some quite remarkable trials. But a few of us, Nick Goodhart and myself amongst them, would have preferred a talk on soaring flight from the master himself.

As the course moved towards its climax things began to go wrong again. On each descent there was difficulty clearing my ears, and frequent pain. I was forced to carry out many of the exercises at lower altitudes. Then my sinuses flared up once more. The top RAF ENT[1] specialist tried his best but there was no permanent cure.

Frank McKenna was kindness itself. I was not to worry. He would organise a replacement whilst I must concentrate on finishing the course as it would always stand me in good stead. Back at Cranfield again I told the sad story to Willie Wilson. Hearing on the grapevine that Auster Aircraft were looking for a test pilot, he arranged for me to visit them.

In the event my visit to Rearsby was a disaster. I had flown an Auster on a number of occasions and had my reservations. Derived from the US-designed Taylorcraft plus, it was a potentially good aircraft, marred by a few unfortunate features such as the throttle and flap controls, and the strange geometry of the control column. Compared with a Tiger Moth or a Chipmunk the handling was disappointing. But a few modifications, and some development flying, could do a lot for its sales potential.

The MD and the general manager seemed to think otherwise. No modifications for them. They were satisfied with the design as it was. Sell as many of them as is possible into a postwar market which was crying out for aircraft. As we sat together in the cramped and ramshackle company offices which had once belonged to the Leicester Flying Club, it seemed to me that the idea that the reputation of their company and its future markets were important – or that they might depend, amongst other things, on the pilot appeal of their first postwar civil aircraft – meant nothing at all.

I travelled thoughtfully back to Cranfield, thanked Willie Wilson for his kindness in putting the opportunity my way, and explained why it was not on. It seemed unlikely that Austers would have any interest in an ETPS graduate or he in them.

"You're probably right," he said, "But it seemed worth a try. I'm only sorry for your sake that it didn't come off."

Pete Lawrence, one of the naval officers on the course, wanted to follow up the vacancy which had come up again at Glosters. I gave him all the contacts, but strangely nothing came of it at the time. Bill Waterton got the job instead, straight from the Central Fighter Establishment, without any test pilot training. Pete joined them in 1951 from English Electric and lost his life soon afterwards, ejecting too low, from a Javelin in a deep stall.

Jim Haigh was married in Bedford at the end of the course. Jumbo Genders and I were present as witnesses and we lunched with the happy couple before they left on their honeymoon. It was the last time I saw Jumbo. A modest man, and an outstanding pilot, he was posted to Aero Flight at Farnborough. He died, like Pete Lawrence, exploring the stalling and spinning characteristics of another swept-wing aircraft. The tailless DH108.

After that it was all over. Logbooks completed and signed up. How to start again? Back to Glasgow University with the aid of a government grant seemed a good idea. The engineering academic year followed a so-called 'sandwich' principle with the long summer vacations working in industry. But the reality of what I was losing hit me really hard when I clocked in at de Havilland Aircraft during the spring of 1947.

Shut away on the production line, armed with a windy drill, I yearned for the Hornets and Mosquitoes out on the tarmac and the open skies above.

A craving which became so acute that I finally put a call through to the chief test pilot's office. John Cunningham answered. At the mention of ETPS he asked me to come and see him immediately. Before we had time to sit down he told me that he wanted a pilot for development flying. Glancing through the window, where a second high speed version of the DH108 was nearing completion, he asked me if I was interested.

It was like Glosters all over again. What I wanted to do most was there for the taking and permanently out of reach. I asked about Doves and Chipmunks – in view of my sinusitis – and his enthusiasm vanished.

I left his office profoundly depressed. How to face life without flying? The airlines might be a possibility. But they held little appeal and the two state corporations only seemed to be interested in pilots with a multi-engined background. That night, while the mood was still with me, I wrote to the Midland Gliding Club and enrolled on a course.

For the next two summers I worked at Boulton Paul Aircraft. Because, I have to admit, Wolverhampton was extremely convenient for gliding at the Long Mynd. It turned out be a most fortuitous choice. During my second year I was to work in the project office; under

Charlie Kenmir the chief aerodynamicist. He could add little to the published information about the fatal accident which had occurred during my previous winter's absence. The two test pilots had been flying together, carrying out diving trials on the prototype Merlin-engined Balliol, and the windscreen had collapsed killing them both instantly. Their replacements had been through ETPS and one of them was an old friend.

Dickie Mancus looked thinner than ever; but it was great to see him again and catch the familiar smile.

"Technical Dave! Welcome back! Charlie said you'd be looking in. Come and meet Ben."

There was a great commotion in the adjoining office. Its occupant was shouting – reading the riot act to some unfortunate on the other end of the phone. He hung up and turned to meet us as we walked through the door. His vitality and the sheer force of his personality filled the little room.

"David Ince," the accent was basic untamed Glaswegian and he spat out the words like a machine gun. "Dickie says you've been to ETPS," his voice shot up an octave, "And what in the hell are you doing in the design office?" It subsided ever so slightly – "Better come over here and get some flying." He grinned at me mischievously and slipped another cigarette into his long ivory holder – "C'mon lad, let's sit down and talk it over."

That was a marvellous summer. Ben Gunn and Charlie Kenmir made a deal. I would work in the project office, act as a flight test observer on the Balliol – which gave me an opportunity to fly it as well – and carry out as much other flying as Ben could usefully organise for me to do. This included allegedly urgent communications and delivery flights in the company Oxford and production testing the Wellington X trainer conversions.

The Balliol was approaching its preview handling trials at Boscombe Down and the two problems which needed urgent attention took up most of my flying time. The air brakes were creating an excessive change of trim. A matter of trial and error – adjusting the upper and lower surface areas – with the limiting speed to be checked at every stage. Easily done but it took lots of flying time and a modicum of simple engineering which suited me very well.

The stall was catch 22! The new advanced trainer spec called for buffet warning and pronounced wing drop. And the Balliol had no warning at all. So Charlie decided to fit breaker strips – short spanwise blades attached to the wing root leading edge, to induce a turbulent wake at high angles of attack. Worked a treat, except that the aircraft no longer dropped a wing, the breaker strips had created such a positive root stall. We tried all sorts, shapes and sizes with no joy at all. We could get one characteristic or the other, but never both together, and Charlie lost his cool. Sod you Balliol! You sort it out David! Eventually I wanted to try breaker strips root and tip but it was ruled out as too dangerous. So it went to Boscombe with none at all and won the contract.

Although we completed the Balliol programme in time, it was hardly down to me, as I took French leave to go gliding. My flight ended at the Caister and Great Yarmouth Golf Club breaking several records. The captain and members were most hospitable. But they alerted the press and two reporters turned up. The cat was out of the bag. Until then, following my telephone call to Charlie Kenmir before getting airborne, I was off sick.

Two days later I arrived early for work, slid unobtrusively behind my desk, and waited for the inevitable. Charlie wasted no time at all. He marched straight across the room grinning with evil delight: "Off sick indeed! It's all over the papers – the press have been after JD and he knew nothing about it – you're in the shit!"

Moments later Ben was on the phone: "What's this you've been up to lad, breaking records and things, JD wants your guts for garters? Come and tell us all about it when he's finished with you." And he rang off shouting with laughter.

J.D. North was the managing director. He had been designing aeroplanes before the First World War. Not that he looked that old. But he rarely smiled or spoke. When he walked into the office that morning I discovered that I had totally misjudged him. He came across to my desk, waving Charlie to join him.

"Hope you're feeling better." There was a twinkle in his eye. "That was a great flight. You can do that sort of thing as often as you like. Provided you let me know beforehand. Then I won't look such a fool when the papers ring up to ask me about it."

Boulton Paul was a small, tightly knit, team. Working with them could not have been better. They had made me feel wanted and appreciated and had helped me to recover my self esteem. At last I was ready and willing to pursue a different career. Test flying, although I did not know it yet, would become a hobby which would put me at the very centre of British high performance sailplane development. Nothing would be wasted. But that is another story.

I looked in on Ben before I left. More than anyone else he had helped me to survive the loss of a test flying career. I wanted to thank him for everything. He looked at me long and hard, handing over a superb reference and speaking as if underlining every word: "You'd better get that degree," he said. "I've got plans for you." He picked up news of my graduation the following spring and rang immediately asking me to join his team. At a personal level I found it desperately hard to refuse.

My time in avionics with Elliott Brothers – later Elliott Flight Automation – produced few flying opportunities. One, related to our contract on the Lightning, was at Martlesham Heath in a BLEU[2] Canberra. The engineering was quite traditional and rather crude, based on an autopilot which could be engaged to drive the whole control system. Actually it worked rather well, the beam capture was smooth with limited excursions from the approach path, and a stable ride right down to the threshold. Enough for us at the time, but it really needed an integrated system with series actuators, for a better evaluation. And that was hardly forthcoming any more than I would be invited to fly the Lightning itself.

Viewed in retrospect the Barnes Wallis episode, which might have resulted in some interesting aviation, seems more like scientific fiction. It began when Air Marshal Sir Victor Goddard, who had been retained by our chairman as defence consultant, came to brief the small avionics team led by Jack Pateman. Sir Victor, with his exuberant hair style and eloquent turn of speech, was an imposing figure. Less happily he was known for his compelling enthusiasms. And his enthusiasm of the moment was a long-range, variable-sweep controlled subsonic transport – the Barnes Wallis Swallow.

We gazed at the great man, as Sir Victor introduced us, and tried to equate his white-haired boyish enthusiasm to an astonishing record. From the geodetic structures of Wellesley and Wellington to dam busting and Tallboy earthquake bombs – with a major contribution in his earlier years to the R100 airship which was so much better engineered than its ill-fated sister, and now this!

In reality they were in deep trouble over stability and control. Having built a simple low speed wind tunnel model, none of the test pilots could fly it, and my own efforts were disastrous. Although it was said to be a key variable geometry project, supported by the Ministry of Supply, Vickers had to pay half the cost. They hoped that we might be able to help. However funding was problematic, our contribution must be on a private venture basis, but success would bring enormous benefits.

The atmosphere cooled noticeably. Private venture was almost a dirty word in our language. It cooled even more when we were informed that a contract had been placed with Heston Aircraft to build a scaled-down glider version. It became positively icy when we were told that one of the Vickers technicians on the project could fly the model without difficulty – that he would be given flying lessons, and when the JC9 was completed he would be its test pilot!

When I reminded Jack about my recent glider test flying et al, and suggested that we might offer my services to Vickers, together with a prototype system, he did not take kindly to the idea. He looked me up and down, and paused as he stuffed more tobacco into his evil-smelling pipe: "Look David, You've got more sense than that. It's not on. You're more valuable to us in other ways than messing around and risking your neck in that crazy device."

In the end the MOS lost interest and it all came to nothing.

Nick Goodhart, perhaps the most forceful and determined of my ETPS colleagues, became project pilot on the Westland Wyvern after Pete Garner lost his life. He had an illustrious naval career, conceived the mirror deck landing system, played a key part in its development, and ended up as a rear admiral. Gliding brought us together again, and I competed against him in many championships, which he usually won. We still remain in touch today.

The survivors meet, from time to time, at various reunions. The fiftieth was special, with a big turnout and there were some jolly encounters. On that occasion I found myself seated at dinner between Dave Davies, who had become rather famous as chief test pilot of the ARB[3], and Harry Dobson. Harry had stayed on in the RAF and retired as a group captain. He was adept as ever at putting his foot in it. Generously accepting that my career in avionics might have had some value, he then proceeded to extol the much greater importance of a service career and demolish the doubtful contribution of a bureaucracy like the ARB.

I could see that Dave, a Welshman with rather a fiery temperament, was getting pretty hot under the collar – and decided to change the subject. "Harry," I said: "Do you remember a certain Wednesday afternoon at Cranfield? You and I were practising golf shots in the sports field behind the mess and someone started up a Meteor outside the hangars. You reacted with such pleasure and delight. I remember it like yesterday: 'That's the most exciting sound in the world. Must always try to live near a jet engine!' That's what you said."

Harry exploded: "Never said that! Not true at all. Live in Norfolk. Hate the bloody things. Can't get away from them – drive me mad!" By now he had forgotten all about D.P. Davies and the ARB.

Pinkie Stark was there that night. After a valuable but surprisingly unsung RAF career, much of it with the Blind Landing Experimental Unit, he too had worked for Elliott Flight Automation. On one occasion we travelled together on a whistle-stop tour of North America. A punishing twenty-two airlines in a fortnight – tremendous pressures, on the ball, and never a cross word, Pinkie was like that.

On the way home we found time to look up an old Typhoon chum, Johnny Brown, a founder member of 193 Squadron and a citizen of

Toronto. We got talking about old times and the unsolved mystery of Johnny Baldwin. Commanding A Squadron at Boscombe Down, after the war, he had invited Pinkie to join him. Later, after he was attached to a USAF fighter wing and reported missing in Korea, Pinkie tried to find out what had happened. Only to be faced with a wall of silence.

Eventually he ran an ex Korea prisoner of war to earth, a Canadian who could have been in the same camp as Baldwin, had the latter ever been captured. On detachment to Edmonton, for Arctic trials, Pinkie was given permission to see this man. "They told me that I could only put one question – and that I must not query his answer. So I asked him if he had ever come across J.R. Baldwin of the RAF while he was a prisoner. He replied: 'No, I did not!' So that was that – and, from then on, I always assumed that he had been killed."

Pinkie wanted to know more and continued his own investigations. In the end it seemed that Baldwin was flying number four in a section of Sabres. They were letting down in cloud over high ground and he called a warning to the formation leader: "Safety height!" They all pulled up, and the others returned to base, but Johnny Baldwin was never seen again.

In our early days of retirement we used to meet at the annual Typhoon and Tempest reunions. Ben would be there too and Pete Thorne and there was a regular Tuesday gathering in the RAF Club which we all tried to attend. Our paths crossed in other ways too. Wonderful guys, without them life would never have been as much fun. Pete was another founder member of 193 Squadron, a modest and delightful man of huge talent. His three AFCs[4] must be quite unique. When commanding A Squadron at Boscombe Down, and at some risk to his reputation and career, he fought against the Swift being adopted as a next generation fighter and was proved completely right. On an exchange visit to the USA he almost bought it out in the desert.

Low, hot and very fast, close to the critical Mach number in his F100A, he had initiated a short period oscillation to check the longitudinal stability about which the USAF was not entirely happy. It took three or four cycles before the motion damped out and the aircraft returned to controlled flight. Surviving, Pete became project pilot on the P1A – prototype for the Lightning. Then later he commanded Farnborough, served as our air attaché in Moscow and retired as an air commodore to work for Martin Marietta (later Lockheed Martin) and the Hunting Group.

Tich Crozier was in a different mould. After returning to ETPS, as chief test flying tutor, he left the service and became a consultant – in his case also for Lockheed Martin. Another Tuesday regular at the RAF Club, he was amusing, sometimes aggressive although it never lasted, and a great raconteur. But there were certain, shall we say, exaggerations about some his stories. Like the following.

Britain's earliest transonic research project – the Miles M52 – was designed for maximum performance. With the low thrust jet engines of that era, the cockpit had to be really small. This put Tich on the short list, almost in pole position, together with Winkle Brown the naval test pilot at Farnborough who had spoken so bluntly about the Typhoon.

Winkle had a great advantage. His position at Farnborough and his fluent German had given him access to a whole range of aircraft, which had fallen into our hands at the end of the war, including the Messerschmitt Me163. This revolutionary machine had one feature in common with the M52. It dropped its wheels on take-off and landed on a skid. But the M52 would have to land much faster. So Winkle ran a series of tests on the Me163 – touching down at progressively increasing speeds, and eventually there was a nasty crash and he ended up in hospital. Tich told us he was sure the project was now his. That he would be the world's first supersonic pilot. He positively revelled in the idea. Until, quite suddenly, the M52 was cancelled.

The second was said to have happened in 1943. Tich was flying for Power Jets. His task on this occasion was to take a Wellington bomber, fitted with an early jet engine in the tail, to the highest possible altitude with all three engines running. He was then to shut down the two piston engines and put the jet through its paces.

At this moment, according to Tich, he was bounced by four Spitfires:

> "They must have looked at their altimeters, decided that a Wellington could not possibly be flying so high, looked with even greater horror at my stationary props – and sheered off to a safe distance. I flew peacefully on and the leader came gingerly back – closed right in on my wing tip – and put his finger to his flying helmet in that time honoured gesture which suggests a significant shortage of marbles."

Tich would finish the story eyes staring – transfixing his listeners (he was good at that too!) with these dismissive words: "And the squadron concerned never reported anything."

One final episode, hardly testing, happened as my flying days were coming to an end. Yet it seems worth recounting for other reasons. It began with an invitation from BAe Systems to join them for the day at Farnborough International Air Show in 2003. There would be lunch, with an opportunity to catch up with some old mates, and a VIP seat for the flying display. However there was a catch. As an original, from way back, they had arranged for me to give a demonstration on the simulator. I would show the audience that their latest Typhoon was incredibly easy to fly. No problem they said. No problem at all.

The viewing gallery was full of pilots from numerous impatient customers, and the usual all moving landscape contained a vast HUD (head up display). Everything I suddenly realised – but everything – would be exposed for them to see. Fortunate indeed that I had spent part of the morning in the cockpit of the static display aircraft, boning up on the essentials.

From the very first moment, opening the throttles, it was brilliant. All that I could have wished for, or imagined, in the days when we were developing the Lightning avionics. Fly by wire, attitude and manoeuvre hold – and much more – with auto safety features thrown in. Aerodynamically unstable – but it handled like a dream and the performance was breathtaking. I longed to try it for real. And they had named it Typhoon!

Whether the final scenario was deliberately arranged, to prevent me ruining it all with my landing, I shall never know.

We – the German test pilot in charge of the simulator and I – were cruising home from a demonstration, which had gone off surprisingly well. My hosts would be pleased. I was feeling rather smug, until the screens suddenly went blank and these heart rending words echoed around the building:

"Gott in Himmel Mr Ince!... You haf broken mein EuroJager!...

Computer is kaput!... You cannot landing!"

I returned to the bar, demanded a large whisky and attempted to gather my thoughts. It had been a marvellous experience, and I was certain that I could have pulled off a reasonable landing especially with yet more help available from the automatics.

Driving home, later that afternoon, I found myself hoping that the future might bring more encounters with the new Typhoon. Since then, I have indeed been involved much more deeply with this splendid aircraft, with Coningsby where it is based, and those who man its first operational squadrons. People who share the same values, the same dedication and team spirit, which motivated us these many years ago. A rare privilege in this day and age. It is an involvement which is reflected powerfully in the final paragraphs of the Epilogue. But also here in the different context of test and development flying today.

Ignoring the very real question: "Is the Typhoon our last manned combat aircraft?" – and the issues surrounding multinational projects – it has certainly ushered in a very different era. Partly due to the infrequent appearance of new designs, partly to the complexity and variety of weapon systems, and the long lead times involved.

As an elderly ETPS graduate I accept that I may be biased. But it does seem to me that the basic airframe/engine/avionics fit needed to provide a satisfactory capability demonstrator, its development and presentation for customer evaluation should continue to remain the manufacturer's responsibility together with those of the prime subcontractors. Equally that all flying, to this point, should be carried out by the firm's (ETPS trained) test pilots.

If only it was that straightforward. For today there is a conflict. The manufacturer, faced with the likely combination of deliberately unstable aerodynamics plus weapon systems to come, wants to create an aircraft which is easy and safe to fly. He seeks to achieve this by means of automatic control systems designed for failure survival. (Another controversial issue but not directly relevant here.) These are also set up to impose certain limits, which the pilot cannot exceed, and in some cases completely exclude him from the control loop. An approach which, as various accidents have amply demonstrated, can actually increase the level of risk involved.

Such restrictions would almost certainly need to be modified – not only for safety reasons but also, and most important, to improve the handling and operational potential. Thus it has become vitally important for service pilots to start flying the demonstrators as soon as realistically possible.

Inevitably these first preview flights, and all further customer evaluation and input, will become a major part of the development testing. In my opinion only a few senior operational people, flight or squadron commanders, should be involved. By definition those who are the most current, and experienced, on the latest combat aircraft in service. It is essential that all of them, or if that is not possible at least a majority, should have been ETPS trained. They should work in close co-operation throughout with the firm's test pilots.

Lastly, all weapon systems development work should be handled by the squadrons themselves. This is where up to date and in depth knowledge of the operational environment and current threats, is most readily available. Although it begs the question about the location and availability of the specialist scientific and engineering back up which is bound to be needed.

Such a scenario suggests a very definite ongoing role for ETPS – not only in training new students – but also in providing refresher courses for those who may have been exposed to a single type, for years on end, with all that this implies. It does however cast a very doubtful light on the future role of Boscombe Down in the evaluation and development of combat aircraft.

At which point I threw my hat into the ring and beat a hasty retreat!!

CHAPTER SIXTEEN

FRIEND OR FOE?

There is only one answer to the "What if....?" question about the permanent commission which I turned down in 1945. There is no sense of regret. Life has rewarded me most fully.

Gliding became a great joy. Apart from years of development testing and evaluation flying, competitions and membership of the British Team Squad brought a new and powerful challenge. Through a stint in airline management, en route to avionics marketing, I met Anne – who became my crew chief – my wife and best friend. And through marriage came two lovely daughters – great girls – who put up with it all and even crewed for me. In turn I was able to support their equestrian activities. For Anne had become a much respected dressage judge; whilst Ginnie and Ros were very competitive.

My last career move was far from aviation. A livestock farming equipment group which needed expertise in handling European companies. This was a direction in which my avionics days had given me some experience. Another fascinating challenge; its responsibilities in Germany brought even closer contact with our former enemies.

It was that, as much as a marked growth in Typhoon reunion activities, which got me thinking about people and the paradoxes of modern war. I was not alone. Talking to my eleven-year-old grandson, he suddenly burst out:

"They were mad Grandpa! Stopped shooting each other. Exchanged presents – ate and drank beer and played football together." He was on about Christmas 1914 and looked quite upset. "Then they got back into the trenches and started it all again."

Who indeed were the madmen? Not those soldiers – those front-line troops – they and those who followed them who were to be swallowed up in the dreadful slaughter of the next four years. The generals? In a sense, yes. Not for conducting a war to which their leaders had committed them, but for conducting it so badly. And those leaders – whether kings, politicians or the dictators of later years – who had failed to follow Winston Churchill's dictum:

"Jaw Jaw is better than War War!" What about them?

Two quotations from Field Marshal Earl Haig – and the fact that they deal with army/air co-operation is immaterial here – reveal quite vividly the utter confusion of the old-fashioned military mind when confronted with significant new weapons. A total inability to grasp their impact and potential.

The first, as CinC Aldershot, one month before the outbreak of the Great War:

> "I hope none of you gentlemen is so foolish as to think that the aeroplane will be able to be usefully employed for reconnaissance from the air. There is only one way for a commander to get information by reconnaissance and that is by the use of cavalry."

Less than a year later, Haig again, by urgent signal to Boom Trenchard[1], commandant of the infant RFC: "I shall expect you to let me know before the attack whether you can fly.... If you cannot fly because of the weather I shall probably put off the attack."

Haig and his generals were already faced with another very major development – massed machine guns and modern artillery, a killing machine more deadly than anything which had been seen before. Prolonged bombardments, against which the enemy defended himself by taking cover below ground, removed any semblance of surprise in advance of an attack. The losses, when the attackers emerged from their trenches into a cauldron of defensive fire, were truly horrific. Yet the senior commanders seemed uncertain, confused, unable to cope, and fresh troops were simply thrown in, time and again, with the same inevitable and ghastly results.

Came the Second World War with better weapons, increasing accuracy and growing attempts, amongst the western allies at least, to reduce the toll of casualties. Some of that effort was undoubtedly due to a realistic appraisal of the manpower resources available. But there was more to it than that. In which, perhaps subconsciously, many fighting men had played a part. Only in the great air offensive against Germany – in Bomber Command alone – would the aircrew killed and missing equate to something like the subaltern generation in that earlier war.

And today, with ultra-precision target finding and weapon delivery, our casualties are infinitely small compared with previous conflicts and we feel utterly distraught about them. Were we to create a graph of killing power and accuracy versus casualties across the last ninety or so years it would show the former tending to infinity as the latter falls towards zero.

The media – especially TV and newspapers with their action pictures, computer graphics and commentary – bring distant battles into our homes as never before. We see and hear the troops at first hand, as they move against the enemy, and even in combat. We see the coffins draped in their Union Flags, the corteges moving through silent crowd-lined streets, the intrusive pictures of family grief and bereavement.

The political and other arguments – justification – equipment – numbers and strategy are played out before us in exhaustive and excruciating detail. More and more questions undermine the certainties, which buoyed us up, through the two great wars of the twentieth century. Small wonder that we feel as we do today.

But there is something else. Those memorials and the endless cemeteries in Flanders, on the Somme, near the beaches and on the battlefields of Normandy, across the world at Imphal and through so many years of pilgrimage and remembrance – have touched us to the core. Those familiar words – so bitter sweet and so painful – have become almost too much to bear. *In Flanders fields the poppies blow – between the crosses row on row... and tell them – For your tomorrow we gave our today.*

And the impact of Remembrance Sunday itself, the precious moments of silence, the poignant bugle calls, the exhortation so infinitely moving.

> *They shall grow not old... as we that are left grow old...*
> *Age shall not weary them... nor the years condemn*
> *At the going down of the sun, and in the morning...*
> *We will remember them.*

The memories, and the dear familiar faces, come flooding back. For me, perhaps above all, those of Normandy in the high summer of 1944. I have been there often over the years, but took my family for the first time on a battlefield tour in 1997, and again in 2008. I wanted to try and show them something of what it was like during those ten dramatic weeks until the major part of Hitler's armies in the west were encircled and destroyed.

First to Omaha, scene of the landings which were shown so vividly in the film *Saving Private Ryan*. Very bloody. There were 3,000 casualties on the beach alone. And so, in some ways, that film was a preparation, if one can ever be prepared, for the first sight of the American War Cemetery at St Laurent – with its endless rows of white crucifixes and Stars of David scattered amongst them.

Then came a most surprising discovery. The German cemetery, at nearby La Cambe, had replaced an earlier American one on exactly the same site. And where, we wondered, were all the Germans who had died in the desperate struggle to escape from the trap at Falaise? Had they been moved here? And if so why?

The answers lay at the entrance to La Cambe itself, written large in gentle words of reconciliation and forgiveness. Which read like this: *The Americans who were first buried here have been taken home... or lie beside their comrades elsewhere... and La Cambe has been given to the German people. So that their loved ones who fought in Normandy... who through a cruel and uncertain fate fought against the liberation and died... may find rest and peace in this place. That it may be forever a symbol of peace between former enemies and the people of France.*

At Pointe du Hoc the brooding remains of a powerful, fortified, coastal battery – surrounded by craters – seems threatening still as if reliving its past. The steep cliffs, the massive concrete emplacements and the silent guns with their long barrels staring blindly out to sea are enduring witness to an act of incredible bravery. Forty years on President Reagan addressed the survivors of the 225 US Rangers who scaled these heights against a storm of defensive fire and knocked them out. Here are some of his words:

> "You were young... with the deepest joys of life before you. Yet you risked everything here. Why did you do it? What inspired all the men of the armies that met here? We look at you, and somehow we know the answer. It was faith and belief. It was loyalty and love. It was the deep knowledge – and pray God we have not lost it – that there is a profound moral difference between the use of force for liberation and the use of force for conquest. You were here to liberate, not to conquer, and so you did not doubt your cause. And you were right..."

Words which so perfectly reflect the mood of those distant days. The sense of purpose, of loyalty and determination, of optimism and fun. The certainty that it is never too late, never too difficult, that one day we shall win.

Our parties – some of them pretty wild – helped us to cope. No doubt the psychiatrists and counsellors of today would have called us flawed – perhaps deeply flawed. But we shared in something far beyond their experience. The camaraderie of those who have dared – who have risked all – who have fought together for a cause which they value above life itself.

There is more. That together we were the best. A belief that absolutely demanded your very best in return, for the Service, for the Squadron, for the sake of your comrades in arms. It was something we couldn't control, immensely uplifting, and occasionally quite alarming.

There is a huge divide between the two images of war. The challenge – the glory, the courage and self sacrifice on the one hand – and the destruction, the suffering and the tragic waste of human lives on the other. That war happens at all is appalling evidence of human failing and weakness. Afterwards comes the guilt – the memorials – the painful moves towards reconciliation and forgiveness.

In 1983 Stern magazine published the first of six articles about the sinking of three prison ships, *Deutschland*, *Thielbek* and *Cap Arcona*, by RAF fighter bombers in the closing stages of the war. Subsequent editorials and readers' letters must have been acutely embarrassing to many Germans. They painted a clear picture of deliberate misinformation to encourage air attacks – of a brutal and pitiless follow up which, on Heinrich Himmler's express orders, was aimed at eliminating all the survivors from the concentration camps at Neuengamme and Stuthoff.

Although not directly involved – for our targets were elsewhere in Lübeck Bay – it brought back powerful memories and guilt hit me hard. Not about friendly fire, but our feelings after hearing about Belsen in graphic detail, the living skeletons, the gas ovens and other horrors.

It is not easy for me to dwell once more on the rest of that day, as I see it now, remote from the tumultuous times of my youth. My grandson would have said: "You were mad grandpa." "Yes George I was – with a different sort of madness." It was sheer hatred. As I briefed the squadron for our next shipping strike there hung amongst us, almost unspoken, a loathing for all things German. We flew with rage in our hearts wanting revenge. Worst of all we demonstrated how anger can grow into the sort of aggression and uncontrolled violence which takes no account of innocence or the reverse. Like the sailors and airmen, at the end of our guns, lumped together in imagination with the guards in the concentration camps.

It was a successful sortie. But war is brutalising and we were certainly brutalised by Belsen as the fighting drew to a close. I'm not proud of that.

How often, as we reflect on the origins of Nazism in Germany do we find ourselves saying: "But for the grace of God…" Had we been there at the time would we have closed our eyes to what was happening? Would we have had the courage to stand up and attack the growing evil which was threatening to destroy our nation? What right indeed have we to stand in judgement?

In war there is no communication with the enemy. They become faceless and propaganda tends to brand them all as evil. Yet, SS and Gestapo apart, we rarely thought about them in any negative sense.

Indeed, if we thought or spoke of them at all, it was usually to admire their fighting qualities. Now I wanted to meet them and learn more about them.

Apart from a few limited contacts, in that artificial period immediately after the end of hostilities, I had to wait seven years for the 1952 World Gliding Championships in Spain. Here, for the first time postwar, there was a German entry. The implications struck me quite forcibly. I found them interesting and not unacceptable.

But the presence of Otto Skorzeny, and of Hanna Reitsch as a competitor, was a different matter entirely. Many Nazis had taken refuge in Spain and the legendary Skorzeny – who had been rather a worry when our Typhoons had been snowbound at Chièvres in January 1945 – had settled in Madrid. With his black eye patch and close cropped hair, he certainly looked the part.

As for the Third Reich's famous woman test pilot, you had to admire her skill and courage, even if she was a bit of a self publicist. Watching her, in animated conversation with Skorzeny, it was impossible to believe that she was beyond politics. Seen for the first time she looked tiny, and fragile, yet it was difficult to feel any sympathy.

Much more to my liking was Heinz Scheidhauer, ex chief test pilot of Gebrüder Horten in Germany, a comfortable and warm personality. When Reimer Horten moved to Argentina, and continued developing tailless aircraft, Scheidhauer had gone with him. And the Argentine team in Madrid was equipped with the latest Horten XVs.

There was a fascinating RAE report on Horten. The two brothers were primarily interested in gliders and thought nothing of diverting German government funds, allocated for military aircraft, to the development of new and better sailplanes. Best of all was the story about the Mustang laminar flow wing. When the technical details and test data were circulated to the German aircraft industry the Hortens used it immediately to build a more advanced version of their Horten IV sailplane.

And this was the company with a radically new twin jet fighter bomber/night fighter, the Horten IX, in advanced development at the end of the war.

So I badly wanted to talk to Scheidhauer. Even if he had almost no English, and I as little German, we managed surprisingly well with lots of sketches and some fairly extreme body language. It was he who had carried out almost all flight testing on the Horten IX V1 – the glider version – and when the powered version was ready bureaucratic officialdom stepped in with disastrous results.

Heinz said that he had been replaced by Irwin Ziller who had zero experience on flying wings or jet aircraft. There were some hard words.

But worse was to follow. On the fourth flight, in February 1945, an engine failed. The combination of poor directional stability, negligible yaw damping, and drag rudders proved too much for this unfortunate man. He failed to follow Heinz's advice about flying wing down towards the good engine, lost control on the approach and crashed heavily. A fatal accident and a sad ending to the Horten IX.

Apart from the cockpit transparency, the engine bulges, the air intakes and exhaust nozzles, the Horten IX was an unblemished flying wing. There were no vertical surfaces of any sort. Apparently there had been talk of a fin and rudder. But it never happened. After learning more about the handling of tailless aircraft from Heinz, I wondered whether this feature might have saved Ziller's life. At the same time Horten's revolutionary design appeared to have all the makings of a lousy weapon aiming platform. Were the Germans clutching at straws, at a crucial stage in the war, mesmerised by the high performance which it promised?

I never saw Heinz again after those short weeks in Madrid. But I have never forgotten him, his frankness and enthusiasm, or the great satisfaction and enjoyment of our 'conversations' together.

My next serious encounter was with a certain Dr K.H. Doetsch in 1954. Karl was one of the German boffins who had been 'persuaded' to come and work at the Royal Aircraft Establishment. Picked up near Oberammergau, his captors had suggested to him that he might otherwise find himself in Russia. So Karl, as they say, 'chose freedom'.

He had been a 'Flugbaumeister'. One of that rare breed, a highly qualified engineer, who was also a skilled test pilot. With his wartime record it was hardly surprising to meet him leading much of the work on auto stabilisation and flight-control systems at Farnborough.

Karl was totally realistic about his situation. Yet the earlier uncertainty of his own position (he had become a British citizen the previous year) made him rather careful about forming any close friendships with his British 'hosts'. To me he seemed rather a cold fish. A very wrong judgement as rapidly became apparent. For we had many interests in common and – although technically he could run rings round me – he was always most considerate. More and more I found myself enjoying his company.

As my role changed to that of seeking new markets and relationships abroad for our avionics business, Germany showed signs of becoming increasingly important. We went in low key first time round at the Hanover Air Show but in a considerably bigger way two years later in April 1966. By that time we had reinforcements. Two new recruits had recently arrived direct from test flying. 'Doc' Stuart from Boscombe Down and Pinkie Stark whose BLEU experience was to prove invaluable. It was over twenty years since Pinkie and I had first met at Wunstorf and here we were heading back there together. We had a good bunch on stand duty and it had all the makings of a promising occasion – work hard, play hard and have fun.

It was Pinkie who, quite fortuitously, brought them all together. He and Doc had been allocated pension accommodation like the rest of us – hotel rooms being almost unobtainable – but the quality was awful. So Pinkie went prospecting and discovered a splendid alternative on the shores of Steinhuder Meer across the water from Wunstorf.

Each evening they guided us over a confused network of woodland tracks to a rambling timber shack overlooking the lake. Behind the bar stood a black-bearded giant of a man, in times past he must surely have been somebody in the Kreigsmarine[2], surrounded by smoked sausages and sides of bacon and dispensing all manner of alcoholic refreshment with great good humour.

It was a haven of guttering candlelight and human companionship, unspoilt and almost undiscovered, a world away from the noise and crowds of Hanover. A wonderful place to unwind. And when you were hungry his kitchen would produce a massive spread of eels, meats, gherkins, rye bread and butter.

Much later, as the light faded outdoors, mine host would remove his prized and ancient blue serge cap from its place above the bar and make an announcement in ghastly anglicised German: "Meine Herren! Ist vild und sturmich nacht – und ven ist so – I put on mein cap jawohl!" Whereupon he rescued his piano accordion from amongst the empty bottles and broke into the first of many drinking songs. His cap went on without fail every night that week, and our repertoire of German songs grew substantially in musical terms, even if the words were mostly beyond us. There was no one to hear in the depths of the forest, with water on three sides, and I often wondered whether we were led into singing some of the forbidden ballads from the Hitler years – without any malice at all.

At the show I had the privilege of escorting General Johannes Steinhoff – head of the new German air force – round our exhibits. It was impossible not to notice his badly burned face. The result of a pothole in a hastily repaired runway as he was taking off in his Me262 – a member of Galland's 'Squadron of Aces' – in the last weeks of the war. Undoubtedly one himself with 197 victories, his questions were incisive, and he knew exactly what he was about. An ex enemy you could not but admire.

Following that show I again got in touch with Karl Doetsch. He had returned to Germany, as Professor of Aeronautics at Braunschweig University, after an exceptional contribution to UK aviation for which he had received various honours and awards. During the second of several visits, and his family always welcomed me with open arms, he insisted on another trip to the workshops of Akafleig[3] Braunschweig where the students were building an ultra high performance fibreglass sailplane. It was a thoughtful gesture because he knew and, to a degree, shared my gliding enthusiasms.

On the previous visit we had motored into the Harz mountains and Karl had looked longingly towards Broken, the highest peak in the range, which now lay behind the Iron Curtain. This time I was with him on my own: “Karl,” I said, “What is it about you and Broken?” And then it all came out. In his early flying days it had been customary, perhaps obligatory to perform aerobatics above that special mountain. Now it was impossible and he made no effort to hide his resentment. He saw it as a brutal obliteration of a youthful and romantic memory. There was more: “This may hurt.” He looked slightly defensive: “Without the Nazis I could never have achieved my dearest wish – never have flown an aeroplane – never have become what I am today.”

As I struggled to find the right words – they came to me suddenly – simple and yet so true: “And what about me Karl? In various ways it’s the same for me too.” Karl lived into his nineties, staying in remarkably good shape, and long enough to see the reunification of his country. I hope that he made that journey to the top of Broken more than once, by road, rail, or even better by air, and that it brought him the greatest of pleasure. He was good friend.

My job in the 1970s continued to take me all over Western Europe, including Germany, where I was responsible for a new subsidiary company in the Bavarian town of Waldkraiburg, some sixty kilometres east of Munich. A strange place, with its heavily reinforced concrete buildings hidden in the depths of a pine forest, until you delved into its history. Waldkraiburg had been a major source of munitions production in the days of the Third Reich.

On my first working visit there was visible apprehension. What had we in mind for them? Were their jobs secure? Our answer to the latter was a resounding yes, provided they pulled their weight, for we were keen to develop the company. As for me, with my RAF background, how would the Bavarian country folk react to their new boss? After all those years might they still regard me as a *Terror Flieger* and would that be a barrier? That said, I need not have worried, their welcome was astonishingly warm.

Our immediate concentration on the market itself, and the success of their products, meant that Rolf Kleindienst the sales director and his staff were very much centre stage. They demonstrated a remarkable degree of loyalty and commitment to the new owners, and to our objectives, and so helped to create a very positive attitude throughout the whole company.

Rolf had been wounded at Stalingrad and was amongst the last to be evacuated by air. He wore an artificial right hand and never allowed it to interfere with an active life. An excellent skier, and a skilled rally driver in his day, he was the most polished and expert motorist I have ever met. With him speed was almost synonymous with safety! A decent loyal man and straight as a die. He must have been a first class NCO in his Wehrmacht days.

There was one problem and it fell right into Rolf's court. The company's sales force was entirely made up of commissioned free agents. Post Nazi employment law protected the small men (agents) from exploitation by their powerful companies. They had never had it so good. When we wanted to add some additional products, they rebelled, refused to handle them and the ring leaders demanded to see the group chairman and managing director. That meeting duly happened and got very heated. But Rolf had done his homework. Legally we could appoint our own specialist salesmen and sell the disputed products over their heads. On hearing this they climbed down and afterwards, as we continued talking together, they apologised almost to a man. First round to our sales director.

Eventually he knew as much about my wartime past as I did about his. It must have been in his mind as we were driving to dinner one evening. He turned to me while we were still in the forest: "Mr Ince, I must show you something special." We drove on until, approaching the end of the trees, a canal appeared running parallel to the road, and a railway bridge obscured the view ahead. Rolf pulled up just beyond the bridge, alongside a massive concrete wall, like the entrance to some medieval castle. It was built into a high bank, seemingly part of the bridge approach. "Here is the door to the flugplaz," he said.

We got out of the car and walked amongst the trees. For several hundred yards, leading away from the road, the ground was torn and cratered like a battlefield. Huge chunks of concrete lay half buried in the ground, tilted at all angles. Then some gigantic hoop-shaped bits and pieces – one which was almost complete – like an open tunnel mouth. In the silent depths of that forest, filled with the scent of pines, we were standing amongst the remains of an underground airfield.

It could hardly have been better sited with road, rail, and canal access literally on the doorstep. And, for munitions and aircraft, there was Waldkraiburg and the Messerschmitt factory at Weiner Neustadt not so far away. But that was mere speculation. Nobody seemed to know about the intended operation of that strange airfield, the type of aircraft, or the method of launching and recovery.

Rolf could only tell me that the Americans had spent weeks and months, and many tons of high explosive trying to destroy it. Now, so the rumour went, at the height of the cold war, they were sorry that it no longer existed.

I looked at the man I had come to like and to trust implicitly: "Rolf it is special – very special – thank you for bringing me here." I paused momentarily: "When they were building this airfield you and I were still enemies." "Yes," he said and smiled: "But that was in the past and now we are friends. It is very good for us both."

Herbert Kutscha was the distributor, based near Heilbronn, for a Belgian company which had recently joined the group. We were introduced to each other at an exhibition in Frankfurt. "You two will have plenty in common," they said. "Flying fighters on opposite sides in the last war."

Herr Kutscha was a slight, rather insignificant-looking character. Hair on the long side, exactly so, and one of those droopy Mexican-type moustaches. Trying to be with it. At first sight I wasn't sure that I liked him. In sheer devilment as we shook hands, and before I could stop myself, the words were out: "A good thing we never met in the air – or one of us might not be here now!"

Later I got to know him rather well. Mainly because he wanted to sell out to our group, and still continue as managing director, and I had to run a rule over his business.

In the air we had more in common than either of us had realised. For Herr Kutscha, the relationship always remained like that on both sides, had been an active glider pilot. But the real eye opener came when he invited me back to his house for a drink. In due course he produced the *Book of German Aces*, turned the pages to 'K', and there was a younger version of my host staring me in the face. He had flown Me110s in the Battle of Britain, then 109s on the Western and Russian fronts, and chalked up forty-seven victories. When I handed the book back to him, he grinned, as if to remind me of my remark at the Frankfurt show: "So," I said "You also think that I would have been the one to die."

We talked far into the night and he was surprisingly frank about his enemies. Ranking the RAF well above our American allies and reckoning that he was lucky to have survived in his Zerstörer. The Russians he classed as rubbish. He had encountered Tempests and Griffon Spitfires, mostly around 10,000 feet or below in the closing stages of the war, and reckoned that his Gustav was completely outclassed. Although he never said it in so many words I sensed that he was rather bitter at his failure to get a posting onto Fw190s or the final and more advanced Ta152. He assured me that he had never been in combat with a Typhoon.

Despite our differences, and the formality of our relationship, the thing that bonded us most strongly – and I mean bonded – was a shared joy in flying and our good fortune that we had fought our war in the air. In the end he asked too much for his business and continued as our Belgian company's distributor until he retired. Perhaps it was just as well for Herr Kutscha was a bit of a loner and very determined. Those qualities, which had produced a Luftwaffe fighter ace, would have made him exceedingly difficult to control.

Manfred Deckart, manager of the Westphalian Central Co-operative in Münster, was like a breath of fresh air. My hotel the night before had been on the northern outskirts of the town. The surroundings looked like an old airfield; and a map confirmed that it was one of the Rheine group which had confronted us back in 1945. It was a warm summer's evening and I walked round the perimeter after dinner and retired in reminiscent mood. The following morning my meeting with Herr Deckart started in a cool if not unfriendly manner, until I happened to mention my airfield hotel, and he really opened up.

What had I been flying, that I knew about the Rheine group of airfields? Typhoons! So I must have been in his sights, and he in mine, during that dramatic spring some thirty-five years ago. He had been called up under age, as a trainee flak gunner, in the last winter of the war and it was enough for him that we had fought on the same sector. From then on he behaved as if we had been comrades in arms.

It was a powerful reminder of the wartime attitude of the Luftwaffe towards their opponents in the air. The stories of aircrew – particularly fighter boys – being entertained on German airfields before being handed over for interrogation, are well known.

Less familiar were the actions of the flak crews, also part of the Luftwaffe, in saving many a pilot's life when he was shot down at the height of a ground-attack mission. From the SS, so recently in his sights, there could be a lethal reaction. But the flak units would insist that he was their prisoner and spirit him away to safety. In a situation where we had overwhelming air superiority, and they were visibly losing the war, it was quite remarkable.

When, inevitably, we went off to lunch together, Herr Dekart suggested that we avoid one particular restaurant and that we kept our voices down when we spoke in English. No, it was not a question of German antagonism towards former enemies. Munster was a BAOR garrison town and some British squaddies had gone on the rampage the night before. Local feelings were running high.

Back in his office he handed me a file which contained a wealth of information about livestock farming in Nordrhein Westfalen – together with a personal introduction to the co-operatives in each of the other

Lander. His secretary had been putting it all together while we were at lunch. A great kindness on his part and most helpful. Rolf was delighted. And for me, coming shortly before retirement, it was a very enjoyable and satisfying way to round off my travels in Germany.

Looking back over those years I met many people. But the ones I have recorded here stand out. They have played an important part in helping me to arrive where I am today. Honouring the fallen, the memory, and the whole brotherhood of the Typhoon has become an absolute priority – as has our Entente Cordiale with the people of Basse Normandie. Other Typhoon veterans, and the French, have been working at this for a long time. They have achieved a great deal. But they are weary, many are no longer with us, we are getting thin on the ground and there is more to be done. It is an urgent calling that I, and others, feel compelled to obey.

And our foes, surely no longer, certainly not for me. Those words of peace and reconciliation, leading into the German cemetery at La Cambe, say something with which I profoundly agree. The time has come – indeed is long past – when we should be in contact with the *Gemeinschaft der Fliegers* – the German Aircrew Association. At the very least to exchange fraternal greetings with the 'Alte Kameraden'. There is an urgency here too. Pray God that it may happen soon[4].

EPILOGUE

The Typhoon and Tempest Association (T and T) was set up by Ken Rimell, a professional photographer, who looked after publicity for the Tangmere Aviation Museum in his spare time. In 1983, having recently recovered a ditched Typhoon from Pagham harbour – he brought us together, more than 200 strong, for the first time since our squadrons had been disbanded. It was a great occasion – to be followed by twenty years of annual reunions at his Museum of D-Day Aviation – first at Apuldram near Chichester and subsequently in a building at Shoreham Airport. Until, painfully and quite unexpectedly, Ken and his partner, Barry Field, were forced to move out and the contents were sold.

Despite everything, Typhoon and Tempest continues. Barry, splendid man that he is, has made his home available for further reunions. He and Ken, helpers and wives, have given us so much over the years – and they intend to keep going until the last veteran hangs up his clogs!

Across the channel in Basse Normandie, some two years after the formation of T and T, Jacques Brehin, an agricultural engineer and part-time farmer, was about to start his first dig. His interest in the Typhoon and those who flew them had begun in 1944 when, as a boy of eleven, he saw a crash on his father's farm, and witnessed the efforts of families nearby as they helped to save the badly injured pilot.

Two months later Jacques' dig was finished. Ken Rimell went over by air, with a number of supporters. An RAF Regiment burial party flew in from Germany. F/Sgt Reginald Thursby's family had been located and he was finally laid to rest, in the military cemetery, at St Charles de Percy near Villers Bocage. In the evening we gathered at the Bayeux Museum for a Vin d'Honneur.

That event gave birth to L'Association pour le Souvenir des Ailes de la Victoire de Normandie (ASAVN), of which Jacques is president. It led on to the idea of a Typhoon Memorial, which was successfully completed and unveiled at Noyers-Bocage in 1990, followed by the Roll of Honour in 1994 and an additional monument in 1999. All, in large measure, due to Jacques and the unwavering support of many Typhoon veterans led by General Paul Ezanno – Thursby's CO at the time of his death – Denis Sweeting who served on the same squadron, the Canadian Chad Hanna and Roy Crane.

As the years passed our numbers inevitably declined. ASAVN and T and T were both badly affected and yet seemingly unaware. Do nothing, and the result of all that dedication and caring would simply fade away, and die with the last survivor. Time was not on our side. We had to act quickly.

Our special one-off reunion which took place in May 2007 at Middle Wallop, home of the Army Air Corps, was a great success. The main themes – thanking the French in Normandy and 'Passing on the Torch' to the new Typhoon squadrons – produced a most generous response from both services. They provided speakers, a splendid air display, and Air Chief Marshal Sir Clive Loader CinC Air Command was the guest of honour.

'Typhoon to Typhoon' laid on by the RAF, as a presentation to members of the Armed Forces Parliamentary Scheme at the Imperial War Museum, had taken place some six months earlier. The opening was simple and to the point. Three of us bonding with our Typhoon opposite numbers of today.

It seemed a remarkable coincidence. Had our plans for 'Passing on the Torch' been leaked? No matter. Apart from the benefit of progressing our relationship with Coningsby, the publicity might well assist our fundraising. If it helped the RAF as well, we were all for it. With hindsight it proved to be a most enjoyable evening. The bonding was real – for they were great guys – and we were delighted when the service chiefs won hands down in the speeches which followed. There was even time to meet afterwards, in the RAF Club, and put it all to bed over a few drinks.

'Typhoon to Typhoon' had other benefits. Group Captain Bob Dixon, who had looked after us so well during our time in London, agreed to host a table at Middle Wallop. Beforehand when my daughter Ros, setting up the powerpoint displays, was in trouble over last-minute French translations Bob came up trumps. He put us in touch with the wife of a leading French display pilot and air show manager who provided them in no time at all.

The younger ones did so much to keep the show on the road. It is great to have their support – at home or abroad. For the logistics, especially the driving and navigation in foreign parts and, pax Ginnie, for her fast reaction when Dad tries to fall off his shooting stick! The pleasure of their company is what matters and the opportunity to tell them like it was. At the acts of remembrance it is so good to have them with us.

In the run up to Middle Wallop generous donors had already covered our costs and put what was to become the new Typhoon Entente Cordiale Trust (TECT) into surplus. A beginning, but sufficient to encourage a new way forward, a new dynamic, to safeguard and build on our much valued relationship with the French. That surplus would be held by the trust in the name of the whole Typhoon force – the eighteen squadrons of 1944 – but specifically as a bursary in remembrance of Reg Baker, charismatic and much loved leader of 146 Wing, who was killed in the Battle of Normandy.

As our special reunion drew to a close there was increasing evidence of its success. Not least in the very clear understanding that we would be most welcome to visit Coningsby and take 'Passing on the Torch' a stage further. It was a great moment for George Wood, Derek Lovell, Johnny Shellard and myself – and for our willing helpers.

At the fiftieth anniversary celebration of Father George's ordination to the priesthood we had decided to set up the trust, to appoint ourselves as the first trustees, and organise the Wallop event. As chairman I had asked my friend, AVM Sandy Hunter, president of the 609 Association, to be our patron. He has been a tower of strength ever since. At Middle Wallop Sandy went public – M/C for the day, running the show immaculately. Two meetings later – including a fascinating visit to Coningsby – 'Passing on the Torch' was in the best of health, up and running.

ASAVN may have a problem with our declining numbers. But their own efforts have gone from strength to strength – locating crash sites, arranging funerals, memorial plaques and blessings – and tracing families that they too might honour their loved ones. These individual ceremonies, so moving in their simplicity, form a vital part of the remembrance weekends, together with Mass in the local church and a pivotal gathering at the memorial.

An unforgettable experience. The colours, the words and the music, the names picked out in gold, the three bold arrowheads locked together above the flame of remembrance. They embrace us all – the fallen, the comrades whom we see no more, the survivors in the twilight of their years, the members of ASAVN and the people of Basse Normandie. A very special Entente Cordiale – infused with new life by those who stand proudly beside us – representing the squadrons of RAF Coningsby.

Overhead perhaps another arrowhead shape sweeps low in salute, the great air intakes a distant reminder of something treasured, something loved. Then it too has gone – reaching upwards in a thunderous burst of flame – until only the memory remains and the image of glowing afterburners fading to nothing high above.

To you from failing hands we throw
The Torch; be yours to hold it high!

It will happen one day. For they have kept faith. They have done a great honour to those of an earlier generation who fought in the Battle of Normandy and onwards to Victory in Europe. We admire them hugely as they take up the Torch. Proud beyond words that they should wish to be associated with us in this way.

APPENDIX

Tactical Air Support – A Critical Overview

DISASTER, BOOTSTRAPS AND MORE

On 1 April 1918 the newly embodied RAF included some thirty fighter and fifteen reconnaissance squadrons. Its predecessor the RFC had grown rapidly, under the impetus of war, concentrating on army co-operation in the widest sense. Close support by fighter and fighter-bomber aircraft, attacking the trenches, had become a recognised if highly hazardous pursuit. Reconnaissance and artillery observation were firmly established.

Some important indicators had begun to emerge. The new and valuable evidence of enemy intentions – which were so clearly visible from the air – despite every effort at camouflage and concealment. The vulnerability of strafing aircraft to machine-gun and rifle fire under static battlefield conditions; and their success in breaking up and destroying enemy troops and supply columns on the march. The latter, as happened in 1918, when the massive Anglo-French air assault played such a crucial part in bringing the great German spring offensive to a halt. And not least the matter of air superiority – without which all other activities would be severely restricted or impossible.

By the end of hostilities the air arm was largely deployed in supporting the army. And its future needs in fulfilling that role seemed pretty clear. Except they were never met.

After the Treaty of Versailles the RAF had to fight for its survival and the case for strategic air power, which helped to win the day, created a very different set of priorities. The bomber – which in the opinion of the Air Staff would always get through – and to a lesser extent the interceptor fighter, came to dominate RAF thinking. The dive bomber, a vital part of the armoury in Germany, the USA, and Japan, was ignored. With its flavour of army support it must have been considered politically dangerous.

For the same reason presumably the RAF bomber and fighter squadrons of the 1920s and 1930s were only given perfunctory training, in what had ceased to be a primary role, nor could aircraft be spared in any numbers. When war broke out two army co-operation squadrons equipped with Hawker Hector biplanes, and five with the recently introduced Westland Lysander, were expected to provide whatever ground-attack sorties the army might need. It was a forlorn hope.

Then came the Fairey Battle. A day bomber – and to the Air Staff 'day' meant that it had to be single-engined. (Not to be confused with the Blenheim which was derived from a private venture design.) But the spec could only be met by a vast monoplane – which needed a far more powerful engine than the Merlin – leaving Faireys to struggle with the impossible.

By 1937 there was no doubt at all. The Hawker Henley was much better than the Battle. Slightly down in range and bomb load, it was much more manoeuvrable, and some forty to fifty mph faster. The outer wings – identical to those of the contemporary Hurricane – could have been fitted with the same eight machine guns. All in all it had the makings of a decent dive bomber.

Why the 200 built at Glosters were modified for target towing is a question which has never been satisfactorily answered. Was it Air Staff fear of the dive bomber? Or the problem of closing down Battle production at Stockport? Or that of making more urgently needed Hurricane manufacturing capacity available at Glosters? Whatever the reason – and it may well have been a combination of all three plus a bit of political meddling thrown in – it was a dreadful decision for the day-bomber squadrons of the Advanced Air Striking Force.

For the Battle itself the day of reckoning arrived on 10 May 1940. Without any semblance of air superiority, ten squadrons of these underpowered and underarmed aircraft, together with five Blenheim squadrons of the BEF[1] Air Component, represented the total offensive capability facing the German forces in the west.

With a top speed of 241mph, one fixed gun and just one rear-mounted defensive gun, the Battles were dead meat when they encountered enemy fighters. But the outcome, when they tried to take out the Meuse bridges, was utter disaster. Guderian, the great panzer general, took a calculated risk and brought his light flak units forward to surround them whilst his main armour was still moving up through the Ardennes. It was an astute move and it worked well.

The obsolescent Battles and their unsuspecting crews met the full destructive firepower of massed German 20mm and 37mm light flak for the first time, mostly in low level attacks, and were decimated. Even when they reverted to dive and medium level bombing the casualties still mounted. After just five days fighting they were withdrawn from daylight ops, together with the Air Component's Blenheims, except in the most dire emergency.

The magnitude of the catastrophe is reflected in the fact that the Battle squadrons lost 137 aircraft, equivalent to over eighty-five per cent casualties. The Westland Lysander also was shown to be far too vulnerable, in its traditional army co-operation role, with some forty per cent destroyed. Only the Hurricanes in their day fighter role proved anything like up to the job – and two of the seven squadrons were still converting from Gladiators.

Looking at the broader picture it has been argued that Bomber Command was too preoccupied with its minimal forays into Germany, and Fighter Command with conserving its forces for the Battle of Britain, to offer any help in France. Further that the two CinCs had lost their sense of history, or they would have remembered the aviators of spring 1918 and done likewise, with a reasonable chance of bringing the German offensive to a halt. A difficult argument to swallow in the very different circumstances of 1940. After the fall of France, together with the virtual destruction of the BEF Air Component and the Advanced Air Striking Force, it was a matter of starting all over again.

The first and most significant step was a change of heart at the highest command levels, brought about by the shock success of the Luftwaffe's tactics. Demonstrated above all by the massed Stuka attacks, closely coordinated with the armoured spearheads, which had broken the gunners – elite of the French army since Napoleonic days – at Sedan. The French had a saying that as long as the artillery 'held', the infantry would 'hold'. At Verdun in the Great War it did. At Sedan it broke.

Second only to that crushing defeat was the failure of aerial reconnaissance to detect Guderian's panzers – as they moved up through the Ardennes for the hammer blow at Sedan – whilst the BEF and a whole French army were lured into Belgium and Holland against a very visible secondary thrust to the north. This shocking failure must have been a major factor in the reorganisation – which brought the Hector, Lysander, and a few Blenheim squadrons together under a new Army Co-operation Command 'to organise, experiment and train'. Within a further year, in mid to late 1941, the vulnerable two-seaters were being replaced by Tomahawks and then by Mustang Is. Fighter-recce had arrived.

In 1941 a mixed South African/RAF Air Component, supporting the ground forces, made an important contribution to victory against the Italians in East Africa. Demonstrating once more, albeit with a motley collection of aircraft from the biplane years – Vincent, Hardy, Audax, Fury, Gauntlet, Gladiator plus some Wellesleys and Blenheims – that ground-attack could still be made to work. And even better when a few Hurricanes were briefly available to provide local air superiority. The senior officers concerned subsequently called for the development of dive bombers plus long-range fighters to attack aircraft on enemy airfields.

But old ideas die hard and in Greece the air commander was pulling in exactly the opposite direction. Refusing to support the Greek army, where the real crisis lay, and frittering away the efforts of his twelve or so Wellingtons and Blenheims in so-called strategic bombing against Italian targets. In the end he was more or less saved from creating an international incident by the collapse of the Greek campaign in May 1941.

It was the Desert Air Force (DAF), working hand in glove with the 8th Army in Cyrenaica that set the pace for inter-service co-operation. This started at the top – with land and air headquarters and ops rooms alongside each other – and developed from there downwards.

Fielding a high proportion of fighter squadrons DAF went on to demonstrate ground support in both attack and defence. In June/July 1942 these fighters and just three squadrons of fighter-bombers (Kittyhawks and Hurricanes), brushing aside heavy losses (some squadrons lost 100 per cent in six weeks), played a vital role in helping to bring the Afrika Corps to a halt at the first Battle of Alamein.

Less than nine months later, after the tide had turned irresistibly in the Allies' favour, their efforts culminated in a splendid set piece series of rolling fighter-bomber attacks during the assault on the Mareth Line in Tunisia. Relays of two-and-a-half squadrons at a time every fifteen minutes, coordinated with the artillery, for two-and-a-quarter hours. Even the follow-up strafing was targeted to take out the crews of those anti-tank guns which might hold up the advancing armour.

As early as 1941, when Fighter Command moved over to the offensive, Hurricanes on the Channel Front had begun to carry out shipping strikes with their four x 20mm cannon – learning the rules of a dangerous game. Playing cat and mouse with the flak ships – like circling just out of range until the fire died down, as the enemy changed magazines, then in and away as fast as possible.

In the autumn of that year the first Hurribomber sorties were flown, within weeks of each other, in Cyrenaica, from Malta, and over the Channel. Two squadrons (the only two) of Westland Whirlwinds – carrying 2 x 250lb bombs apiece – were next to join the Hurricanes on their hazardous missions. Mostly low level against merchantmen escorted by flak ships. Sometimes penetrating right into enemy harbours, along the channel coast, and the losses were correspondingly high. Dive-bombing had become the recognised alternative, when the defences were too strong, but there seemed to be a reluctance to exploit it at this stage of the war.

Top: Whirlwind with 2 x 250lb bombs. A great aircraft, with many advanced features. Dogged by a lack of Peregrine engines due to high priority demand for Merlins.
Bottom: Hurricane IV. Heavily burdened, leading the way in fighter RP ground-attack, and at some cost.

The Hurricane IID, a tank buster with two Vickers 40mm cannon, was tried out by the DAF from mid 1942 to early 1943. Effective in knocking out isolated groups of tanks – the maximum speed of 286 mph was said to make it far too vulnerable against the flak defences of larger concentrations.

One wonders whether its big cannon should have been tried out on the Typhoon, as a higher accuracy back up for RPs. There would have been a lot of factors involved. Interesting to discover how a cost/benefit analysis might have looked versus RPs.

Last in the Hurricane ground-attack story were the rocket-equipped Mk IVs which became operational, several months before the first RP Typhoons, in June 1943. Carrying 8 x 60lb RPs they could not manage much better than 170mph!

Their attack on a pair of important lock gates at the end of the Hansweert Canal broke all the rules. Flying very slow aircraft, against a heavily defended target, they were briefed to go in low level. The squadron commander, newly appointed, had never flown on ops but insisted on leading the show. He could not find the target, and orbited several times, before committing himself. The result was inevitable. The CO and another pilot were shot down and killed and every aircraft was damaged. It was totally inexcusable at this stage in the war.

The survivors, with a new and experienced CO, were put onto Noballs[2] – braving the flak again and again, trying to go down vertically in their ancient steeds, a hard way to build up RP experience. In all there were three squadrons equipped with Hurricane IVs and some unlucky heroes were to continue flying them on ops until late spring in the following year. It was also said that some Typhoon squadrons took to loitering at around 170mph, near the enemy coast, hoping to catch those who might be tempted by the thought of an easy Hurricane kill.

Following the Dieppe raid, the first Typhoon wing was disbanded in August 1942 because its performance characteristics could not be fitted to the existing pattern of fighter sweeps and escorted light-bomber ops over northern France and the Low Countries. Its performance at altitude was inadequate for use as high cover and it was too fast low down for bomber escort. The Typhoons had previously survived one conference at Fighter Command in June 1942; on the understanding they could operate independently to provide a sweep covering withdrawal of the main force.

The three squadrons were now relegated to low level daylight interception against bomb-carrying Fw190s. Undeterred by that setback Denys Gillam, Bee Beamont and others, continued to demonstrate the effectiveness of the Typhoon in ground-attack at every opportunity.

Their efforts were rewarded when the first fighter-bomber wing was formed in the winter of 1942-1943. From then it was all go for the Typhoon, as the Spitfire IX was capable of holding its own against the Fw190, and the invasion of Normandy came closer. More squadrons were formed, and progressively equipped with bombs and rockets, taking over from the Hurricanes and Whirlwinds.

RARE AND VITAL SKILLS – TRAINING TO WIN

Meanwhile, the pressure was really on, to create and train another tactical air force in time for the invasion. The first order of battle for 2nd TAF was issued on 25 November 1943. At that time it included a light bomber group – two composite groups comprising some thirty Spitfire and Typhoon squadrons, hived off from a reorganising Fighter Command – seven Mustang-equipped fighter-recce squadrons from Army Co-operation Command and the same number of Auster Air OP squadrons. Set up initially as 'The Tactical Air Force', some five months earlier, the formal separation from Fighter Command did not occur until that November date. With less than six months to go the composite groups had to be expanded by a further twenty squadrons. Although most of these already existed it was a massive training task in relation to the fast changing operational requirements.

Operational training had effectively become a two-stage process. Hard to say whether this was deliberate or not. Starting at AFU, with a strong bias towards the 'straight' fighter pilot, this provided a much better foundation than we gave it credit for at the time. Our instructors trained to teach 'stick and rudder', but not applied flying, showed some reluctance to detail the latter exercises in advance. Their efforts were much more in the nature of 'watch me and do as I do' and yet somehow it worked. Not perfectly but reasonably well.

Moving on to a fighter-recce OTU, there was the sheer delight at being let loose on a modern single-seat fighter. Authorised low flying. The importance and the challenge of pinpoint navigation. Satisfaction at bringing back a good set of reconnaissance photographs. Success at gunnery. For me, thanks to my subsequent transfer to Typhoons, the best came last, like a third OTU stage at the group support unit. Sorties led by an experienced leader who really put you through the hoops – battle formation, endless crossover turns, tailchasing, mock combat and ground-attack – so that you were forced to fly your aircraft to the limit. You landed back, wringing in sweat, with a marvellous feeling of satisfaction, like the end of a hard fought rugger match. The Typhoon flight at 84 GSU was a great bonus.

Those memories helped to pinpoint the strengths and weaknesses of operational training. Aerial photography, and standard attacks on enemy bombers, were effectively taught because the techniques were well defined and backed up by proper illustrated detail. Most important and valuable of all was what, much later, came to be known as lead/follow training, under the control of experienced, highly motivated, instructors. Close to what I had experienced at 84 GSU.

Ground-attack and fighter-recce required an additional training element which seemed to be missing. That of combining two types of applied flying on a single sortie – a specific operational task together with defensive tactics against enemy fighters and flak. Difficult to organise but vital in creating additional awareness and reducing potential casualties.

Overall the main shortcoming, indeed weakness, was in tactics and training with bombs and RP. This seemed to stem from the fact that the OTUs – unlike the elementary and service flying training schools which operated to established methods and standards – were always chasing a changing requirement, technically and numerically. And there was resistance to change. One pilot who joined his squadron two months before D-Day, claimed to have flown ninety per cent of his training sorties on fighter exercises, whilst over eighty per cent of his first ops were dive-bombing. At some point in this process his CO suddenly accepted the fact that he was leading a ground-attack unit. But it was too late. He was moved on shortly afterwards!

Ground-attack called for a major change in a system geared to the output of 'straight' fighter boys. So full marks to the visionaries who recognised the urgent need to train leaders in the many aspects of this new skill, and to do so in some numbers, during the run up to the invasion. At the heart of this effort was the Specialised Low Attack Instructors School, set up by Denys Gillam at Milfield at the end of 1942, and the infant Fighter Leaders School formed at Chedworth as an element of 52 OTU in early 1943. FLS moved with its parent to Charmy Down, and then Aston Down, before breaking away, as an independent unit in its own right, and moving to Milfield in January 1944 where it absorbed SLAIS. An exercise in which Batchy Atcherley played a not inconsiderable part.

The vital contribution, to fighter ground-attack leadership training, undoubtedly ran from the beginning of 1944 until FLS became part of the Central Fighter Establishment at the end of that year. By then the job had largely been done. The war was in its closing stages and, two months later, a few 2nd TAF squadrons were actually being disbanded.

It was also said that there were plenty of fighter leaders from the Middle East who were experienced in army support. But that was a false premise. They were hardly evident in the Typhoon squadrons of 84 Group and the terrain, in any case, was very different to that of the western desert. Moreover the German armies, which had become exceedingly skilled at camouflage in the face of allied air superiority, exploited those differences to good effect. For all that, one wonders why Desert Air Force knowledge and skills could not have been more widely used in the training role. A touch of the 'not invented here' perhaps?

Certainly by D-Day there was no shortage of leaders well trained in ground-attack. What proportion of these had been through FLS as opposed to being 'trained' and promoted on the squadrons, it is difficult to say. But the latter certainly happened in my time and indeed to me.

As to the value of FLS – those who attended the courses were already experienced operational pilots. Most seemed to benefit from the exchange of ideas – put into practice in the air – and a few had the opportunity to fly and evaluate enemy aircraft. But this did nothing directly to develop the operational skills of the chaps they went on to lead, which was equally true of those leaders emerging from SLAIS.

For the 'new' boy all the evidence suggested a failure to set up and sustain a minimum OTU capability – to support it with a sound and developing syllabus, and to stop it being eroded by short term squadron needs. Continuity, however limited, even when pilots or aircraft were in short supply, would have been far better than closing units down. Operational skills and tactics were what mattered and took time to assimilate. Instructors, almost invariably, were 'resting' operational pilots who had been given no training for their role at an OTU. Type conversion was not a problem, but an inability to recognise the extent, and the penalties, of 'on the job' operational training certainly was.

In the autumn of 1943 two OTUs were re-designated as combat training wings, and soon after as tactical exercise units. 1 TEU was disbanded in July 1944 – leaving 3 TEU only. Until it too was disbanded in December 1944 to become 55 OTU – at the same location – and using the same aircraft and personnel. The OTU syllabus now included weapons training and tactics. Excellent in principle. At squadron level, however, there was almost too little war left to assess the results. Which might well have been very positive.

In an ideal world a fighter ground-attack OTU should have provided the following exercises at the very least:-

Flying aircraft to its limits	– aerobatics
	– one-to-one air combat
	– lead/follow
Weapons training	– air-to-air gunnery
	– air-to-ground gunnery

- dive bombing <>
- low level bombing <>
- firing RPs <>
- section ground attacks <>

Navigational exercises
- low and medium level cross countries <>
- low and medium level target finding <>

Tactical training
- battle formation
- bouncing by instructors <>
- minimising risk from flak <>
- meteorology in relation to flak and enemy fighters <>

In the experience of many pilots those exercises marked <> were rarely included. Was this another example of subconscious resistance to change?

Armament practice camps were an additional form of post-operational training. The squadrons rotated through them in turn, coming off ops for two weeks at a time, for intensive RP and bombing practice. The results of each sortie were readily available, and the individual trends looked generally positive, so APCs were considered to be a good thing. But just how good?

For this was a highly subjective judgement, unsupported by any measured trend analyses or final results in squadron terms, based entirely on the overall averages achieved over the whole training period.

It can be said however that the limited figures rescued from 193's visit to Fairwood Common in September 1944, suggest some fifty per cent improvement in average dive and low level bombing accuracy. A considerable increase in hitting power[3] of which there was some evidence when we went back on ops. As for the Squadron RP result, the record shows a disappointing 27 yards, of which more anon.

In addition all this has to be seen, and recognised, as a performance high immediately after a squadron had passed through APC. Beforehand of course, and progressively afterwards (due to casualties and the departure of tour-expired pilots), it would have gradually degenerated.

Which leads to the thought that if all those destined for ground-attack could have been put through the equivalent of an APC, before joining a squadron, the overall performance would have been much improved. However you view them – as a potential OTU extension or a squadron upgrade and despite the limitations of the day – the armament practice camps were most valuable.

There was another facet to the operational training story. By 1942, it had been established that single-seat fighters were capable of handling army support and reconnaissance, which had been the preserve of light bombers and other specialist aircraft like the Lysander. Not only that but they sustained lower losses, were easier for other fighters to escort, and could look after themselves much better in combat.

From that moment it could be argued that there was a growing requirement for a new breed of fighter pilot. One who, with respect to his forebears, could navigate himself really accurately, find pinpoint locations and seek out an enemy on the ground.

Whether to reconnoitre, to photograph, or to attack was immaterial in the broader training context. Those were complementary skills, which could be added on as required. Perhaps the time had come for tactical army support OTUs and front-line units to combine the functions of fighter-recce and ground-attack. The Typhoons of 146 Wing had demonstrated the idea, at least in part, with their photo-recce sorties, and it appeared to offer many advantages.

Interesting, in later years, to discover how much the A&AEE at Boscombe Down was involved in evaluating new weapons – in trying out possible tactics for their use – and how little if any of this reached the squadrons. RPs and napalm were classic examples. Perhaps the system of scientists reporting to the Ministry of Aircraft Production, created an impenetrable barrier, for which a short cut needed to be devised in time of war. Perhaps their most significant findings were routed via CFE and/or SLAIS, to 2nd TAF or group headquarters, and suffered communication problems beyond. It is certainly true that opportunities were missed.

While they were busy evaluating two-tier RPs and the like, the squadrons were carrying a load of redundant hardware. The original trials had been conducted with Swordfish. Slow at best, slower still when festooned with RPs, so that rails were needed to guide the missiles until their aerodynamics could take over.

True of the Swordfish, but not of the Typhoon, although it has been claimed that the latter could not have operated with zero-length rails, earlier than the Tempest, which was evaluated with them in spring 1945 – thanks to the arrival of a new and improved RP propellant. Whatever the truth, and with all credit to the help from A&AEE, the fact remains that the RP Typhoon had to carry that extra weight, drag and loss of manoeuvrability for the whole of its operational career.

Boscombe had immediately recognised the difficulties of RP aiming and accuracy which had been solved so effectively by Bill Tacon with his

Beaufighter. The need to eliminate slip or skid and above all to set up correct combinations of range (R), speed and angle of dive (a°). The modification, already described, which rotated the reflector sight image through 90°, so that the range bars could be used to set up a depressed RP sightline, was an excellent idea. Although adjustable for dive angle only, it helped considerably.

Could more have been done before the GGS (gyro gun sight) took over? The lateral thinker might visualise angle of dive markings on our pristine canopies, miniature standby altimeters (displaying H) mounted close to the sight itself (R=H/sin a°), and so on. It would have been most unwise. Pilots were under enough pressure already, during an RP attack, and would have been totally overloaded. The demands on peripheral vision and mental agility would have been self defeating.

With the technology of the day the best solution, as ever, was a combination of the modified reflector sight – APC (yet again! plus some exercises identifying angles of dive and range) – leaders setting up good positioning for the attack, precise and accurate flying and, I can say this because I never fired an RP in anger, sheer guts.

As for the GGS (a great idea) essentially it set up a sightline based on the measured angle of dive modified by range. The latter was generated by setting an RP 'equivalent wingspan' – based on typical ground-target dimensions – and using the throttle twist grip (see GGS on Spitfire XIV in Chapter 14). The initial design using the bottom diamond – 'bottom diamond aiming' – was replaced by 'centre spot aiming' which produced a dramatic improvement in accuracy. From then on it was reckoned that direct hits were to be expected. Sadly, like zero-length rails, the GGS arrived too late.

The problem with napalm was worse than we suspected. A two-way communication failure. A&AEE never knew about our operational trials, the squadron attack on an enemy strongpoint near Arnhem, or the subsequent demonstrations before we were disbanded. The lack of any feedback from Boscombe Down, to confirm and support my own findings on the s'Hertogenbosch range, undoubtedly contributed to the rather uncertain results from our sole napalm attack. Although, fortunately for us, the effect of our new weapon was very demoralising.

Napalm was to become an emotive subject in later years. Largely due to its indiscriminate use in Vietnam. Had it arrived earlier on the scene there seemed to be no good reason why it should not have become a key weapon in our close-support armoury. Flame throwers were used by the armies on both sides. So why not a flame-throwing bomb against enemy soldiers? A low level close support show, using napalm followed by high explosive, would have been quite devastating.

The day we discovered an Me109 production unit dispersed around the forts at Antwerp was a reminder of what we might be up against in combat – and even more so when the squadron assembled its own Gustav and brought it to full flying condition.

In fact there was no established training programme on enemy aircraft. It happened in fits and starts throughout one's service career. The beginning, at ITW, concentrating on aircraft recognition only – with the familiar three-view black silhouettes for study – and then exposed briefly in tests. For me, despite my alleged defective eyesight, it was never a problem. I believe that most of us would have achieved high marks had we been regularly tested.

During my attachment to 613 Squadron we visited Wittering, or rather the satellite at Collyweston, to see the German circus. It was an impressive set up because the two airfields had been merged into one. But the visit itself was rather a damp squib. Apart from the twins, Me110, He111, Do17 and Ju88 which were well represented, there was just one Me109E and no Stuka. To our great disappointment the whole fleet was treated like a collection of expensive toys. No flying display, no engine runs and we were barred from climbing aboard.

The verbal briefing brought out a number of points with which most of us were already familiar. We picked up more about the negative g advantages of the fuel injection system on the 109's Daimler Benz engine. Try to escape by pitching nose down into a dive with your Hurricane or Spitfire and the Merlin would cut. Not so the DB601 and the Hun had you at his mercy. The redoubtable Miss Shilling at RAE Farnborough was known to be working on an interim mod and the Merlin 61 on the Spitfire IX would provide a first production solution. This apart, we gathered that comparative tests had shown the Spitfire – in its various marks – to be better all round than the contemporary Me109s, a view not universally accepted until the later arrival of the Spitfire IX. The German fighter also suffered from very heavy controls at speed. Worst of all was the disturbance created by the slots opening, in a random manner, at high angles of attack which could make aiming extremely difficult in combat. Take-off and landing characteristics, with that very narrow undercarriage, were not good and the view was dreadful.

More than two years later, at Antwerp, I knew a deal more about the Luftwaffe. Some of it from following up any published information available. Much more from listening to the thoughts and ideas of those who had met it in action – chaps like Mike Bulleid, Charlie Hall and Toddy – and through those long and fascinating one-to-one sessions with Neville Thomas.

Our late model Me109G seemed a strange mixture. The worst features were still there – modifying the narrow undercarriage was obviously too difficult – but the dreadful canopy and windscreen with their intricate framing and flat side panels had only been marginally improved. It was very much an 'electric' aircraft, with those beautiful flight instruments, and a demand oxygen system years ahead of ours. But the airscrew control switch, on top of the stick, must have been a terrible fiddle in combat. It was as if pressure, for more and more production, must have played havoc with a balanced development to produce a better fighting machine. We might have to watch the 109s' turning performance versus our Typhoons. But otherwise we dismissed them – including the higher powered Gustav – as no threat at all.

The Fw190, which had been around for almost three years, was very different. Better performance, well harmonised controls, very high rate of roll and a decent one-piece sliding canopy. Charlie Hall, who flew one at AFDU on his fighter leader's course, raved about it and Farnborough, in the shape of Winkle Brown, was most impressed. That high rate of roll so dangerous when you wanted to escape in a dive – once the speed and hence the g forces were too much to attempt anything dramatic in pitch – was a worry. We viewed what we heard about the Fw190 with some respect.

If I remember correctly information on the Me262, and the tailless rocket-propelled Me163, began to filter through during the German offensive in the Ardennes. When a V2 set an oil storage tank alight in the Scheldt estuary, about that time, it was no surprise to see a single Me262 low down on a dawn reconnaissance sortie. Equally true of the Me163s when we encountered them distantly in the following March, we were well aware of their short duration and vulnerability when the fuel ran out.

Once these new aircraft were flying operationally, there was a good flow of combat extracts, which could be found in the wing ops room. From these it was possible to build up a picture of the strengths and weaknesses of our impressive new adversaries; and a few clues about catching them at a disadvantage.

I am indebted to Johnny Shellard, of 263 Squadron, for this account of combat with a couple of Me262s on 26 April 1945.

> "The three of us were pulling away after an RP attack on a train, and preparing to cover our leader who, hit by flak, was about to make a forced landing. We could not have been more vulnerable as the two jets bounced us. The first aircraft overshot, tried to turn with us, and incredibly kept changing direction, so that each Typhoon was able to get in a good long burst! I then raised the nose and fired at the second EA which was climbing steeply away with the wicks turned fully up. As

he disappeared, out of sight and out of reach, we watched the leader spiralling downwards in flames until his aircraft hit the ground and blew up.

"At debrief we were mystified by the tactics of the enemy pilot. It was obvious that we could outturn him, and would have no difficulty in obtaining sufficient deflection, and he could have gone skyward at any time beyond our ability to keep with him. Yet he chose to stay with us and changed direction erratically. He appeared to have an inability to turn without losing height. But we also wondered if the pilot had been wounded, or the aircraft damaged, to explain this lack of action.

"As for our leader, he was rescued from an angry crowd by Luftwaffe officers and taken to the nearby Me262 base. Where it is reported that he had a jolly time with them before going on to a POW camp."

There was little information about the new 30mm cannon and JG1 – the first He162 Volksjaeger unit – was just operational at the end of the war. It made a few sorties, even made some dubious claims, and one was shot down by a Tempest. The Arado 234 was cloaked in secrecy. It was not until 1997, visiting the museum shop at Arromanches, that I discovered a book about the very first high altitude photo-recce sorties by a jet aircraft. Two of the preproduction Arado 234s had captured most of the beachhead on film, including our advanced landing grounds, and we knew nothing about them.

I have written much about flying on ops already. But perhaps some of it needs to be said again. The moment of truth. Of challenge and uncertainty. Of the need to belong and be accepted. Of fear and fulfilment and the subtle awakening of squadron pride. A time to learn as much and as fast as possible, from your fellow pilots, and from every sortie. To be possessed by a determination to help the ground troops who were fighting such a bloody war compared with your own. For this was the way to success. And success it certainly was. The evidence is there, in the war diaries of the Typhoon wings, from Normandy to Schleswig Holstein and eastwards to the Elbe. It is recorded for all time in the signals from ground commanders at every level. Close support really worked.

Even so there were many lessons to be learned. In the Great War, as we have already seen, ground fire from rifles and machine guns was most feared by the strafing fighters. For the ground-attack aircraft of 2nd TAF it was light flak. Those same multiple 20mm and 37mm guns which had wreaked havoc amongst the vulnerable Battles of the

One German reconnaissance result very near home. Our advanced landing ground at St Croix sur Mer. A story lost for many years after the war.

Advanced Air Striking Force in 1940.

By comparison our Typhoons had speed, firepower, manoeuvrability and an airframe which could take an immense amount of punishment. But we always treated light flak with the greatest respect. Wing shows, described in outline already, were a classic example. Anti-flak covering fire and the main attacks following each other as fast as possible, and from different directions, in order to confuse and saturate the defences. Weapon deliveries to be in their descending order of vulnerability from flak, bombs low level; RPs 30° dive; dive-bombing last of all.

VCP/FCP[4] and Cab Rank[5], so often thought of as the ultimate in army close support, were less used in Western Europe than might have been expected. The reason was simple. Keeping aircraft on standing patrol, waiting for orders, was inefficient and wasteful. In theory at least Cab Rank was reserved for situations involving a brief and highly concentrated succession of strikes. Such as might be required to support an attack, or to break up an enemy counter attack. In practice these conditions hardly seemed to apply.[6] It was all rather confusing.

'Rover', the system used in Italy, was a definite step forward. Each formation was briefed for a target before take-off. On arrival overhead they made a single orbit, allowing the controller time to divert them on to an alternative (Cab Rank) opportunity, and this would take immediate priority. No call from Rover and they attacked the original target. In which case there was the disadvantage that the element of surprise might have been lost.

Cab Rank could be very effective, but sometimes there were problems in pinpointing and identifying the target – to a greater extent than on other missions – in the absence of good 'close in' navigation features. There could be other confusions, with artillery marking using coloured or white smoke. And the enemy was not above adding to the difficulties by putting down his own decoys. There was surely a case for air-to-ground 'pathfinder' marking of difficult targets, using smoke rockets or napalm, with fast follow up to retain some element of surprise.

There was also the question of switching the Cab Rank effort quickly to vital sectors along the front. The American tank formations, on their breakout from Normandy, solved the problem with direct radio communication between the leading tanks and the supporting 9th Tactical Air Force fighter-bombers. And to avoid problems of mistaken identity they carried red canvas roof panels.

One of the constraints on close support was Tedder's 'curse of the heavy bomber'. When, as happened very occasionally, the heavies bombed short and hit our own troops, the bomb line was pushed forward in a panic response. Sometimes thousands of yards. It was frustrating to be barred from attacking the enemy by an edict which bore no relationship to the accuracy of fighter ground-attack.

Whenever the battle went mobile, and the ground forces started to advance, we were faced with a similar band of enemy territory in which no air attacks were permitted. And the faster their progress the broader it was. Thus, when the Hun was at his most vulnerable, forced onto the roads in daylight, the bomb line afforded him its greatest protection. It was another powerful argument in favour of direct radio communication with the forward troops.

Looking for targets of opportunity – particularly in conditions of mobile warfare – was full of uncertainty. Sometimes escaping transport

Typhoon with prototype, steel, RP rails. Heavy, high drag, and bad news for air combat. Aluminium ones were slightly better.

would be almost unprotected. But the light flak was never far away – there could be new and totally unexpected concentrations – and flak traps like that experienced at Beauvais. Our tactics had to take account of these difficult and different conditions. A rapid advance also increased the flying distance to the battle area, until drop tanks became essential, creating a conflict between range and hitting power.

The RP-equipped Typhoons were reduced from carrying eight rockets (twelve maximum on two-tier installations) to four plus two forty-five-gallon drop tanks. For the fighter bombers it was a question of tanks or bombs. Typhoons had been known to operate with a single 500lb bomb under one wing, and a drop tank under the other, but it was very rare.

Mobile warfare also meant more armed reconnaissance. Broadly the alternatives were to go in on the deck trying to avoid any known defended areas (not so easy in a fluid situation), or just above the light flak ceiling of 4,000 feet. At this level formations of eight aircraft tended to be the norm.

Low down it was better to operate sections of four, or even pairs, particularly if the weather was bad. Sometimes you might catch and hit the enemy in a single flying pass. But to pull up immediately, on encountering a train or road convoy, was simply asking to be clobbered. Much better to press on out of range and come back in a dive, line abreast, at right angles to the length of the target. These tactics enabled the whole formation to attack simultaneously – faster in and out – with a better chance of swamping the defences. Fewer flak guns would be able to engage each individual aircraft and even less would be presented with non-deflection shots.

Low level bombing using high explosive with eleven and twenty-five-second delay fusing was argued about at great length. Badly delivered, as we have seen, they bounced over or through the target.

146 Wing's 'Bomphoon' squadrons, choosing between the two methods of low level delivery, tackled the problem in totally different ways. One went to great lengths – including the study of stereo pair photographs – in order to arrive at the bomb-release point in level flight and as far below the top of the target as possible. The others almost invariably made their attacks, in a shallow dive, aiming at the base of the target. Both techniques worked well in practice and there seemed little to choose between them – or in the level of risk involved – given a determined attack, with minimum warning. In both cases it was considered better to use twenty-five-second delay fusing.

During the Great War aerial reconnaissance had forced the armies to move by night in an effort to conceal their intentions. In World War II, once the Germans had lost air superiority, they were forced to do the same – in order to avoid destruction by Allied ground-attack aircraft. There was a greater penalty. They could not observe the invasion build up, and the Allies mounted a highly successful deception plan, in which the tactical air forces played a major part.

As a result some fifteen German divisions were held in the Pas de Calais, to await the second landing which never came, and were thrown piecemeal into the battle as the crisis worsened.

Whatever the arguments about RP accuracy, the Typhoon vs. tanks engagement at Mortain in August 1944 epitomised the concept of close air support on the battlefield backed up by good intelligence and reconnaissance. The totality of that operation demonstrates the progress that had been made.

The German plan for a concentrated panzer assault westwards to the Atlantic coast, with the intention of cutting off the American spearheads pushing south was revealed in full by the codebreakers at Bletchley Park. On the first day, combat air patrols over its airfields prevented the Luftwaffe from intervening, US medium bombers attacked all movement on the approaches to the battlefield, and 2nd TAF Typhoons supported by Thunderbolts of the US 9th TAF went for the German armoured formations. Although the fighting continued for another seventy-two hours or so, before the Germans finally gave up, that first day broke them. By the end, almost by air action alone, the last vestiges of offensive capability in the German 7th Army and Panzer Group West had ceased to exist.

During the Battle of Normandy and afterwards, until the end of the war in Europe, air superiority was taken for granted by the allied armies. By day they moved at will, convoys nose to tail, as if the Luftwaffe did not exist. There was no attempt at concealment. 2nd TAF squadrons were concentrated on the best airfields, in large numbers, aircraft parked close together.

On the other side things were very different. Camouflage was as masterly as it was essential. Almost nothing moved in daylight, unless the Hun was in full retreat. Once on the road his transport attempted to keep well spaced out, dashing from cover to cover. Foxholes and vehicle pits, a desperate attempt to provide some protection from air attack, had been dug into the verges alongside all the principal routes.

It was similar at night. There was no difficulty identifying the battle zone. The lights of the allied supply columns – the Yanks were said to be by far the worst offenders – led forward until they were suddenly extinguished, and from there on was nothing but darkness.

Thinking about that lopsided environment raised all sorts of questions. For the Typhoon squadrons in particular – was it possible that we had been tied too closely to an army which had become dangerously dependent on air power? Had the wheel turned full circle, reproducing some of the worst features of the Wehrmacht/Luftwaffe relationship which had been so damaging to the German air force?

The answer must emphatically be no. We were part of a tactical air force and army support was our job. The RAF had other commands and massive resources elsewhere. Within 2nd TAF itself the Spitfire IXs, an increasing number of Mk XIVs, and two wings of Tempest Vs were there to hold the ring with the Luftwaffe. Sufficient to say that the Germans learned as much, when they tried to achieve local air superiority, during von Rundstedt's last winter offensive in Ardennes.

Of course the Typhoons did get an occasional fighter sweep when the Luftwaffe was in its more active phases. But these were few and far between. Never really enough to satisfy the desire of any pilot worth his salt, flying a single-seat fighter, to prove himself in air combat. Even those of us deeply committed to ground-attack were not immune.

But the real point of issue, it seemed in retrospect, was the balancing act needed between battlefield air superiority and effective ground-attack. For the needs of the army could best be met once the enemy air forces had been driven onto the defensive. If the Luftwaffe had been stronger, in the last year of the war, the pattern of Typhoon ops might have been different. As for the Germans, they had learned to live without air superiority, and that held some lessons too.

One cannot end a brief resume like this without considering a further scenario. What might have happened if there had not been those two atom bombs. If the Japanese had not surrendered.

Tempest V first demonstrated the feasibility and benefits of zero length rails. An opportunity lost for the Typhoon.

With the end of the war in Europe Wing Commander Beamont had returned from his POW camp in Germany and was forming a Tempest II wing at Chilbolton for action in the Far East. I got wind of it and put in an application to join him – emphasising my additional photo-recce and napalm experience – with high hopes that I might be accepted. Within two months or so it was dead duck.

Meeting him over the years, visiting Morton Valence from ETPS when he was carrying out Meteor development testing, at Warton to discuss Lightning avionics and for the last time at the Farnborough International Air Show in 2003, was a continuing reminder of what might have been. Although we had hardly spoken of it all.

I remember that last occasion so well. Bee's Chilbolton Wing was part of the baggage which I had carried around with me during those early chaotic months after the war – something which I had longed to do – a regret and a yearning for more operational flying. But that was long ago and my feelings had certainly changed. Yet something fired me up that day. Perhaps the realisation that this might be a last opportunity – he looked ill and wanted to talk – and to do so might bring him some comfort. Whatever it was, as the air display thundered away overhead, I bared my soul.

I enthused about the Tempest's handling and performance – the comfort of that big, two-row, sleeve-valve radial up front, the joy of those spring tab ailerons, of RPs with zero-length rails and the huge benefit of aiming them with a gyro gunsight, and of napalm and forward oblique cameras. Not least that the splendid combination of aircraft and armament – skills and experience – under his command would have created the ground-attack unit of all time.

Bee listened in silence and then: "It's quite a thought. And you may be right. But what about being shot down attacking Japanese troops? It was bad enough against the SS. With the Japs I just dread to think. We were lucky that it never happened to us."

He always was a realist.

ENDNOTES

Chapter One

1. Smith, Group Captain Duncan. *Spitfire into Battle* (John Murray Publishers Ltd)
2. PSP: Pierced Steel Plank. A temporary runway system based on interlocking, lightly corrugated, perforated steel sheets.
3. ABTA: All Bombs Target Area
4. Panzerfaust: Hand held infantry anti-tank weapon.
5. 'France' from *Selected Poems* by Siegfried Sassoon (Faber & Faber Ltd)

Chapter Two

1. Hurdy-gurdy: Hand cranked musical instrument with keys.
2. Dundas, Group Captain Sir Hugh. *Flying Start* (Stanley Paul and Co. Ltd)
3. *Queen Elizabeth*. New Cunard Liner.
4. OTC: Officers Training Corps
5. FTS: Flying Training School

Chapter Three

1. Molotov Cocktail: Crude bomb – flammable liquid in bottle.
2. OCTU: Officer Cadet Training Unit
3. KRs: Kings Regulations
4. ACIs: Army Council Instructions
5. Motley: Mounting for anti-aircraft Bren gun.
6. Hegedus de, Adam. *Don't Keep the Vanman Waiting* (Staples Press Ltd)

Chapter Four

1. Grading School: Purpose outlined later in chapter.
2. ITW: Initial Training Wing

Chapter Five

1. EFTS: Elementary Flying Training School
2. Glide Path Indicator: At runway threshold. Amber if approach too high, red if too low, green for correct glide slope.
3. SFTS: Service Flying Training School

Chapter Six

1. AFU: Advanced Flying Unit
2. P38: USAF Lockheed Lightning long-range twin-engined fighter.
3. Marauder: USAAF twin-engined medium bomber.
4. Drem Lighting System: Large circle of lights centred on the airfield –

with 'lead in' funnel – twin flarepath and glide path indicators.
5. Gooseneck flare: Paraffin container with spout and a cotton wick.
6. LMF: Lack of Moral Fibre, i.e., failure to cope with stress or fear.
7. TacR: Tactical Reconnaissance
8. Overlord: Code name for the invasion of Normandy.
9. Tee Emm: Air Ministry publication which taught good airmanship and accident prevention in a light-hearted way.
10. Irving, Lawrence. *Great Interruption* (Airlife Publishing Ltd)

Chapter Seven
1. Clipped, Clapped and Cropped: Wings of the Spitfire Vc were clipped, and the supercharger blades cropped to improve low level performance. It was still ancient and 'clapped out'.
2. Pompey: Slang for Portsmouth
3. GSU: Group Support Unit
4. HE: High Explosives

Chapter Eight
1. B3: A specific Advanced Landing Ground.
2. Chore Horse: Trolley-mounted battery and generator.
3. Servicing Echelons: Engineering units of 2TAF. Identified by squadron number plus prefix 6.

Chapter Nine
1. MT: Motor Transport
2. APC: Armament Practice Camp
3. RPs: (Unguided) Rocket Projectiles

Chapter Ten
1. Gustav: German phonetic letter 'G'., i.e. Me109G or Gustav.
2. Brat: RAF Halton Apprentice
3. EO: Engineer Officer
4. FR: Fighter Reconnaissance, also shortened to fighter-recce.
5. Longbow: Call sign for 84 Group Control.
6. Hang Up: Bombs fail to release.
7. Craven A: Cigarette of the 1940s. Nickname given to Squadron Leader Craven, the airfield controller.

Chapter Eleven
1. MRCP: Mobile Radar Control Post
2. AOC: Air Officer Commanding: Air Vice-Marshal Trevor Hudleston.
3. VCP: Visual Control Post. Controller, an experienced pilot, directed attacks on army requested targets. See also Appendix.
4. AFDU: Air Fighting Development Unit

Chapter Twelve
1. Slipper Tank: Belly-mounted long-range tank.
2. A & AEE: Aircraft and Armament Experimental Establishment

Chapter Thirteen
1. Balbo: Large formation of aircraft. Named after Italian General Balbo who led a series of flights in this manner to promote Italian military aviation.
2. KG200: Luftwaffe Clandestine and Special Purposes Unit.
3. CRE: Chief Royal Engineer
4. See *Project Cancelled* by Derek Wood

Chapter Fourteen
1. ETPS: Empire Test Pilots School
2. BAFO: British Air Forces of Occupation
3. CFE: Central Fighter Establishment
4. SASO: Senior Air Staff Officer
5. RAE: Royal Aircraft Establishment
6. MAP: Ministry of Aircraft Production
7. GGS: Gyro Gunsight

Chapter Fifteen
1. ENT: Ear, Nose and Throat
2. BLEU: Blind Landing Experimental Unit
3. ARB: Air Registration Board
4. AFC: Air Force Cross

Chapter Sixteen
1. Colonel Trenchard, Commanding Royal Flying Corps. Later Marshal of the Royal Air Force, Lord Trenchard.
2. Kreigsmarine: Name of German navy.
3. Akaflieg: (University) Academic Flying Group
4. The long awaited exchange of greetings occurred immediately before the sixty-fifth anniversary of D-Day.

Appendix
1. BEF: British Expeditionary Force
2. Noballs: V1 launching sites.
3. Hitting Power: Calculations suggest that sixteen Tornados with high explosive bombs could, due to their increased accuracy, achieve similar results to those of 400 Lancasters on the first Peenemünde raid.
4. FCP: Forward Control Post (target not visual). Trials after the war, using a photo-recce Typhoon to simulate an attack and record the target, suggested that VCP (Visual Control Post) with a pilot controller could be very accurate. FCP was less so, but did not require a pilot in charge.
5. Cab Rank: where a flight would be called in by a controller, execute an attack, and return to base for refuelling and rearming, while other flights were constantly overhead.
6. Dundas, Group Captain Sir Hugh. *Flying Start*. (Stanley Paul and Co Ltd.)

INDEX OF PERSONALITIES

Including ranks and decorations, which are recorded as accurately as possible.